The Strange Voyage of
Donald Crowhurst

Also by Ron Hall

SCANDAL '63: A STUDY OF THE PROFUMO AFFAIR (with C. Irving
and J. Wallington)

The Strange Voyage of Donald Crowhurst

by

NICHOLAS TOMALIN

and

RON HALL

HODDER AND STOUGHTON

Contents

Illustrations

KEY TO ACKNOWLEDGEMENTS

[1] Peter Dunne/Sunday Times
[2] Donald Proctor (Devon News)/Sunday Times
[3] Peter Beard
[4] Devon News
[5] Devon News/Sunday Times
[6] BBC Television (West Region)
[7] Allan Ballard/Sunday Times
[8] Ron Hall/Sunday Times
[9] Sunday Times
[10] Frank Herrmann/Sunday Times
[11] Kelvin Brodie/Sunday Times

MAPS

Sectional drawing on page 296–7 by Peter Sullivan

PARANOID GRANDIOSITY

"Paranoid grandiosity tends to be well organized, relatively stable and persistent. The complexity of delusional conviction varies from rather simple beliefs in one's alleged talent, attractiveness or inspiration to highly complex, systematized beliefs that one is a great prophet, author, poet, inventor or scientist. The latter extreme belongs to classical paranoia."

Prof. Norman Cameron, Yale
(*Ency. Brit.*)

Authors' Preface

To combine the techniques of the novelist with those of the journalist is to tread on slippery ground. Henry James wrote of the danger to the novelist of the "fatal futility of Fact"; it is even more hazardous for the journalist to be lured into using the devices of dramatic fiction. There is a temptation to suppress inconvenient facts simply because they spoil the shape of the narrative, and to re-create imaginatively thoughts and attitudes of protagonists that can never be known with absolute certainty (how can one tell precisely what was in the mind of a sailor alone at sea?).

As far as possible, we have avoided these temptations. We have tried to record all the evidence, so that the reader, if he disagrees with our judgments, can form his own. We have allowed the story to unfold as a strictly documented chronology, supported by Donald Crowhurst's own copious writings. At times, to make sense of a sequence of events, we have had to speculate about Crowhurst's state of mind, and even about some of his actions, but we have always tried to make it clear when we are doing so, and have avoided reaching firm conclusions except where overwhelmingly supported by the facts.

If, despite this rigorous approach, the book should have something of the flavour of a novel, it is simply because the actual sequence of events had the shape and inevitability of fictional tragedy. When the bare outline was first revealed in the *Sunday Times* of July 27th, 1969, it was at once recognised as a story of deep psychological complexity as well as sensational incident. It captured the imagination of the Press for many days, and Sir Francis Chichester referred to it as "the sea drama of the century". At that time, however, we knew little about the personality of Crowhurst, and had read his logbooks only for external detail. As we investigated further, it emerged as one of the most extraordinary stories of human aspiration and human failing that, as journalists, we have ever had to record.

Although it is basically a story about heroics, there is no hero — but neither is there a villain. Crowhurst, despite his deceptions, was a man of courage and intelligence, who acted as he did because of intolerable circumstances. The fact that he paid a far greater penalty than he need is testimony to his quality. We have fully convinced ourselves that the two main supporting figures in the venture — Rodney Hallworth, the agent, and Stanley Best, the sponsor — were never knowingly parties to Crowhurst's deceptions. (Nor, for that matter was anyone else.) Both have been outstandingly frank in discussing their involvement, and have opened their files to provide us with much valuable source material.

We have had similar excellent assistance from the boat-builders, John Eastwood and John Elliot. Although everyone admits that Crowhurst set off round the world unprepared, it was not the fault of Eastwoods, but of the whole confusion and rush that preceded the voyage (few boat-builders would have even attempted the task in such a short time). Eastwoods have generously agreed that, in the interests of historical completeness, Crowhurst's various outbursts against the boat should be recorded in the book, though often they speak more of his state of mind than of the state of the boat. Most of the faults that did exist would have been avoided if there had been a normal time for building and trials.

We are indebted to many friends and acquaintances of Donald Crowhurst who gave up time to describe aspects of his life and his preparations for the voyage; in particular to Peter Beard, Ronald Winspear, Edward Longman, Bill Harvey, Eric Naylor and Commander Peter Eden. We have received wise assistance in many matters from the Crowhurst family solicitor, T. J. M. Barrington.

We thank Cassell & Co, for permission to publish extracts from *A World of My Own* by Robin Knox-Johnston, Arthaud, Paris, for permission to reproduce some of Bernard Moitessier's writings, and Weidenfeld and Nicolson for permission to quote from *The Image* by Daniel Boorstin. Our thanks are particularly due to the BBC for providing us with transcripts of Crowhurst's tape recordings, and to Donald Kerr and John Norman of the BBC South and West Region who volunteered their own testimony as actors in the drama.

Rupert Anderson, Receiver of Wrecks, Kingston, Jamaica, gave us enthusiastic help during our inspection of the boat after the voyage, as did his boatman Egbert Knight, who spent two days working with us in blistering heat. Captain Richard Box, of RMV *Picardy* which found Crowhurst's boat, provided invaluable information.

On the immediate task of writing the book, we are indebted most of all to Captain Craig Rich, who spent several weeks investigating every aspect of Crowhurst's navigational record, and prompted many important conclusions. Peter Sullivan was responsible for the detailed drawing of *Teignmouth Electron*, and Michael Woods for the maps. Robert Lindley, the *Sunday Times* correspondent in Buenos Aires, investigated Crowhurst's secret landing in South America, and Chapter Thirteen is based on his account. Ruth Hall undertook the difficult task of deciphering and transcribing Crowhurst's logbooks, and offered many valuable suggestions, as did Claire Tomalin.

Of our colleagues at the *Sunday Times*, our thanks go first to Harold Evans, the editor, who initiated the writing of this book, and spared us from our regular duties while it was in preparation. Robert Riddell, secretary of the Round-the-World race, made his files available to us. Dennis Herbstein, William Elsworth Jones, Philip Norman, Murray Sayle and Jacquey Visick helped us with their own memories of reporting the race. Edwin Taylor and David Gibbons of the *Sunday Times* Art Department designed the picture presentation. Pamela Gordon and Caroline Ritchie researched and typed the text of the book with unfailing energy and accuracy.

We have had invaluable assistance from various experts in relevant fields. One of the judges in the Round-the-World race, Michael Richey, has read the manuscript and offered useful technical comments. So has Dr Glin Bennet, of the Department of

Mental Health, University of Bristol. However, responsibility for the book's conclusions is, of course, entirely our own. Both in nautical and in psychiatric matters we have tried to compromise between the strictly accurate technical expressions and terms comprehensible to ordinary readers.

Above all, our thanks must go to Clare Crowhurst. After the ordeal of many months' inquisition by journalists of every description, she was none the less prepared to re-live all the details of her life with her husband, and every circumstance of his voyage with an honesty and an intelligence that were remarkable. It was not necessary for her to be so frank about a story that must cause her great distress. She clearly felt that Donald Crowhurst was too considerable a man to be remembered with the falsely heroic euphemisms or demeaning sneers of routine journalistic accounts; he needed the whole truth to receive the understanding he deserved. She has read our manuscript for factual accuracy, and although she does not agree with some of our interpretations of her husband's character and actions, has approved publication. We have said this is a story without a hero. The heroine, however, is certainly Clare Crowhurst.

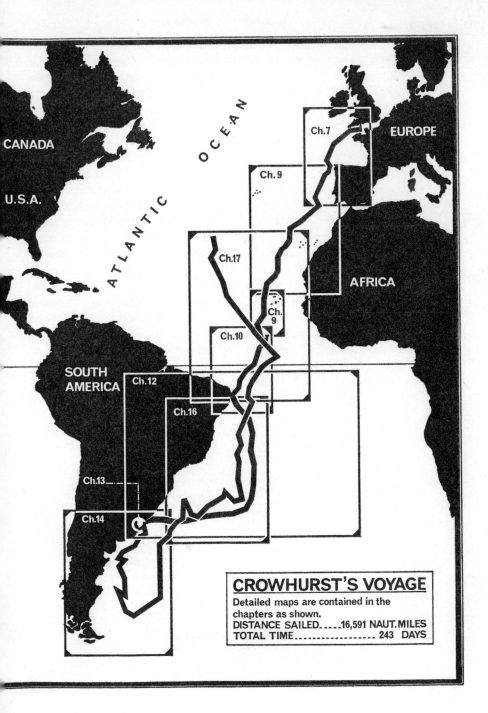

CANADA

U.S.A.

OCEAN

ATLANTIC

EUROPE

AFRICA

SOUTH AMERICA

Ch.7

Ch.9

Ch.17

Ch. 9

Ch.10

Ch.12

Ch.16

Ch.13

Ch.14

CROWHURST'S VOYAGE

Detailed maps are contained in the
chapters as shown.
DISTANCE SAILED......16,591 NAUT. MILES
TOTAL TIME.................... 243 DAYS

Prologue

Captain Richard Box, master of the Royal Mail Vessel *Picardy*, bound from London to the Caribbean, was roused early from his bunk in mid-Atlantic. A small sailing yacht had been spotted, and as this was an unusual place to find such craft, the Chief Officer thought the Captain should have a look at her. The time was 7.50 a.m. on July 10th, 1969; the position was Latitude 33° 11′ North, Longitude 40° 28′ West, about 1,800 miles from England.

As the *Picardy* came closer, Captain Box realised that the craft was a trimaran, and she was ghosting along at scarcely more than two knots, with only a mizzen sail raised. There was no one on deck; her crew was presumably in the cabin, resting or sleeping. Captain Box altered course so that his ship would pass just round the stern of the yacht, and decided to wake whoever was on board. He sounded his foghorn three times, loud enough to awaken the deepest sleeper. Still no response. The trimaran, which he could now see was named *Teignmouth Electron*, continued smoothly and silently on her way.

Perplexed, Captain Box stopped his engines and ordered a boat to be lowered. The situation needed to be properly investigated;

whoever was sailing *Teignmouth Electron* might well be ill, and unable to come on deck. The Chief Officer, Joseph Clark, and a crew of three were lowered in a boat down the side of the *Picardy*, and then chugged the few hundred yards over to the trimaran. Clark stepped on to the wide deck of the trimaran, poked his head into the cabin, and then disappeared for two minutes. The boat was completely deserted. He climbed out again, and gave his Captain a thumbs down signal.

Clark realised immediately that the *Teignmouth Electron*, abandoned in apparently excellent order, presented a complete mystery. The cabin was untidy. Two days' dirty dishes were in the sink. Three radio receivers, two of them disembowelled, stood on the tables and shelf, and radio parts were strewn in confusion everywhere. To one side a soldering iron was balanced precariously on an old milk tin — evidence that the boat had not been hit by any sudden wave or storm. An old, dirty sleeping bag lay on the forward bunk. The supplies of food and water seemed to be adequate. The boat's equipment was in reasonable order, but the chronometer case was empty. The smell in the cabin clearly indicated, to an experienced seaman, that no one had been living there for several days. On deck the life-raft was still firmly lashed in place, the helm was swinging freely. The lowered sails were neatly folded, ready to be raised, and nothing on deck gave any clue to an accident.

Clark next examined three blue-bound logbooks he found piled on the chart table, as if awaiting inspection. They had been methodically kept. The last entry in the navigational log, he found, was for June 24th, more than a fortnight earlier. The last entry in the radio log was for June 29th. At this point it became obvious that the *Picardy* had encountered not only a mysterious tragedy, but one that—with the meticulous logbooks, the missing chronometer, and the apparently tranquil boat—was an uncanny repetition of the famous mystery of the *Mary Celeste*. Ninety-seven years earlier the *Mary Celeste* had also been found inexplicably deserted in the mid-Atlantic—and ever since people have been trying, without success, to discover what had happened to those aboard her.

Meanwhile on board the *Picardy*, someone had remembered the name *Teignmouth Electron*. Wasn't she one of the yachts in the Golden Globe single-handed round-the-world race? Someone else had an old *Sunday Times* cutting with drawings of all the race entrants. There it was: *Teignmouth Electron,* a trimaran ketch. Sailed by Donald Crowhurst, an electronics engineer from Bridgwater, Somerset. Departed Teignmouth, Devon, on October 31st, 1968. Last to set out, but put up a remarkable time round the Roaring Forties to Cape Horn. Now the only yacht left in the race, headed triumphantly for Teignmouth, where she would win a £5,000 prize.

It took about an hour and a half to hoist the trimaran aboard the *Picardy.* The deckhands had to get the heavy derrick rigged, take down the small boat's mizzen, and raise her with care on to the forward cargo hatch. Captain Box sent off a cable describing his mysterious find to the head office of his owners, Furness Withy, in London. They in turn informed Lloyd's and the Navy, who immediately asked the U.S. Air Force to start an air search of the area to see if Crowhurst could be found.

By now it was 10.30 a.m. in mid-Atlantic, early afternoon in London, and although he set course to search, and directed his crew to look for a swimmer, Captain Box was not hopeful that this mysteriously disappeared sailor would be picked up. He was, by now, examining the logbooks himself; if the dates they gave indicated the time Donald Crowhurst went overboard he could certainly not have survived, in those waters, for so long. To all enquirers, including Donald Crowhurst's wife Clare and his agent Rodney Hallworth, Captain Box however merely cabled that the whole thing appeared a complete mystery.

The next day the *Picardy* abandoned her search, and so did the Americans. During the following week, as the vessel sailed towards Santo Domingo, Captain Box read through the three Crowhurst logbooks. They contained, as well as simple navigational and radio details, long personal meditations. There, surely, he would find some clues that would reveal precisely what had happened?

He never found any answers. In fact, the more he read the more insoluble the whole affair seemed. He could find no sign of any impending disaster. The navigation seemed almost over-precise, and the figures indicated—at a quick glance—a successful routine voyage. All the radio messages had apparently been neatly documented. But he did find, on three pages of the last log, evidence that something mysterious and terrible had taken place.

Furthermore, hidden amongst the scrawled philosophical meditations there were odd, cryptic phrases: "Alas, I shall not see my dead father again . . . Nature does not allow God to Sin any Sins except One—That is the Sin of Concealment . . . It is the end of my game, the truth has been revealed and it will be done as my family require me to do it . . ." which complicated the situation. They showed this wasn't a conventional sea mystery, and the missing man wasn't a conventional sailor. An investigation of his strange voyage, and what made him decide to sail round the world, would only begin to reveal the truth. Perhaps the only way to solve the mystery of what happened aboard *Teignmouth Electron* would be to relate the whole story of Donald Crowhurst's life, from the beginning.

One

The Bravest Boy of Them All

Donald Crowhurst was born in India, in 1932. His mother was a schoolteacher, his father a superintendent on the railways, and they lived the uneasy life of second-generation colonials, slightly looked down upon by the military and administrative British, in their turn distinctly superior to the coloured Indians. A photograph of Donald survives, which shows him sitting upon a wicker table in his parents' garden at Ghaziabad near Delhi; his face is pert and cherubic, his hair extraordinary: it hangs down over his shoulders. This style was decreed by Alice Crowhurst because she had hoped for a daughter rather than a son. The boy was very close to his mother in early childhood. As she was religious, so was he. He heard the voice of God speak to him about his mother in church but, when he was about six, it stopped. Why, Donald asked resentfully, did God say no more to him about mummy? From that time onwards his religious fervour and his especial closeness to his mother waned.

At eight, hair now cut short, he was sent off to an Indian boarding school. The custom at the time was for little boys to leave their parents for barbaric, nine-month-long school terms, but he survived the ordeal well. His first report commended him for "an excellent first term", and awarded him a row of orthodox "Very Fairs", "Fairs" and "Goods" in most subjects, particularly Old Testament Divinity. The young boy did not agree with these conventional assessments. Next to each he scrawled his own, self-lacerating comments: "Bad", "Very Bad", "Disgraceful", "Very Bad", "Failed".

In a catechism he was given at this time there are more Crowhurst annotations of a similar nature. "If we have done wrong or harm to anyone," he wrote, "we must confess this to the party concerned first, and then to God. No other confession is ever necessary. Once we have experienced God's power in our lives we can talk to God—direct—each one of us." There is another photograph of him at this time, holding a sailing boat. The boat is only a casual toy, but he was obviously interested in sailing. He owned a booklet called *Heroes All* which included a tale called "Alone Around the World", about an early lone yachtsman called Alain Gerbault. Its message was as clear as the catechism:

Adventure means risking something; and it is only when we are doing that that we know really what a splendid thing life is and how splendidly it can be lived . . . The man who never dares never does; the man who never risks never wins. It is far better to venture and fail than to lie on the hearthrug like a sleepily purring cat. Only fools laugh at failure; wise men laugh at the lazy and the too-contented and at those who are so timid that they dare undertake nothing.

His father, John Crowhurst, was a taciturn man, who performed his duties on the North Western India Railway with competence if not distinction. Alice Crowhurst remembers this marriage as entirely idyllic and her husband as gentle, kind, and always considerate. Others remember him as more complex. According to them there were times when he would visit the railway club after work, drink heavily, and return home truculent and potentially violent. He acted distantly towards his son, performing fatherly duties in a formal manner but never with great ease; he would take Donald for the occasional fishing trip, throw a ball and teach him cricket, but they never had much to say to each other.

When Donald Crowhurst was ten, his parents moved to Multan, a small city in Western Pakistan. There is yet another photograph from this period: Donald in school uniform, his face still cherubic, but fixed in an expression of ferocious determination. The boys who knew him testify that he was the most self-assertive, courageous boy they had ever known; he was so brave, it was odd. He would always lead them, racing up the local water towers which rattled in the high winds off the desert, tripping round the six-inch cat-walks at the top, and mocking them as they shivered in terror half-way up the ladders. If thwarted he could be violent. An Indian watchman who caught him hunting birds in the Multan engine shed found himself suddenly faced with the ten-year-old's airgun. It wasn't loaded, but the gesture succeeded. "All right, all right, Sahib. You carry on shooting."

Family life could be equally tumultuous. The Multan neighbours remember the young Donald being hurriedly handed over the garden wall because his father was coming home drunk. When John Crowhurst got back he started to wreck the deserted house. "Where's my wife? Where's my son?" he shouted, while Donald lay in bed next door enjoying the fuss, keeping his friends awake half the night with vivid stories, imitations, and jokes. Donald was ebullient, sharp with his tongue, a superb mimic. When in the mood he could charm anyone with his warmth and wit. He was as clever as he was brave. Above all, he was brilliant with his hands; he could always fix things.

After the war, Donald Crowhurst was sent back to England to become a boarder at Loughborough College. A letter from the fourteen-year-old schoolboy to his parents was unusual only in its attempt to reassure his mother. Note the doubling of consonants in two of his words. Donald Crowhurst was never good at spelling; the consonant-doubling trick* stayed with him all his life:

Dear Mum and Dad,
    Ta for your letter, it relieved me a great deal to know all is well at home. I received the tennis raquet, its a real beaut. Have you seen it yet? . . .
    I remember the days you taught me, and curse, and as you say, I rebell. But its not against you, its against myself. How I bless *you* for what you taught me, I am *still* reaping the benefit of scraps I remember of what you taught me. How I wish you'd

* We have usually corrected spelling and punctuation in quotations from Crowhurst's letters and writings. His characteristic mistakes were, however, useful clues for reconstruction work in this book: even in typescript it was possible to distinguish Crowhurst's own writing from material drafted for him by his publicity agent and others.

had my full co-operation and that I knew *all* you taught me . . .

Its typical of the Indian in authority nowadays to mess about with your papers for so long. If you do come by boat I hope you don't feel seasick!! I should immagine its worse in an aeroplane! . . .

Well Bye Bye for now

Your everloving Son
Donald

In 1947, the time of India's Independence and Partition, John Crowhurst brought his wife back to England. He put all his retirement savings into a small sportsgoods factory in the new territory of Pakistan which was to be run by a Pakistani partner.

Mr Crowhurst was Alice's second husband, and she had married him late. Her first husband, the dashing Captain David Pepper of the Indian Army, she now remembers only as a man "who made my life a misery with drink and chasing after women". By Captain Pepper she had a first son, Deryk, with whom the elderly couple first went to live on their return to England. Deryk was at this time in the British Army, with a Russian wife and one son Michael.

After a short while, the Crowhurst parents bought their own small house at Tilehurst, near Reading. A letter from Alice Crowhurst to a relative demonstrates both her emotional character and the problems of being poor, cold, and servantless in post-war England after a life in India which, whatever its adversities, was lived on a heroic scale:

My dear Florence,

Hearing from you has thrown a sort of soothing balm over my numb, dazed brain and crushed spirits and made me resolve to pull myself together and face up to things instead of sinking down to the depths as I've been doing lately . . . My husband said to me: "Now we've got the dining room ready could you manage if I got employment? Things in India are going all wrong and I'm afraid my hopes regarding doing wonders with my Sports Business won't materialise. I cannot get an Import Licence." . . .

Within four days he was (*what* do you think, Florence and Robert?) doing a *porter's job* in the co-op jam factory in Reading — I almost went off my head, for over a fortnight daily expecting him to be dead, and could do nothing whatever but prayed

onald Crowhurst: 'I am going because I would have no peace if I stayed'

Donald Crowhurst in the garden of his parents' Indian home at Ghaziabad. The long hair, which he wore until seven years old, was decreed by his mother, who had hoped for a baby girl

John and Alice Crowhurst with their baby son, Donald

Aged seven, with his first sailboat

As a schoolboy, living in Multan (Pakistan)

Donald on his seventh birthday, just before his hair was cut short

The young adventurer. Learning to fly as an Acting Pilot Officer in the Royal Air Force, an[d] trying his hand at motor racing at Brands Hatch

and prayed for him to be given the health and strength. He brings home between £5 and £3-10 every week and gets up at 6 and returns about 7 every evening going part of the way by bus and walks about 20 minutes. He is 51, and landed in England sick at heart and soul-weary. After he and I were expecting him to get even a clerk's job, it was cruel to think of him learning to be a porter — with *his* intelligence, capability, honesty, sincerity of purpose, powers of organisation and love of humanity and the gift of handling men — used to having hundreds of men under him, and now he has to be *one* of a gang of 6 *under* a foreman!!!

Imagine the state of affairs in the house — I too dazed with a sort of band round my heart and a vice tightly clamped round my head — to do what I wanted — and feeling sick — literally — all the time, and sick at heart too, because everything requires to be repaired or mended and painted — particularly the kitchen — and my arm and thigh are so wracked with rheumatic pains and my wrists and fingers suffer so, that I find its all I can do to just carry on . . .

We're both agreed that even if we cannot give Donald his heart's desire to take the Aeronautical Engineering Course at Loughborough — we cannot break into his GLC and he must be kept there till July next year, whatever happens. I wrote to Donald (whom we will have with us for Xmas) at school and have told him, and all he says is he better join something at school and qualify to enable him to choose what he wants to do in the RAF, as that will be the best thing for him to do now after he's passed his GLC!!!! Poor dear, brave lad — God Bless him.

Your loving cousin,
Alice

The year continued, with the Indian sportsgoods factory finally burned down in Partition riots, and John Crowhurst trapped in his porter's job. By Christmas the family had decided their son must definitely leave Loughborough as soon as he had passed his School Certificate. On March 25th, 1948, John Crowhurst fell dead from a coronary thrombosis while digging at the bottom of his garden.

The troubles of the family, which had been critical, suddenly became overwhelming. At sixteen, Donald Crowhurst took his truncated school career philosophically. His one major regret, so he told his wife later, was that his father died before he could get to know him properly. For the first time, since the return to England, they had begun to talk to each other without restraint. For the first time Crowhurst realised that his father, though crushed by circumstance, was a man of considerable intelligence. The shock of the death threw him into his preparations for the coming exam; his diary of that time is filled with admonitions about studying harder. He also had his first serious love affair with a girl at Loughborough. One of his particular beliefs in later life was that sixteen is the crucial age in anyone's life—by that time the child demonstrates what he will become.

Crowhurst took, and passed, the London University School Certificate (still shining at arts subjects, and doing only moderately at science). He then joined the Royal Air Force, starting studies in electronic engineering at Farnborough Technical College. Meanwhile Mrs Crowhurst lived on, in increasing distress, at Tilehurst. A letter from a distant relative in May 1948, puts the position with chilly clarity:

Dear Cousin,

As promised, I send herewith a loan of £5.

We have visitors until Saturday, and then over the week end: so that it would be inconvenient to entertain you until after the middle of next week.

As to Deryk, if I heard you aright on the telephone the £5 is for your and his fare to London, whereas you have told us that he is very well off. We cannot understand the position. Surely he could find a reasonable priced hotel not too far from India House? This would be more convenient for him and more agreeable to us.

Please always write rather than telephone, as you are very difficult to understand on the telephone* and perhaps I have got it all wrong.

If you personally can come to us next Thursday for a few days be sure and bring your ration card. We hope you are getting on alright. We have been looking for a letter from you and wondering how your story is going on . . .

Shortly afterwards, Deryk left his wife. Despite the world-wide

* Alice Crowhurst still speaks with a strong Anglo-Indian accent.

accounts of Crowhurst's voyage he has never contacted any of the family.

* * *

During the next half-a-dozen years, Donald Crowhurst enjoyed himself in the Royal Air Force. He passed his technical examinations, learned to fly, and was commissioned. As a recruit, he had written a youthful essay on "The Necessity of Faith" for his education officer, which presumably had some importance for him, as he kept it carefully in his personal file. It was a typical schoolroom exercise, culminating in the ingenious if cynical conclusion that one should "have faith in the insignificance of Faith". One passage in particular makes an interesting comparison with his later thoughts on the subject:

> The two questions that vex mankind more than any others are perhaps "Why do I live, and what am I when I live no more?" ... Could not the strife to find purpose in life be motivated by the pleasure man derives by endeavouring to show himself (in his own eyes, anyway) equal to the force that drives him and by virtue of his mental strife, overcome this force and drive himself?

(The education officer, in prim red ink, had commented: "Very fair. If you adhere to the views you've expressed you'll find it not easy to take the knocks which will come your way, but you will avoid pitfalls in which lots of other people will flounder.")

But at this time his main preoccupations were far from theological. He had enough money to play the young officer, racing around in a large old Lagonda he managed to buy second-hand. His friends say that as a young RAF officer he had the same mad-cap power to inspire affection and imitation he had had as a boy in Multan. They called him "Crow". Always the wildest, bravest in any group, a compulsive risk-taker and defier of authority, he led his gang of fellow students at Farnborough in riotous saloon bar living. It was always Crowhurst who proposed exploits. He was always the one who bought the first round. His mind moved so much more swiftly and decisively than those around him that it was a nonstop performance: flirtations, intellectual knock-out arguments, insane show-off stunts and practical jokes followed each other at bewildering speed. "Hullo folks!" he would cry, Goon Show style, and everyone would grin weakly and feel things were hotting up. "Let's paint a telephone box yellow (everyone piled into his Lagonda) . . . Who can drink the most gin backwards from a beer glass? . . . I've just built an electric motor boat, who wants a ride? . . . I hear that sniffing mothballs increases potency, let's try!" To anyone immune to such charm it could be infuriating. His friends followed admiringly. It was not so much what he did that impressed them, it was his warmth and the way he made their lives seem more vivid.

Now middle-aged, these men remember him with awe. With some he kept the friendship going long after by surprise visits, his car racing up to their front doors (usually at three in the morning), just as a break in some impromptu cross-country journey. "Hullo folks!" They would cheerfully wake for him, hand out coffee or booze, and let him perform.

He embarked on a passionate love affair with a girl called Enid, whose fickleness kept him mildly in thrall for the rest of his life. To her, Crowhurst wrote mawkish poetry:

Enid's Crow

In the book of life and fate they set a page aside,
Wherein the names of all who loved Enid are by time enscribed,
Look! — What name foots the yet short list?
The ink upon the parchment scarcely dried?

Crow! The faith in his once staid emotions deeply shaken,
Finds some weeks pass by in which his love is for amusement taken,
And then, as always seems to be the case with dogs, affection no
    more
Affords amusement. Time then for a tortured soul to be left
    foresaken.

Profound emotions ever stir and choke
His heart, tear roughly at his mind, and cloak
All senses with that strange and subtle blend of
Bliss and misery all thoughts of her evoke.

The Autumns pass — Death's cancelling line obliterates his name
He joins the oblivious multitude, who all life's tortuous game
Has played; through all the years remains as when first pen
Wet parchment, that tender love he felt for her — the same.

28

Enid was not as scornful of Crowhurst as this mournful verse might suggest.

In the end, Crowhurst was asked to leave the RAF. No one is quite certain why this happened. According to his agent Rodney Hallworth it was because of an incident one night when he rode a powerful motorbike through the sleeping barrack rooms at Farnborough. Another story is that he went off racing at Brands Hatch in his Lagonda on the day of a vitally important parade, and the Station Commander noticed his absence. Whatever happened, it was not serious enough to prevent him promptly enlisting in the army, again being commissioned, and again becoming the leader of a group of racy subalterns, this time at Arborfield, near Reading. He was taking an army course in electronic control equipment.

He was still buying the first round of drinks. He smashed his Lagonda into a bus in the middle of Reading. He was caught two or three times driving without insurance, had his licence confiscated, and continued driving none the less. One night in Reading he tried to borrow a car for the trip back to Arborfield. He was leaning over the engine to connect the ignition wires when a policeman came up behind him. The usual embarrassing dialogue took place:

Constable: "Excuse me sir, is this your car?"
Crowhurst: "Yes, of course, officer."
Constable: "Would you mind telling me the licence number please?"

At this point Donald started running. He leaped into the Reading Canal, but was unfortunately caught on the far bank. In court, a fellow officer testified that they'd all had a beery evening, and he had bet Crowhurst five pounds that he couldn't steal a car for a jape. The escapade cost him a five pound fine at Reading Magistrates' Court and, because the police were at that time conducting a campaign against car thefts, his photograph was sent up to the Scotland Yard Criminal Records Office.

It would have been in keeping with Crowhurst's character to have boasted about this mild indiscretion, but as he grew older something made him socially prudish. He never told his wife or family about it. It was also sufficiently embarrassing for the army authorities at Arborfield to ask him to resign.

Out of the army in 1956, Crowhurst decided on a new ambition: to gain entrance to Peterhouse, Cambridge. They told him he need only pass his Latin qualifying exam to get a place there. He never managed to pass the exam, but in the meantime earned his living by doing research work at Reading University laboratories. He was twenty-four, and considered not only a dashing local figure, but something of an intellectual. A part of this impressive public personality was a set of basic ideas about life, which he would often expound to his friends. He thought, for a start, that life was best looked upon as a game, played in friendly fashion against society, authority, and God (if God existed, which he doubted). This was "life's tortuous game" that he had cited in his poem to Enid. He also thought cleverness was the most important virtue, and stupid people were not particularly worth taking trouble with. He was gradually working out a theory that mind was independent of people's bodies; in a few centuries we could exist without any bodies at all. To the extent that he was religious, his religion was scientific precision: if a thing was true, it must be supremely logical. It must "compute", that is to say it must be so precise that it could be fed into a computer with productive results.

*   *   *

Clare Crowhurst met her future husband at a party in Reading early in 1957. Everyone was consciously bohemian, but although Clare was from Ireland, she had become used to such society in her three years in England. Donald, none the less, mildly surprised her. He came up to her and told her fortune. "You are going to marry an impossible man," he told her. He also said he would never again leave her side. Next evening he came round to take her out, the evening after that, and the next. On the second evening, after seeing *Carousel* at the local cinema, they were walking home when they noticed an old bedraggled prostitute standing in the street. Most of Clare's friends would have automatically recoiled from this local scarlet figure. Donald merely said "Poor old soul. How terrible she should have to earn her living that way." It was a sort of tolerant, sophisticated kindness Clare had not encountered before. She was impressed.

He courted her all that spring and summer. He took her boating at Oxford, and pointed out the hotel where, he said, they would spend their honeymoon. Clare laughed. It was a new approach, but it made an impression. As with many other apparently impulsive things which Donald Crowhurst proposed, that prediction about the hotel came true. They did spend their honey-moon there.

"This is important," says Clare Crowhurst. "Donald had this definite talent. He would say the most amazing things, but then no matter how crazy they seemed, he would be clever and ingenious enough to make them come true. Always. This is a most important point about his character."

Clare Crowhurst comes from Killarney. Her father was an Irish Catholic who farmed just beside Killarney golf links. Her mother, an Anglo-Irish Protestant, was a member of the Talbot family, socially markedly different from her husband. But, says Clare, she loved him deeply and led a very happy, if hard, life. (In his more expansive moments Donald Crowhurst used to confess he was related, through his mother-in-law, to the Guinness family.) When happy, and relaxed, Clare Crowhurst is very Irish, with a wide grin and a jolly way of moving her body. When something reminds her of the tragedies in her life and she has to take hold on herself, the stern Protestant blood of her mother takes over. She becomes visibly thinner, tauter, more formidable. Her voice rises several notes, and her "English" accent overwhelms the Irish.

They were married on October 5th, 1957, at the Roman Catholic Church of the English Martyrs, in Reading. (There was much joking amongst Donald's friends about the English martyr.) For a year they lived with Alice Crowhurst, and their first child James was born. At about this time Crowhurst began sailing seriously.

Then he found a job with Mullards, the electronics firm, and they moved away. The Mullards job, in prospect, was very exciting. Crowhurst was given a car and expected opportunities to do exciting original research. As it turned out, he worked merely as a specially qualified commercial traveller, explaining the intricacies of other men's inventions to impatient customers. He detested the routine, scorned the necessary company politics, and the deathly daily journey to and from the large impersonal London office. After a year he had a car crash. He was repri-manded, took the reprimand badly, and told his superiors very vividly what he thought of them and the job. Then he left.

Donald Crowhurst was now twenty-six. He had started three promising careers and each had collapsed. He was not, and never wanted to be, a good company man. After Mullards, Crowhurst worked for a while in Maidenhead and then, in 1962, found a job in Bridgwater, Somerset, as Chief Design Engineer with another firm, Electro-dynamic Construction. It was merely a way of passing time and earning a living, for he had already decided this wasn't the way he was destined to get rich. What he must do was set up his own business, and sell his own electronic inventions. He spent his time conjuring up new and strange devices and imagining markets for them. This was his habit during the whole time Clare lived with him: to get away from people into a solitary room, to tinker with wires and transistors, to solve problems and create gadgets. Many of Donald Crowhurst's friends referred to him — like the English wartime scientists — as a boffin. The word, with its slightly dated connotations of lonely brilliance and esoteric heroism, says much about his character. It was the most important of the many roles he played to himself and the world. He would emerge from an eight-hour session alone in a workroom with a vacant happy expression, scarcely aware he had a wife, a family, or a non-electronic life.

At about the same time he bought a small, blue, 20-foot sloop called *Pot of Gold*, which he kept at a boatyard near Bridgwater. Sometimes, instead of retreating into his workshop he would scuttle impulsively off to sea. It was, for him, the same kind of solace.

The device which Crowhurst decided would make his fortune was called a "Navicator", a radio direction-finding device for yachting navigation. The Navicator is a well-designed instrument, although there is nothing outstandingly original about it. There are many direction-finding gadgets on the market (indeed, any transistor radio, twisted until a signal is at its loudest, can be used to fix a very rough position) but when first produced the Navicator was among the most convenient of them. It was housed in a neat plastic container that looked like a pistol, with a compass incorporated, so that the entire operation could be done with one hand. Donald, says his wife, had deliberately chosen such an unambitious product as the foundation of his business because he knew the more ingenious devices that he envisaged would be more difficult to market. He decided to call his firm Electron Utilisation.

For three years the Crowhursts lived in a small village just outside Bridgwater, called Nether Stowey. It is a beautiful place in the Quantock Hills, colonised by successful businessmen and professionals from Bridgwater and Taunton who have tidied it up into an almost over-picturesque little community. The Crowhursts were probably at their happiest in Nether Stowey. By the time they left they had three more children; James was followed by Simon in 1960, by Roger in 1961, and Rachel in 1962. Electron Utilisation was still an exciting prospect, there were constant workshop sessions, sailing expeditions, or impulsive rambles up into the Quantock Hills. There were also sympathetic neighbours, the locally unconventional, the more-or-less intellectual. The centre of the local social life was the Amateur Dramatic Society; Donald shone in their theatricals, and made a point of making himself indispensable by reconstructing their lighting system. After play readings or rehearsals, half-a-dozen of the brighter sparks would stay behind, to drink or talk, and generally set the world to rights.

"Donald Crowhurst was the most open-minded man I've ever met," says John Emmett, one of the leaders of this group. "He would talk about anything, anywhere. He was, for instance, a very unsuperstitious man. He was always scornful of religious people. And he finally carried Clare with him in that, I think, although she had already drifted away from Catholicism before she met him. Even so, if someone said something like 'What rot this astrology nonsense is!' he'd pause, and think, and say that nothing could be dismissed with such certainty. After all, it is a well-known scientific fact that the moon can affect people's emotions. Could it not be possible that the stars, in some remote fashion, do so too?"

It was at these late night talk sessions that Donald would once again expound his various theories of life as a game, or the mind existing without the vulgar encumbrance of the body, of truth as something which computed. Clare, who usually had to baby-sit, tended to stay at home.

*　　　*　　　*

Later, in Bridgwater, Crowhurst established a smaller coterie of two married couples, the Winspears and the Beards, whom he would round up on the spur of the moment for expeditions, dinners or elaborate games. Ronald Winspear appealed to the intellectual side of his nature, Peter Beard to the boisterous. Crowhurst needed them both, and their attendant wives, to indulge these two sides of his nature, and they were content to let him show off in front of them because they enjoyed his vivacity and adventurousness. Ronald Winspear is a physicist at Hinkley Point Nuclear Power Station; Peter Beard, born and bred in the

Bridgwater rural working classes, ex-Coldstream Guardsman, is now doing very well making a cheap self-steering gear for yachtsmen.

Obviously, this coterie was not a very cohesive group; intellectual discourse and boisterous antics do not mix easily. When Crowhurst and Ron Winspear plunged deep into discussions of metaphysics or workers' co-partnership, Peter Beard looked bored. When Crowhurst embarked on adventure with Peter, or was telling the whole bar how he was worth £40,000 and would thrash any man who doubted him, Ron Winspear would look disapproving. In particular, the Beards and Clare Crowhurst did not get on.

When asked about Donald Crowhurst, the two men friends offer interestingly contrasting opinions. Peter Beard says: "The thing about Donald was that he thought himself God. Everything in his life revolved about his belief in himself, and he was always so quick and clever he could make others believe in him too. He thought he was so wonderful—and he was, a smashing bloke, a genius. But he wasn't God, and that's why all his troubles were his own fault."

Ronald Winspear says: "I did not worship Donald Crowhurst; I *recognised* him—as the most vivid and real person I have ever met. When he tried to impress people, selling himself, there was something a little second-rate about him. But when he knew he didn't need to perform, he would relax and simply be impressively alive. Donald was not a man to go into business with. But he was one very much to be admired."

The problem for a man as intelligent as Donald Crowhurst— and there can be no doubt that he was very intelligent indeed—is that living in a rural, provincial town like Bridgwater, there were too few people to exercise his intelligence against. It became largely a means to show off in front of others. If Crowhurst had managed to get into Cambridge, his intelligence would have been disciplined, and humbled, by equally clever rivals and friends. At the same time he would not have felt the frustrations of the provincial intellectual, constantly thinking that he was worthy of better things than his confined world could offer, and looking on the larger world with envious scorn.

In the one field where he had a disciplined training, electronic engineering, Crowhurst was highly sophisticated, and impressive in his original ideas. For someone with an engineering background he was also surprisingly literate. Though only patchily read, he was well able to use literary devices in conversation, argument and writing.

On the other hand, he lacked the intellectual control and restraint that derives from a more formal general education. In his writing he often seemed unable to distinguish between good and bad. He would write well-constructed, lively prose that was marred by simple mis-spellings and sudden plunges into banality. Similarly, as a mathematician and engineer, he would tackle advanced problems in a confident and inventive way—but then would get a simple addition sum wrong. His failures would drive him into prolonged depressive sulks, which he could only break out of with another burst of manic high-spirits.

A character like Crowhurst will be familiar to anyone who has read the novels of provincial life of H. G. Wells, or C. P. Snow. Like their small town intellectuals, he had a strong sense of resentment against the bigger world that had not opened its gates to him. The characters in both Wells's and Snow's novels some-times won success in the big world, and this mellowed and educated them. Crowhurst was desperate for a similar success, but had not—as yet—learnt the rules of that particular game.

* * *

In 1962 Donald Crowhurst's mother became a problem to the family in an unexpected way. While staying with the family the bewilderment and distress of her confined life suddenly over-whelmed her. Donald, bringing in her breakfast on a tray one morning, saw his mother place a pile of sleeping pills on the palm of her hand and stuff them into her mouth. Before he could reach her, they were swallowed. She was rushed to hospital, where the pills were pumped out of her. She has lived in various hospitals, and a home for old people near Bridgwater almost ever since.

After a few years Donald decided to ask his mother to sell her house at Tilehurst, and to use some of the profits from the sale to launch his own firm, Electron Utilisation. This she readily agreed to, and the capital was enough to start manufacture of the first batch of Navicators. He threw himself into the firm with violent energy, convinced it would be a success. He visited London and tried to establish firm marketing arrangements there, advertised in all the yachting magazines and even ventured off to the Continent on selling trips.

A year or two later he had a chance to exercise his ambition for local power by standing as a Liberal councillor. He was asked to be a candidate for the Bridgwater Central Ward, and won the election with an image he skilfully projected of himself as a businessman with all the management skills required to solve Bridgwater's industrial problems. His election manifesto was a mock computer programme. "You may think you are logical, but DARE YOU do this test?" it shouted at the voters, and took them through a series of political questions with alternative answers leading to different numbered sections. Needless to say, the truly logical voter had, inexorably, to vote for the supremely logical, technological, financially experienced candidate: Donald Crowhurst. Liberalism computed.

Around this time, Crowhurst bought himself a new Jaguar car. He drove it far too fast, and after six months had another crash. The car turned over, and he received a nasty gash on his forehead. His wife detected a change in his personality after this crash. He became more moody, less efficient at business, and spent long hours in the living-room at Woodlands staring sulkily at the carpet. If things frustrated him he would burst into violent fits of temper. A drawer that lacked what he was seeking would suddenly be up-ended, its contents strewn all over the floor, while Donald stamped around the room. With his children, however, he was always gentle. Each time he arrived home they would run up the drive to meet him. He would pick up all four in his arms and walk into the house with them, telling stories to the giggling bundle as he deposited it, softly, in a living-room armchair. They worshipped him.

He became interested in the supernatural again. He still professed to be a complete sceptic; God was not for him. However he now tried a couple of table-tapping sessions with the Winspears and the Beards, and also experiments in thought transference. One day, so Mrs Beard says, he took her up to The Mound, a lonely hill above Nether Stowey, and told her he believed in black magic, and she must become his blood sister. He gave her his shirt to wear, murmured incantations, cut his arm, and smeared some blood on her wrist. This, he said, bound her to him for life; she would discover special markings that proved it. Four days later, she says, a row of weals came up on her wrist. Whether it was all a joke, or Crowhurst playing God, or all in deadly earnest, Pat Beard did not enjoy the experience.

On another occasion someone bought a pack of Tarot cards,

and Donald began telling people's fortunes. Late in 1966, just as *Gipsy Moth IV* was approaching Australia, Crowhurst and his friends tried out the Tarot pack on Francis Chichester. Card after card came up predicting death, drowning and disaster. Crowhurst, fascinated, kept turning up more and more cards, watching Chichester head towards catastrophe. Suddenly Clare, who took it very seriously, cried out that this kind of jape was very distasteful — would everyone please go home?

*　　*　　*

Initially Crowhurst's firm, Electron Utilisation, had looked a success. He rented a small factory and employed six full-time workers. The design of the Navicator attracted the attention of Pye Radio which began take-over negotiations and paid Crowhurst £8,500. However this deal went no further. Pye, with boardroom troubles of its own, pulled out. The money that Crowhurst had received helped to keep the firm prosperous for a while, but soon things started to go wrong. Crowhurst left his factory, moved his operation in the Woodlands stables, and reduced his workers to one part-time electronics assembler. He was never able to make lasting marketing arrangements to sell the Navicator efficiently, and spent most of his time scraping round for enough capital to buy the components needed, particularly the Navicator compass, which he had to buy ready-made at £3.10.0 a time.

Searching for other financial support, Crowhurst was introduced to Stanley Best, who became his backer in Electron Utilisation, and ultimately sponsored his attempt to sail around the world. Best is a Taunton businessman who has succeeded in precisely the way Crowhurst hoped to. He has achieved this with a very different temperament and method: dogged, methodical sales of petrol and caravans have made him a rich man. He has a lot of capital to invest, and in 1967 he lent £1,000 to Electron Utilisation to tide it over what Crowhurst considered was merely a temporary tight patch. The loan lasted into 1968, but troubles multiplied, marketing partners came and went, and the temporary tight patch continued.

It took Stanley Best a long time to realise that Electron Utilisation was not, after all, a firm that was going to make him a second fortune. Crowhurst's persuasive dash kept his confidence long after the balance sheets flagged.

"I always considered Donald Crowhurst an absolutely brilliant innovator," he says. "In a workshop or laboratory he was superb. But as a businessman, as someone who had to know how the world went, he was hopeless. He was so much on the move all the time he never appreciated what was really happening. He seemed to have this capacity to convince himself that everything was going to be wonderful, and hopeless situations were only temporary setbacks. This enthusiasm, I admit, was infectious. But, as I now realise, it was the product of that kind of over-imaginative mind that was always dreaming reality into the state it wanted it to be."

This was a neat summing-up of Crowhurst the Bridgwater businessman; it was to be an even better summing-up of Crowhurst the aspirant hero.

Two

The Great Race

Late in May 1967, Francis Chichester sailed single-handed home into Plymouth to fame and considerable fortune. The British public had unpredictably decided to create him a hero, as in the past it had singled out Scott (of the Antarctic), Hillary (of Everest) and Bannister (of the Mile) for national adulation. A quarter of a million people lined Plymouth Hoe that evening, virtually every small craft in the district formed into a vast welcoming armada, national television schedules were abandoned for hours of live coverage, a knighthood—already conferred in Australia—was hastily dubbed at Greenwich, and the book that quickly followed was one of the most profitable best-sellers for years.

The extent to which Chichester's circumnavigation caught the public imagination had surprised everyone connected with the voyage, not least his newspaper sponsors, the *Sunday Times*. Chichester, it is true, had sailed round the world faster and more stylishly than anyone before, and had restricted himself to only one stop. But there was nothing essentially new about the feat: it had first been done as long ago as 1895–98 by Joshua Slocum and had been repeated by several others since—all making several

39

stops. American news-magazine essayists, puzzled as always by British reflexes, attempted lengthy explanations of the phenomenon: with the Empire gone and with no money to send men to the moon, the British had reverted to the purer, nobler, uncomplicated heroics of conquering the elements. As we shall see, the motivation of men involved in this kind of adventure and the mechanics of public response to them are scarcely as simple as that.

The *Sunday Times* had at first been somewhat hesitant in supporting Chichester's voyage. It had initially turned the idea down flat (as had the *Daily Mirror* and the *Daily Telegraph* when it was first offered to them). Eventually it agreed to buy—for £2,000—half the newspaper rights in only half the voyage, as far as Australia, with an option to renew. Public interest was so low in the early months that the price seemed none too cheap, and indeed the other newspaper sponsor, *The Guardian* (in one of its periodic economy drives) had to drop out when Chichester was only half-way round. However the *Sunday Times* continued its sponsorship, Chichester fever—encouraged by his regular and lively dispatches—began to take hold, and by the time the cheering quarter-million were gathered on Plymouth Hoe it was clear it had got itself one of the newspaper bargains of the century. As a result, the newspaper was afterwards well-disposed to further seagoing adventures. This was particularly so after Harold Evans, the only *Sunday Times* editorial executive who had displayed early enthusiasm for the Chichester venture, became the newspaper's editor. But the problem, after the saturation of salt-water narrative that Chichester had inspired, was finding new variations on the theme.

* * *

There was one surprising absentee from the welcome-home armada for Chichester. Donald Crowhurst admired Chichester inordinately. He had bought and studied all his books and had been following his trip closely; but some jealously sceptical spirit made him avoid the last moment of triumph. Instead of travelling the short distance to Plymouth, he spent part of the day sailing in the Bristol Channel with Peter Beard before returning home to watch it on television. The two men had listened in a scornful mood, as hour upon hour of commentary had poured from the yacht radio. Crowhurst pranced mockingly around the deck, parodying announcers, cheering crowds and mayoral welcoming committee. What, he asked, was all the fuss about? Chichester wasn't the first man round the world. He clearly had a hopeless boat. And he'd stopped off for a long rest in Australia. The only remarkable thing about the voyage, declared Crowhurst, was Chichester's old age.

Donald Crowhurst claimed, even then, to have the ambition to sail alone and *non-stop* around the world—which really would be a "first" that would add his name to the immortals. He had, he said, conceived the idea four years previously. It was true that in the meantime he had also flirted with other maritime projects without actually putting them into effect. He had thought of imitating Thor Heyerdahl's primitive, unguided and well-publicised raft flotations, and even more of reproducing Alain Bombard's lone trip from the Canaries to Barbados on a diet of raw fish and plankton, which appealed simultaneously to his love of the dramatic and the scientific. But from the time of Chichester's return, it was the idea of a non-stop circumnavigation that increasingly dominated his thoughts.

The continuing lionisation of Sir Francis and the evident financial success of his venture can hardly have damped Crowhurst's enthusiasm. For Chichester, there were mounting commercial royalties, endorsements, and lecture and television fees, to say nothing of the income from a dozen translations of his book and the new impetus given to his small map and guide-book business. By now, Electron Utilisation Ltd was faltering, and Crowhurst needed an heroic achievement for more reasons than one.

*   *   *

His response to the Chichester voyage was by no means unique. It is, after all, natural enough when something is achieved to look for ways of going one better. Apart from simply trying to make the voyage faster (which Chichester's earliest imitator, Alec Rose, had no hope of doing), the only way of capping his achievement was to go round the world without stopping.

By the end of 1967, at least four yachtsmen were taking practical steps to do precisely that. They may all have been over-optimistic even to consider the possibility. Chichester himself, it must be remembered, for all his great experience, had difficulty even in reaching Australia; and Rose was forced into an unplanned stop at New Zealand as well as calling at Sydney. Success would require a boat, seamanship and personal qualities of the highest order, plus a good deal of luck. But Chichester had demonstrated that the rewards, spiritual and temporal, from such a venture might more than outweigh the risk.

The first man with a workable scheme was an ex-naval submarine commander, Bill Leslie King, who was making firm plans within three months of Chichester's return. Realising that much would depend on the boat itself, he approached Colonel "Blondie" Hasler, the man who some years previously had given the big impetus to solo sailing by inventing a self-steering gear designed to operate on all points of sailing. Hasler was asked to help prepare the perfect boat for a circumnavigation, which was to be specially built; he agreed to design the rig, and selected Angus Primrose as the best man to design the hull. The resultant craft, rounded and smooth with a flush "turtle-back" deck was appropriately reminiscent of a submarine, apart from the incongruous superimposition of two junk-rigged masts. Building of the boat—named *Galway Blazer II*—started at the end of the year, and as early as the Boat Show in January 1968 it was announced that King already had newspaper sponsors, the *Daily* and *Sunday Express*.

Even before King's scheme got under way, a twenty-eight-year-old merchant navy officer, Robin Knox-Johnston, was also trying to get a boat specially built for a non-stop circumnavigation. He started discussing designs in April—seven weeks before Chichester's return—and soon had a builder. But after spending months trying unsuccessfully to raise the money he had to drop the plan. Undeterred, he decided before the end of the year to attempt the voyage in *Suhaili*, the tiny 32-foot teak-hulled Bermudan ketch he already owned. The boat was, on the face of it, most unsuitable. She was too small and slow, and her high, vulnerable deck-house produced shudders from more experienced sailors. Only two things could be said in her favour: she had been well-tried on a voyage from India, where she had been built for Knox-Johnston four years previously; and she was remarkably well-balanced and easy to sail.

Once his mind had been made up, Knox-Johnston made the wise move of bringing a London literary agent, George Greenfield, into the project. Greenfield's agency, having flourished for some years, not least on the fortunes of the Enid Blyton books, had more recently come to make a speciality of adventurers—yachtsmen, explorers, mountaineers and the like. In the whole complex process of hero-creation, there is no more adept exponent than Green-field. Chichester, himself, was one of his clients. At the time of the Knox-Johnston approach, the agency was working on the build-up of Wally Herbert and the British trans-Arctic expedition. Greenfield immediately saw excellent material in the determined young man with his boy-next-door charm and started to set up sponsors. His judgment was impeccable as always: Knox-Johnston throughout the project turned out to have an uncanny gift for saying and doing the right thing; not least in actually completing the voyage.

As we shall see, stability of mind proved to be a crucial factor in subsequent events. Robin Knox-Johnston, like his boat, was the best-balanced of all those who set out. His only eccentricity, for one so young, was an unfashionable tendency to very right-wing and blimpish views, but even they are not uncommon among adventurers and heroes. Before and after his voyage, he was sent to a psychiatrist so that the mental effect could be studied. "I am delighted to say," wrote Knox-Johnston after-wards, "that on both occasions he found me 'distressingly normal'."

Nobody could accuse the next yachtsman to declare his hand, Bernard Moitessier of France, of being "distressingly normal". Amongst long-distance sailors he was already a legendary figure. He had sailed many thousands of miles in the Pacific and had in 1966 completed the (then) longest non-stop voyage by small sailing boat—14,216 miles from Tahiti to Spain via Cape Horn, accompanied by his wife, Françoise. A sensitive and literate writer, he had written two classic books of the sea: *Un Vagabond des Mers du Sud* and *Cap Horn à la Voile*.

Like Crowhurst, Moitessier had a colonial background—he had been brought up in French Indo-China. But there all similarity ends. Moitessier, a strong, wiry man, is by temperament a true romantic with an almost mystical feeling for the sea. And the thing he hates above all on board a sailing boat is anything to do with electronics.

Moitessier had formulated his plans for the voyage before the end of 1967; he spent January in Paris at the French Boat Show, making detailed preparation of his equipment; he then left for Toulon to begin several months of careful work fitting out his boat, *Joshua*, for the voyage. *Joshua*, five years old, with tens of thousands of miles behind it, had been built as tough and rugged as a trawler and, though bearing the scars of a hard life, it was still absolutely sound. She had a great welded steel hull painted red, two chunky masts of solid wood, and a primitive self-steering gear which may have lacked the sophistication of a Hasler, but looked infinitely less delicate. *Joshua* possessed, wrote Moitessier, the secret of all good boats: "Solid, simple, sure—and fast on all points of sailing."* No boat could have been more different from the one in which Crowhurst eventually set sail.

Finally, at the end of 1967, John Ridgway, a formidably fit captain in the Special Air Service, was applying for leave to make his own attempt. He had already achieved fame in 1966 by rowing across the Atlantic with Sergeant Chay Blyth, and had become something of a professional adventurer. He had no particular distinction as a yachtsman, and his sloop, *English Rose IV*, was notable only for its small size (30 feet). He seemed to regard the trip mainly as an exercise in physical survival, and on that level, at least, nobody could have been better equipped.

*   *   *

That was the line-up in January 1968—the old salt who loved pottering about in boats, the determined young man who wanted to do something for Britain, the romantic Frenchman who needed to commune with the sea, and the professional adventurer who wished to display his toughness. Crowhurst's motivations were less easy to define. They were certainly not unconnected with the decline of his business, which by now had reached a crisis that even he had to acknowledge. But, as before in his life when conditions were hostile, he was looking for a dramatic gesture, seeking to make a permanent mark on a world that did not appreciate him. The way he set about the task was characteristically flamboyant.

It had already been decided that Sir Francis Chichester's boat, *Gipsy Moth IV*, should be embalmed in concrete at Greenwich, as a permanent memorial to his epic voyage. Some of the money for the job had been raised, and construction of the shrine was about to begin.

Crowhurst telephoned the Town Clerk of Greenwich to explain that it would be madness to put *Gipsy Moth IV* to sleep, and he had a better idea. He followed it up in mid-January with a letter. If they would only let him have the craft for a year, he argued, he

* *Cap Horn à la Voile*, Arthaud, Paris, 1967.

would sail non-stop round the world and then hand over all the money he would undoubtedly gain from the feat. The letter concluded:

Firstly let me say that I know myself to be competent to undertake this voyage in a seamanlike manner. I believe there is not a single hazard attendant upon my proposal that I have not considered, whether it may lie in the yacht, in the elements and the sea, or in myself. There are risks in such a project, but I ask you to share them with me not only because they are acceptable but also because our tradition as a seafaring nation demands that we accept them.

The tone of the letter was pure Crowhurst, and most convincing. However, Mr Doble, the Town Clerk, did not respond. He wrote a formal reply, stating that he didn't feel his council had any discretion in the matter. He passed Crowhurst's letter, and the buck, to the Cutty Sark Society, which was responsible for putting *Gipsy Moth IV* on display. The Society decided to take no action. Their plan, which also involved two local councils and Lord Dulverton, the owner of *Gipsy Moth IV*, was already too firm to change.

However, Crowhurst continued his campaign. Some weeks later he telephoned the Cutty Sark Society, and spoke to Frank Carr, Chairman of the Ship Management Committee. This exchange was far more colourful. Both were men of strong vision and feeling, with a penchant for rhetoric. They talked on the telephone and Crowhurst expanded his original offer to an immediate £5,000 donation, plus any prize money won, plus insurance cover of £10,000.

Frank Carr told Crowhurst, privately, that he didn't think the boat was a very suitable one for the voyage, quoting Sir Francis's own scathing criticisms of her. He thought it unwise to risk such a notable heroic symbol at sea. As to the offer of prize money, he pointed out that the Cutty Sark Society had already committed £17,000 to building the dry-dock at Greenwich, and Crowhurst's offer scarcely touched this amount, let alone the value of the boat.

Crowhurst, in the meantime, was acquiring some powerful allies. While selling Navicators at the Boat Show in January 1968, he diligently lobbied influential figures. Angus Primrose, the co-designer of *Gipsy Moth IV*, as well as designer of Bill King's *Galway Blazer II*, remembers being approached. He was highly impressed by Crowhurst's enthusiasm and yachting knowledge. Ultimately, the yachting journals took Crowhurst's side: Anthony Churchill in *Yachting and Boating Weekly* and Bernard Hayman in *Yachting World* thundered ferociously that boats, even famous ones, were meant for sailing, not for museum displays, and that Donald Crowhurst's enterprise was worth more than pleasing a lot of curious schoolchildren.

The final result of this battle of wills was unpleasant for everyone. Crowhurst lost his boat and Frank Carr lost the goodwill of the yachting public who responded with seafaring enthusiasm to the journalistic protests, and contributed meagrely to the *Gipsy Moth* Fund.

Although Frank Carr, and all others concerned, had openly mounted the obvious arguments against Crowhurst's proposals, it is possible that behind these was an even more powerful argument. Sir Francis Chichester, though not the formal owner of the boat, had been consulted; he had asked his friends about Donald Crowhurst. None of them could give him any evidence of the man's competence beyond his own bland assertions. So Crowhurst's scepticism was returned with devastating effect. Sir Francis's instinctive suspicions never waned; they played an increasing part in the Crowhurst story.

If the Cutty Sark Society *had* accepted Crowhurst's offer of an immediate donation, where would the money have come from? Or if he had a boat specially built, who would finance it? Crowhurst had not the slightest idea, despite his grandiloquent claims. The problem was clearly exercising him, because in his personal diary of the period he painstakingly listed every press baron and virtually every industrial philanthropist in Britain. He wrote down, for instance, the home telephone number of Lord Thomson of Fleet, discovered the name of his valet, and ascertained the exact time when Thomson normally rose in the morning. Precisely five minutes after that time, he telephoned Lord Thomson's home.

"Is that Paxton?" he said to the valet in his most peremptory subaltern's voice. "This is Donald Crowhurst and I want to speak to Lord Thomson."

According to Crowhurst's own account, Lord Thomson was just at that moment descending the stairs to breakfast. The bold approach succeeded: Thomson took the receiver. Crowhurst then proceeded to suggest to him that it would be a marvellous idea if *The Times* or the *Sunday Times* sponsored a non-stop voyage round the world. Or perhaps even a *race* round the world. And he, Crowhurst, would very much like to take part as he was sure to win. And perhaps Lord Thomson might like to help him with his entry?

Lord Thomson cannot now remember the conversation. It is not unusual for lobbyists and even cranks to try to approach him on his private telephone. If they get through, he hastily tells them to contact the appropriate editor; or simply does not listen. Certainly, on this occasion, he did nothing about the suggestion. But, by coincidence, only two weeks after Crowhurst's call, the *Sunday Times* did announce a round-the-world race. Crowhurst was thereafter convinced that the whole thing was his own idea — and in several subsequent letters he referred to himself as the originator of the race. Considering the coincidence, he had some reason.

*   *   *

The genesis of the *Sunday Times* race, however, was quite different. It is worth describing in some detail, because its rather odd formulation was to become an important component in the events that led to the Crowhurst tragedy.

In early January 1968, George Greenfield told Harold Evans, the *Sunday Times* editor, about his new young protégé, Robin Knox-Johnston. He wanted the newspaper to sponsor his voyage in the same way as it had sponsored Chichester. Evans listened sympathetically, but deferred his decision.

A month later, with Greenfield still pressing for an answer, Murray Sayle, the *Sunday Times* reporter who had handled the Chichester story, was assigned to take soundings. Bill King's plans were already public knowledge, and Sayle quickly picked up rumours of other probable starters, now growing in number. He also sounded yachting opinion about likely performances.

Sayle reported back — quite wrongly as it turned out, but understandably — that the one who certainly wouldn't win was the unknown young Knox-Johnston in his scruffy little ketch. The boat he tipped as most likely to succeed was a catamaran sailed by an Australian-born dentist called Howell, known in yachting circles as "Tahiti Bill".

So the *Sunday Times* started to get interested in Tahiti Bill. The trouble from a journalistic point of view was that coverage of the voyage, even a non-stop one, would inevitably be too similar to that of Chichester; and there had already been signs that the readers were surfeited. It was at this stage that Sayle and the head of his department, Ron Hall (one of the authors of this book), came up simultaneously with the idea of holding a race, though they had different views about its organisation. Sayle argued that the only thing that mattered to the hero-worshipping public was who got back home *first*. Hall argued that for the event to have the proper flavour of a race, competitors must have an equal chance; and since, for various reasons, they would all be setting off at different times, victory would need to be calculated on an "elapsed time" basis. The prize, in other words, should be awarded for the *fastest* voyage.

There was another problem. Sayle now knew that there would be at least half-a-dozen yachtsmen attempting non-stop circum-navigations that season, and some were already making arrangements with other newspapers, magazines and publishers. What if one of them refused to enter — and then completed the voyage first? The *Sunday Times* race would lose all point.

With this in mind, Sayle and Hall sat down that afternoon in early March 1968 to draft the rules. The first conflict was easy to resolve: why not have two prizes, one for the first and one for the fastest? The first home, it was decided, would be given a trophy (it acquired its name, though not its substance, there and then: the Golden Globe). And there would be a £5,000 cash prize for the fastest voyage.

The other problem was more difficult. It was got round by not requiring the contestants formally to "enter" the race at all. If someone set out, and had the dates of his departure and arrival recorded by a national newspaper or magazine, then he would automatically become eligible for the prize or Golden Globe. The event was therefore more in the style of the famous Northcliffe prizes for air pioneering than of the *Observer*'s Transatlantic Single-handed Race, with which it invited more immediate comparison.

The advantage of this arrangement was that nobody could *not* take part; it was, as someone said, rather like a horse setting off for a canter across Epsom Downs and suddenly finding itself taking part in the Derby. The disadvantage was that the *Sunday Times* could not, strictly speaking, require any "vetting" of participants for technical and mental suitability. They might be accused of irresponsibly encouraging the unqualified to take risks. However, as the next best thing, a prestigious panel of judges was set up under the chairmanship of Sir Francis Chichester.* Their job was not only to make sure that the voyages were properly completed without putting into port and without outside assistance, but also to use their influence to advise of the dangers and dissuade rash competitors from setting out. As it happened, a number of starters were successfully talked out of going, including a youth with a home-made yacht in the Outer Hebrides, who nearly had to be made a ward of court.

Of those who did start, the only one who gave pause for thought was the Atlantic rower Chay Blyth, who, with only a few days' sailing experience, set off in an ordinary production cruising yacht in emulation of his rowing compatriot, John Ridgway. Even so, it would have needed a brave vetting panel to refuse an entry to a man who had survived the Atlantic for ninety-two days in a rowing boat, on the grounds that he was a danger to himself. As for the plausible Donald Crowhurst, it is certainly unlikely that any vetting panel would have turned him down. He had, after all, only recently convinced half the yachting world that he was the ideal man to sail *Gipsy Moth IV*.

Some final refinements were made to the rules. Because it was thought dangerous to encourage anyone to arrive in the Southern Ocean before the end of the southern winter, or still not to be past Cape Horn before the beginning of the following winter, starting dates were restricted to June 1st to October 31st, 1968. The October deadline played a crucial part in the Crowhurst story.

The start and finish of the "elapsed time" race had to be a port in the British Isles. But to make sure that Moitessier, if he insisted on starting from Toulon, would be included, the Golden Globe for the first man home, was left open to anyone sailing from any port north of 40° N. (This proved unnecessary. One of the first tasks in setting up the race was to despatch Murray Sayle to France to persuade Moitessier to bring his boat to England. The Frenchman explained that he was going for the good of his soul, and didn't want to be part of any race; but he finally relented, on the whimsical ground that he liked Sayle's face.)

On March 17th, 1968, the *Sunday Times* announced its race, and

* The members were: Mr Michael Richey, Executive Secretary of the Institute of Navigation, M. Alain Gliksman, editor of *Neptune Nautisme* and well-known French yachtsman, Mr Denis Hamilton, Chief Executive and Editor-in-Chief of Times Newspapers, and Colonel "Blondie" Hasler (who later dropped out because he felt too closely identified with the King voyage).

it created a flurry of interest in the yachting press. Within four days Crowhurst had declared himself a competitor. He was described for several months in the editorial columns as the "mystery yachtsman", because he seemed to be keeping his plans very much to himself. In fact there was no mystery about it. At that stage, he still did not have a boat, nor any money to have one built.

Three

The Revolutionary Boat

        For two months after the announcement of the race, Donald Crowhurst continued, even intensified, his doomed campaign to borrow *Gipsy Moth IV*. Lord Dulverton, the boat's legal owner, was lobbied, but bleakly refused support. With persistence born of his wounded feelings, Crowhurst again contacted the Cutty Sark Society. He wanted his "competence, and physical and mental stamina" to be put on trial. He wrote to Frank Carr:

That you should have serious reservations about my ability to carry my plan through is understandable and indeed sound. A method by which the point may be proved would appear to be a short passage of a few hundred miles simulating single-handed conditions under observation. It would seem fair that two observers should be selected, one each. Obviously they must be men whose integrity and knowledge of the sea we can both accept, and I would readily agree to yourself as one, should you wish it. If it seemed that I was endangering the yacht due to lack of skill, the observer could of course act as crew. The issue could be settled by the appropriate committee if a difference of

opinion remained, though I would hope that this was unnecessary.

This could be seen as the salesman's habitual device of a free-
trial-without-obligation. But it was also part of Crowhurst's urge,
at times of rejection, to prove himself by formal examination,
almost by ordeal. When his father died, and lack of money
catapulted him out of Loughborough, his childish diary was filled
with daily admonitions about his coming School Certificate; he
must *work harder*. When he was asked to leave the army he was
obsessed with the idea of passing the Latin exam and making
Cambridge. When the Mullards job failed, it was Electron Utilisation and sailing. When Electron Utilisation failed, it was circumnavigation. Each newly sought challenge both concealed failure,
and put off the final judgment. He was gay and supremely convincing while he lived with such obsessions, but they were obsessions none the less.

Throughout his disputation with Frank Carr and the Cutty Sark
Society, Crowhurst had repeatedly and unblinkingly asserted that
he regarded *Gipsy Moth IV* as "the most suitable boat for the
voyage in existence". Did he really believe this? Apart from his
brief chat with Angus Primrose, the only direct information he
had about her was what he had read in Chichester's book, which
had poured pages of abuse on her design and behaviour. This
wasn't, therefore, a detached judgment; it was a belief created
by his need to sail round the world. When, for whatever reason,
Crowhurst had set his mind on some course of action, he would
employ remarkable dialectical skill to justify his decision to the
world—and to himself.

As he at last sensed defeat in the *Gipsy Moth* controversy, Crowhurst was also finding out if he could have a boat specially built.
Once again, he had absolutely no doubt about the kind of boat he
wanted; but it was a totally different breed from *Gipsy Moth*. He
had suddenly become a partisan of trimarans.

It was a questionable choice for single-handed cruising; many
yachtsmen regard trimarans as unsafe unless the helm is continuously manned. Their performance at sea—very fast before the
wind, but poor to windward—is totally different from traditional
monohulls. They do not capsize easily, but if they do they stay
upside down. But Donald Crowhurst was soon drafting long,
didactic letters to the yachting journals justifying the use of

trimarans for round-the-world racing in even less equivocal terms than he had previously used for *Gipsy Moth*. The most remarkable thing about his new-found enthusiasm was that—although he had some experience aboard twin-hulled catamarans—he had formed his views on trimarans without ever having sailed in one.

*　　　*　　　*

It was, by now, the middle of May and time was ticking on towards the October deadline. The first two competitors, John Ridgway and Chay Blyth, were within a few days of setting sail, and Knox-Johnston was in the final phase of preparation. A second seasoned French yachtsman, Loick Fougeron, had joined the race and was preparing to set out for England. He, too, had a well-tried, steel-hulled boat. Crowhurst, still without boat or sponsor, remained euphoric. Time and again he told friends like John Emmett or Peter Beard that he was going to be the man who first sailed unaided round the world. What Chichester had called the "Everest of the Sea" was, he said, designed for him to conquer.

Meanwhile, Stanley Best, examining the Electron Utilisation account books with his methodical eye, had finally decided he must pull out. He therefore asked for his money back. For a while the two men corresponded and argued over the situation, Crowhurst eternally optimistic and sparkling with fresh ideas, Best adamant but—in his fashion—understanding.

It was by a calculated afterthought to one of these letters on May 20th, that Donald Crowhurst pulled off the greatest persuasive coup of his life. In some way that Best, always the most unimpressionable of men, still cannot fully understand, Crowhurst convinced him that his best possible financial investment was to put up the money for a boat to sail around the world.

Crowhurst's letter, which again conveyed the self-confident manner of total competence he could bring to any project, set out with great clarity the advantages and drawbacks of trimarans:

... There are technical hazards in such an attempt that can be carefully evaluated so that procedures can be worked out to deal with them well in advance. And with modern equipment one's survival is almost certain, even in the very unlikely event of serious difficulty ...

The really exciting prospect is the possibility of a trimaran equipped with various safety mechanisms that I have designed for use in trimarans. (Trimarans are, as you probably know, a new and rather controversial type of boat having three hulls.) . . . What does emerge quite clearly is that the trimaran is a highly suitable platform for the electronic process control equipment. The only equipment available so far is crude and works along entirely the wrong lines.

The trimaran is a light displacement craft built of marine ply and/or glass fibre, costs per bunk being about one third those of traditional yachts. Interiors are spacious and well lit in comparison and the continuation of the boating boom will ensure that the trimaran will become the caravan of the sea, once doubts about safety are removed. Apart from the fact that (to date) they stay capsized, they offer many other advantages over the keel boat, notably that they can be sailed about three times as fast, and that unlike a keel boat they are virtually unsinkable. If the practical utility of the equipment I propose can be demonstrated in such a spectacular way as in winning the *Sunday Times* Golden Globe and/or the £5,000 prize and it is properly protected by patents, the rapid and profitable development of this company cannot be in any doubt. Let me say at this point that having been to sea in small boats over a period spanning almost thirty years you can rest assured that commercial considerations alone would not induce me to make this attempt. I have gone into the problems and risks in detail, and am able to say that I am very confident of success . . .

On the basis of the declared entrants I could win both trophies, as I have already secured the approval of two boat-yards to a plan enabling work to begin at short notice on a trimaran of well proven basic design with the necessary self-righting features built in. My estimates indicate that the boat would only cost about £6,000 so that with yacht mortgage facilities the outlay is very modest in comparison with the returns, which do not merely accrue to this company but include film rights, communications and story rights and advertising revenue. The details I have given here are known to very few people and are sought after by the yachting press with some avidity, so I would ask for your co-operation in treating them as confidential.

It was a subtly persuasive letter. Its reference to the "caravan of the sea" was a neat appeal to the caravan dealer Stanley Best;

so too were the hopes it offered to rescuing his otherwise barren investment in Electron Utilisation. There were some rather stretched claims — such as his "thirty years" of sailing experience — but the basic argument of the letter was both fair and well thought out. There is no doubt that, at the time, Crowhurst really believed he could put the whole thing into effect: safety devices, electronic process control equipment, patents and all. Even the cost of £6,000, though it later almost doubled because of rush and modifications, was what he then had every reason to expect.

Stanley Best now says he cannot understand what made him agree to the project. "My wife tells me I must have been mad," he says. "I, who have always invested in a certainty or a rigorously calculated risk, suddenly jumped into this mammoth undertaking, which I didn't really comprehend, with only the shadowiest prospect of a proper reward. It was, I suppose, the glamour of the idea, the publicity and the excitement — and the persuasiveness of Donald. He was, when all is said and done, the most impressive and convincing of men."

In fact, the risk that Best undertook was not quite so great as might seem. He promised to underwrite all the costs of the boat, but other sponsors were to be sought to share the expense. Also it was agreed that if anything went wrong with the voyage, Stanley Best would have the option to sell the boat to Electron Utilisation Ltd. It was, says Best, only for tax reasons. But the repurchase clause was later to weigh heavily on Crowhurst's mind. He knew that its effect, if the voyage failed, would be to force his firm out of business.

*   *   *

Crowhurst had been negotiating with several boatyards about a possible trimaran commission. He finally chose Cox Marine Ltd of Brightlingsea in Essex to build the three trimaran hulls and L. J. Eastwood Ltd of Brundall in Norfolk to assemble the hulls and fit out the boat. The major problem was time, and this was why the construction job was split. Cox regretted that they could not do everything in time for the October deadline and proposed Eastwoods as a sub-contractor. Eastwoods were sufficiently idle to take on a major rush job. They agreed to do it for minimum profit and with maximum effort.

Two partners ran the firm. One, John Eastwood, is a quiet, slow-spoken man with a rustic beard and a lifetime's experience as an engineer and boatbuilder. In 1962 he had given up an important job with Perkins Diesels to set up his own little boat-yard and had found that although it was not the most secure or profitable of enterprises he found the work to his liking. "It is sad that what one enjoys doing most almost inevitably makes the least money," he says. "But luckily, I believe—and so do most of the men working with me—that it is better to enjoy the satisfaction of building boats than to go reaping easy money elsewhere. Oddly enough, I judge myself to be a little like Donald Crowhurst. I love developing ideas, but I am not so good at routine work and administration. To me, all that is boring, and my mind is rushing ahead on new ideas."

His partner, John Elliot, is more extrovert and less expert. He was the salesman, publicist and business organiser of Eastwoods, and quickly saw what an opportunity for attracting attention to the yard such a job would be.

As they got down to the details of designing the boat there was an interesting development: another trimaran joined the *Sunday Times* race. It was entered by a naval officer, Commander Nigel Tetley, and was so large and comfortable that he and his wife had been living aboard her for several years. It was a craft of the "Victress" class, designed by the American trimaran pioneer Arthur Piver. At that time, Piver trimarans were the most tried and tested in existence, their reputation marred only by the recent death at sea of Piver himself—the presumed victim of the one major drawback of trimarans, their inability to right themselves after a capsize.

Crowhurst had agreed that his own trimaran would also be based on "Victress" hulls, which could be quickly made on Cox's existing production line. But he had no doubt that he could give Tetley several weeks' start and still beat him. The standard "Victress" had a large cabin and a high enclosed wheelhouse, which Crowhurst thought would be vulnerable to the crushing seas of the Southern Ocean. In his own trimaran he had decided to do away with all this superstructure and substitute a flush deck broken only by a low, rounded "dog-house". There would be some loss of comfort and space—but a hero could surely put up with that—and the boat would be faster and safer. And he had a score of other ideas for adapting the "Victress" to round-the-world sailing.

*   *   *

At this moment Donald Crowhurst was, in Peter Beard's words, "grappling with problems and therefore euphoric". It was the biggest test he had ever encountered and he was producing daring solutions. In the theoretically impressive working out of all possible disasters and the design of electronic gadgets to avert them, he was buried in the most intoxicating workshop session of his life.

It is necessary when thinking of all this to forget the ultimate disaster, even to forget that when he set sail his vessel was so unprepared that all his magical electrical equipment was incomplete and useless. Almost every account of a successful adventure contains in its early chapters instances of over-optimism, confusion, and pushing salesmanship. Once the happy ending is reached these early setbacks only look like evidence of determination and integrity. The beginning of the Crowhurst adventure is similar: it is only the ending that has soured people's memories.

During this period any visitor to Woodlands was confronted with the Crowhurst grand piano in the living-room swamped with maps, plans, charts, diagrams and manifestos. Crowhurst would stride up and down, excitedly explaining it all. He had even worked out in precise mathematical detail who would win the race and why. His tabulation—which was left behind among his papers—was a remarkable essay in optimism and self-persuasion. It "proved" that he would not only make the fastest voyage, but also that he would overtake all the earlier starters, arrive home first, and win the Golden Globe.

Entrant	Likely max. speed	Highest probable average speed	Departure date* (P = probable)	Duration (days)	Arrival date*	Place
Ridgway	7½ kts	4 kts (95 mpd)	June 1	295	Apr. 1	(7)
Blyth	7½ kts	4 kts (95 mpd)	June 1	295	Apr. 8	(8)
Knox-Johnston	7¼ kts	4¼ kts (108 mpd)	June 14	260	Mar. 3	(6)
Moitessier	8½ kts	5 kts (120 mpd)	July 21 (P)	234	Mar. 14	(5)
Fougeron	7 kts	4 kts (95 mpd)	July 21 (P)	295	May 18	(9)
King	9¼ kts	6 kts (144 mpd)	Aug. 1 (P)	194	Feb. 14	(4)
Crowhurst	15 kts	9 kts (220 mpd)	Oct. 1 (P)	130	Feb. 7	(1)
Tetley	15 kts	8 kts (192 mpd)	Sep. 1 (P)	146	Feb. 12	(3)
Howell	15 kts	8 kts (192 mpd)	Sep. 14 (P)	146	Feb. 10	(2)

* Departure and arrival dates are reproduced as written by Crowhurst, though they are not always consistent with his estimate of place, or the duration of the voyage. Actual departure dates were: Ridgway, June 1st; Blyth, June 8th; Knox-Johnston, June 14th; Moitessier, August 21st; Fougeron, August 21st; King, August 24th; Crowhurst, October 31st; Tetley, September 16th.

As it turned out, Crowhurst's estimated average speeds were right only for Moitessier and Fougeron. The other monohulls all averaged less than he expected; but he was most wildly wrong with the multihulls. His blind enthusiasm for them was at this stage so high that he imagined Tahiti Bill Howell's catamaran and Nigel Tetley's trimaran could average nearly fifty per cent more than Chichester's record-breaking 131 miles per day. As for himself, he thought he could average a phenomenal 220 miles per day—and even this forecast was presumably conservative, because in the original draft of the table he had at first estimated himself at 290 miles per day. Later during his preparations, his estimates became slightly more realistic; when he set sail he took with him charts marked with target speeds, putting the duration of his voyage at 194 days, still substantially better than Chichester.*

*   *   *

As he had noted in his table, Crowhurst was expecting to set sail on October 1st. Eastwoods had promised to finish the entire job by the end of August. For such a firm, with at most two dozen workmen to call on, it was not only a great rush, it was a commercial gamble. They, like Stanley Best, were lured by the challenge and the potential publicity of the project.

Until the delivery of the hulls from Cox's, they could not start work. But at least this part of the project kept to schedule; the hulls turned up on the promised date, July 28th, and Eastwoods launched into their task. A few days previously, Crowhurst had visited the yard and told John Elliot of all his latest brainwaves. Then on the weekend of July 27th to 28th, Eastwood, who had just finished a rushed summer holiday, drove down overnight to Bridgwater to work out the technical details.

Their meeting, which lasted the entire Sunday from nine in the morning to nine at night, saw Crowhurst at his best—assured, inventive, and totally in command.

"I must say that at this point I was most impressed," says Eastwood. "Donald seemed to know precisely what he wanted. He had a good technical background and an imaginative mind.

---

* Howell was at this time competing in the *Observer* Transatlantic Race. Although he did better than all but one of the multihulls and came fifth, he averaged little more than 100 miles per day. Disenchanted with the general behaviour of his catamaran he decided to withdraw from the round-the-world event. Tetley, who very nearly completed his round-the-world voyage, averaged 111 miles per day, slightly less than Moitessier.

We went through everything and it all seemed absolutely clear and relatively straightforward. Of course, subsequently there were troubles; he kept having new ideas which were impossible to carry out and test in the time, but which were often brilliant."

The two men that day discussed every aspect of the proposed design. Description of the more technical details is left to an appendix at the end of this book. But their general flavour can be gathered from the ingenious system Crowhurst had worked out for righting the boat in case of capsize, which he regarded as the central technical idea of the entire project. This is how he said it would work.

If the boat started to heel over dangerously, electrodes in the immersed float would send a signal to a central switching mechanism in the cabin. The switching mechanism (which Crowhurst proudly called his "computer") would pause for a second to make sure the immersion was permanent—then it would click into action. An electrical circuit would be completed, which would fire off a carbon dioxide cylinder connected to a hosepipe disappearing up the hollow mast. At the top of the mast would be a large rubber "buoyancy bag". Under the pressure of the carbon dioxide, the bag would break loose from some of its lashings and inflate, thus preventing the boat from turning completely over.

At this stage, the trimaran would be bobbing about on its side, tipped slightly beyond the horizontal, supported by a partly immersed float at one end and the inflated rubber bag at the other. A large wave might possibly knock the boat upright from this position, but in case this did not happen another system would come into play. On either side of the cabin would be a Henderson water pump, permanently connected to the adjacent float. The appropriate pump would be operated by Crowhurst to fill the upper float with water—which would have the effect of pressing the bottom of the boat slowly downwards until the mast became level with the sea. It would now need only the merest ripple to send the trimaran bouncing upright again. As a final refinement, the connections of the Henderson pump could then be reversed to empty water from the flooded float, and all would be back to normal.

When describing all this, Crowhurst would hasten to add that a capsize was, of course, highly unlikely, because the "computer" would also constantly be checking for earlier signs of danger. Unusual stresses in the rigging, for example, would be electronically monitored, and if anything went amiss warning lights would flash on and alarms would sound. Abrupt changes on his wind-speed indicator would be noticed by the "computer" even when he was asleep, and it would automatically slacken the sails. The buoyancy bag was there only as a last resort, but it would, as he had promised Best, make "survival almost certain".

Although the whole arrangement sounded somewhat quixotic, Crowhurst would describe it with such assurance that nobody had any doubt he could make it work. Eastwood arranged to incorporate the pumps and wiring into the design of the boat. The Avon Rubber Company agreed to make the buoyancy bag for a nominal sum. The sober *Yachting & Boating Weekly* described the arrangement as "sensible". And Crowhurst wrote in his publicity handouts that a patent was being applied for, that tests were complete and the equipment was "now operating successfully", and that it was the product of long "development project" by Electron Utilisation Ltd, of which Mr Crowhurst was managing director.

What was not generally understood at the time was that the "development project" had still to take place in Donald Crowhurst's solitary workshop, and that at the commencement of his voyage the "computer" consisted of nothing else but boxes and boxes of switches, relays and transistors—all completely unassembled.

Other technical details discussed at the July 28th meeting were also to become central to the story, but need only brief mention here.

The Henderson pumps, it was agreed, were to have the additional function of pumping out normal bilge water shipped from minor leaks. Since the boat would have ten different watertight compartments, it would have been cumbersome to provide permanent piping to each one. Instead there would be just one long length of Heliflex hose (specially designed to withstand suction) which could be moved at will to any part of the boat. Eastwoods say it was not their responsibility to supply the hose: Crowhurst had not asked for it in his contract.

Because of all the electronic gadgetry, Crowhurst wanted a good power supply for charging his batteries. An Onan petrol-driven generator—a rather weighty bit of marine equipment—was chosen. Generators are notoriously susceptible to damp, and the problem was to find a dry place for it. It was the subject of much discussion that Sunday. Eastwood, in his tentative plans had

placed it high in the boat *beside* the cockpit. According to Eastwood, it was Crowhurst who insisted that this should be changed
—obsessed with the fear of a capsize off Cape Horn, he wanted
all heavy equipment to be placed as low in the boat as possible.
The only position that could be found was in a compartment
under the cockpit, which had to be approached by a hatch in the
cockpit floor. Since the cockpit was to be completely open, an
almost continual battering of solid waves would pour over it in
rough weather, so the hatch would need to be absolutely watertight. Both men realised the arrangement was risky. But Eastwood
reluctantly agreed to try and make it work.

There was another similar problem. As a variation on the
standard "Victress" design, Crowhurst had asked for the inclusion
of watertight bulkheads in each float—which required three extra
deck hatches for the divided compartments. Eastwood had a
simple proposal for the hatch design: he would just use flat round
pieces of wood, each bolted down by twelve wingnuts on to a
rubber seal. It was a quite workable solution, but Eastwoods admit
that they were unable to obtain rubber of the texture desired for
the purpose. The seals were too hard to mould themselves to the
slight unevennesses of the deck. Of the several design faults of
the trimaran, it was here that Eastwoods were most clearly to
blame.

"Our normal supplier had run out of soft rubber," explains John
Elliot. "We rang round everywhere we could think of. But everywhere it had just disappeared, magically. Apparently the motor
industry had developed a sudden thirst for it, and had used all the
supplies. Perhaps if there had been time to try longer, we might
have found some—the best of all comes from Scandinavia. But
that's the trouble with a rush job; you sometimes have to make do
with second best."

All these decisions and omissions affected the eventual outcome.
But it would be easy to judge Crowhurst and Eastwoods too
harshly. The simple truth was that they had all undertaken more
than could reasonably be done in the time, as was to become
increasingly apparent in the next few frantic weeks.

The first serious delay was over plans for the sails and rigging,
which Crowhurst himself had promised to organise. The normal
"Victress" rigging could not be used, because the weight of the
buoyancy bag and the pressure it would exert if the boat capsized
made a shorter, sturdier mast advisable.

Eastwood hoped at last to settle the matter at a meeting Crowhurst had called at Cox Marine in late August. Two sailmakers and a rigging designer were supposed to be in attendance, but Crowhurst's arrangements had gone wrong and they did not turn up. In the end, Eastwood himself had to convert Crowhurst's rough ideas into a detailed plan. Two alternative schemes were swiftly drawn up, and Crowhurst made his choice.

The visit to Cox's was also to have been the occasion for Crowhurst's first sail at the helm of a trimaran; a "Victress" was nearing completion at the yard and he expected to be allowed out in her. However, his request was refused. The trimaran had just been sold; the new owner was pressing for early completion; and Cox's felt they could not risk someone else's boat on the sea, particularly with a beginner.

* * *

Eastwood and Elliot complain that during these vital middle stages of building they did not see enough of Crowhurst, though they saw rather too much of him at the end. They still feel that he seemed too casual and absent-minded during this period, and they could never get clear instructions from him.

Crowhurst, however, had enough other problems to deal with. He was trying, for instance, to set up some arrangement for keeping Electron Utilisation ticking over in his absence. He had arranged for a friend to take over the sale of Navicators in London, on a shared-profit basis, and hoped this might produce an income of £10 a week to keep Clare and the children from starving during the voyage. There were financial arrangements to be made with Stanley Best, who now, in effect, controlled Electron Utilisation. Best provided a second mortgage on Woodlands to pay off some of the debts, which put Crowhurst's last tiny vestige of reserve capital in pawn.

As late as September 18th to 25th, Crowhurst was driving almost every day to Bristol to brush up on the one aspect of sailing at which he already had considerable expertise. He had enrolled at the Technical College for an intensive course in radio-telegraphy procedures, because the Post Office required all nautical radio-operators to have a certificate of competence. Whatever else happened on his voyage, his morse-coded messages would be meticulous.

There were also more ebullient and expansive things to do. This is the moment when the remarkable figure of Rodney Hallworth, ex-crime reporter of the *Daily Mail* and *Daily Express*, proprietor of the Devon News Agency, public relations man, local news gatherer and prominent local citizen of Teignmouth, appears on the scene. Hallworth is a large man, with a large face, and everything he does is larger than life. Anyone who has seen Charles Laughton playing Henry VIII could instantly imagine him. His expansive figure, clad in white shirt, mesh vesting, and a cream linen jacket, is encircled by the thick leather belt of his grey flannel trousers. His ability, acquired while on the *Daily Mail* Scotland Yard beat, to drink pint upon pint of bitter without missing a thing is an example to all less redoubtable newsmen.

He has written an excellent book, *The Last Flowers on Earth*, which is an account of an expedition to Greenland: but his real talent is for spine-chilling crime reporting. This talent he has since transferred to the less vivid, but equally demanding discipline of dramatic local news stories. As will be seen, his capacity to transform half-a-dozen scrambled cable words into a coherent and tear-jerking account of Donald Crowhurst's lone struggle against the hostile elements was little short of genius. There was genius too in the way he managed to fulfil his various roles as public relations officer for Teignmouth Town Council, publicist for local enterprise, hawker of local news stories, and pal of assorted PROs to everyone's mutual advantage.

In his office at Devon News is a reverentially framed photo of an Alsatian dog affectionately nuzzling a swan, and inviting the caption "Best of Pals". (That picture, says Hallworth, has gone "round the world", making pots of money for his agency.) It is symbolic of his trade. Thus: when Crowhurst set off, "Teignmouth's ambassador had started his mission"; while he was sailing, "*Teignmouth Electron* surged like a wild horse over high wet mountains and through valleys of swirling foam"; when he was coming home, "a tumultuous welcome is waiting Donald Crowhurst in Teignmouth"; when he disappeared, "Teignmouth, the town which to some extent sponsored Crowhurst, was grief-stricken". Stock phrases for stock situations—usually involving Teignmouth.

No one could call him a cynic. "I loved that man, I loved him like a brother," he would say of Donald Crowhurst. "I worked myself to the bone for him. When all is said and done, the hardest amongst us newsmen keeps that little softness deep inside. Eh, old boy?" And no one who has heard him talk of God, late at night in the bar of the Passage House Inn near Teignmouth, could accuse him of lacking passionate beliefs: "Religion? Don't talk to me of religion! For I have stood on Dartmoor, with the clouds down and kissing the crag tops, and the trees whispering their lullabies to the southern wind, and the tiny lights of the seaside resorts twinkling in the distance, and I have reached up to put both my arms round the warm body of religion itself! So don't talk to me about religion."

Hallworth first met Crowhurst through the *Sunday Times*, which had commissioned a photograph from Devon News. The photographer, on his return, told his employer that Crowhurst still lacked a publicity agent. Scenting a possible new client, Hallworth arranged to meet him at a midway hotel near Taunton.

"When I first saw Donald in the hotel bar," Hallworth recalls, "he was a bit stiff and officer-class. Conversation went rather stickily. By the time that meal was over we were firm friends, I believe. He slapped me on the arm, leaning right across the table, and told me I'd got the job. When you got him warmed up that man was, amongst many other things, a real swashbuckler. I think, without flattering myself, that I appealed to some aspects of Donald that he couldn't properly satisfy in other people."

At that time there was another agent already working for Crowhurst trying to get him commercial sponsors. There had been several hopes—including a vague possibility that the *News of the World* might sponsor the boat in return for its name on the bows—but in the end there was little more to show than ten cases of Heinz tinned foods and some Whitbread's Barley Wine. So Hallworth found himself trying to raise commercial support as well as handling Press matters.

It is clear that one of Crowhurst's major disappointments was that no firm would agree to be the basic sponsor of his trip. Perhaps he had started his appeals too late, or did not have the intimate connections with yachting business executives. So he had to try to solicit odd items here and there. A yellowing, sea-splashed file of his correspondence was among the other relics left on board the boat at the end of his voyage:

To Alcan Foils Ltd:
In my capacity of Managing Director of this small company, I read *Packaging Review*. On noticing your advertisement in the

ptember 23rd 1968: the launching of Teignmouth Electron at Eastwoods yard, Brundall, rfolk. Afterwards, Clare Crowhurst pours her husband a celebratory glass of champagne

The press agent, Rodney Hallworth: a large man who does everything larger than life

The sponsor, Stanley Best (left) the boatbuilder, John Eastwood

John Elliot, Eastwood's boatbuilding partner with Crowhurst on the maiden voyage

Peter Beard, and . . .

. . . Ronald Winspear, Crowhurst two contrasting friends

last issue it occurred to me that there may be areas of mutual interest that would be worth exploring . . . I have a very good chance of winning not only the Golden Globe but the £5,000 prize as well. If that does happen the publicity would be fantastic, for in saying that this event is the Everest of the Sea, Chichester is admitting that his voyage was no more than a preliminary for the main event . . .

To Plysu Containers Ltd:
My entry . . . is the fastest boat entered for the event . . . If you will meet my needs you can have all the publicity you want free of charge . . . The publicity when I win will, of course, be tremendous.

To Mallory Batteries:
My own view may not be of interest to you, but in case it is I will go so far as to say that Chichester and Rose were no more than preliminaries for the main event, which is not going to be won by King but by Crowhurst. Whatever the actual merit of Ridgway's effort, there cannot possibly be any value in it from your point of view.

The equipment that is going to enable me to win is electronic. The emergency power for the entire system, including communications, is primary cells. The news value of my entry even before the start is going to be greater than that created by all other entries combined because of the highly spectacular nature of the trials I shall be running . . .

Many similar letters lie in Rodney Hallworth's files at Devon News. There were some successes, but in the end Stanley Best had to pay for many of the goods to equip the boat. In the absence of any other newspaper sponsor, the race organisers, the *Sunday Times*, volunteered £500 for newspaper rights, but Hallworth decided he could do better by selling speculative stories from Devon News.

The BBC did buy television and tape recording rights. Donald Kerr, then the Bristol news editor, had sent his reporter, John Norman, to interview Crowhurst as early as May, and had subsequently decided on a small investment: £250 down, and £150 when he returned. They provided him with a second-hand Bell and Howell 16 mm camera (which cost £120), and a Uher tape recorder. Kerr had made what he thought was a modest gamble on an orthodox entrant in a conventional adventurous contest. As he now confesses, it was a decision made on totally wrong premises; it was also—in terms of dramatic news material—the most rewarding decision of his life. Moreover, Donald Crowhurst turned out to be—after twenty minutes' instruction—the most professional film-maker of any single-handed sailor.

By this time only one property remained to be offered to sponsors: the name of the boat. Crowhurst wanted it called *Electron Five*, to publicise his company. Hallworth, in his other guise as public relations officer of Teignmouth, had another proposal. If Donald would agree to start his voyage from there, to harp on his local connection as much as possible, and add Teignmouth to the name of his boat, Hallworth would start a fund-raising campaign. Crowhurst proposed *Electron of Teignmouth*. Hallworth—knowing his PR—insisted on his client's name first. From that moment, the three-quarters-completed trimaran became *Teignmouth Electron*.

*   *   *

Meanwhile at Eastwoods in Norfolk, building was falling further and further behind schedule. The yard first put every man on a seventy-hour week, and finally established a night-shift, recruiting labour from other local yards. Already the August 31st launching deadline had passed, and so had the revised September 12th deadline. Crowhurst asked for a special oversize rudder, to be made in sections, in case his own could not control the boat in the Roaring Forties. He ordered the cupboards to be replaced with shelving for Tupperware plastic containers, which had been solicited from the manufacturers.

He also wrote Eastwoods a stiff letter, complaining that the delays had used up all his carefully allotted reserve time:

> It must be made clear that there will be no further postponement of the launch after 23rd September. If you are delayed for any reason in the smooth flow of work I must be informed, as the entire project is now in jeopardy . . . As a Company and as individuals you have taken on a formidable task; more formidable in many ways than my own part in the project, and you have done it well. The whole success of the project depends on your completing what remains in the time available and doing

it just as well! If my good wishes were of any use you would have no trouble doing so.

Eastwoods replied with an equally stiff letter, arguing that extra work had already run up an additional bill of £900, and payments were further behind schedule than the boat.

On September 21st, two days before the launch deadline, Crowhurst's temper finally snapped, and a noisy argument took place over the telephone. The "Victress" specification required the hulls and decks to be completely sheathed in glass fibre. This had already been done with the hulls supplied by Cox's, But East-woods had been so late in laying the deck—because of the delays in establishing the rigging plan—that they now wanted to save time by simply painting it with polyurethane paint. Eastwood rang to get Crowhurst's approval, arguing that since they had used double thickness plywood on the decks, the glass fibre was unnecessary from a structural point of view, and that in any case the glass fibre skin would be so thin that paint would do just as well.

Crowhurst exploded with anger. His view (which Cox's support) was that the glass fibre was an essential part of the "Victress" design. He got even angrier when he learned that preparations for painting had already reached the point of no return. (There had been earlier attempts at contacting him, but he had been away at his radio-telegraphy course.) All the simmering frustrations of the building period boiled over.

That night, with Donald Crowhurst in an angry, unhappy mood, was the only time during the entire venture when Clare pleaded with him to refuse delivery of the boat and give up the project. Somewhat to her surprise, he seriously considered her arguments. "I suppose you're right," he said, "but the whole thing has become too important for me. I've got to go through with it, even if I have to build the boat myself on the way round." Clare afterwards felt she had put her case too strongly because after this Donald became more secretive about the further difficulties that arose. And there were many more of those.

Four

The Maiden Voyage

Clare Crowhurst launched *Teignmouth Electron* into the river at Brundall on September 23rd. She made a short, graceful speech and swung the champagne bottle delicately against the fibreglass-and-plywood hull. The bottle did not break. John Eastwood took the job over from her, with the reassurance that such an ill omen was not unprecedented. Sheila Chichester had suffered the same failure when she launched *Gipsy Moth IV*.

Afterwards, the tiny cluster of press and television cameramen took pictures of *Teignmouth Electron* riding high on her moorings, still without masts and rigging. She looked businesslike enough, but not very pretty. The colours — white hulls and pale blue deck — were marred by blotches of bright orange for the special deck hatches, and the underside of the wings. Like all trimarans, she was squat and square, an impression heightened by the wide sweep of the deck over three hulls, devoid of guard rails, scarcely interrupted by the small bulge of the cabin roof. If Bill King's boat had looked like a submarine, Crowhurst's looked like a miniature aircraft carrier.

There followed a last week of feverish activity at the yard, stepping the mast, rigging the boat, and fitting all the deck fixtures. By this time Crowhurst and Eastwood were at odds, falling frequently into recrimination and argument while the workmen grew more and more resentful at the flow of conflicting instructions. John Elliot, always the diplomat, would carry Crowhurst off for long, reflective Norfolk teas.

This tension built into two big explosions. One came on October 1st. Crowhurst wanted to sail off immediately, Elliot told him he couldn't; so a document was made up declaring that if Crowhurst took the boat away that day, he alone would be responsible for her condition. The second was a long, tense conference about money. The extra work, said Eastwood, had almost doubled the building costs. Crowhurst questioned this (it was still a matter of dispute between Stanley Best and Eastwoods a year later), but was forced to promise a £1,000 'releasing fee' for the boat, to be paid the next day. Finally, by lunchtime on October 2nd, *Teignmouth Electron* was at last declared fit to sail. Her maiden voyage, from Brundall to Teignmouth, was not a happy one. Crowhurst was expecting to complete the trip in three days. It took two weeks.

*   *   *

Workmen from the boatyard were still completing odd jobs aboard *Teignmouth Electron* as she set off, propelled by her outboard motor, down the River Yare. John Elliot and Peter Beard took pictures with their cine-cameras as windmills and cottages swept by. Even the tranquil Broads have their perils, however. As the boat approached Reedham, swept on by the ebbing tide, the local chain ferry began to cross the river. Crowhurst had two alternatives: to sail on and risk snagging the hulls on the tightening underwater chain of the ferry; or to try to stop. Eastwood thought it all right to go on; Crowhurst thought otherwise. He shouted to the workmen on the foredeck to let go the anchor and bring the trimaran to an abrupt halt. It was simple bad luck that as *Teignmouth Electron* stopped the tide swung her sharply round and smashed her into some pilings on the river bank. The plywood skin of her starboard float was holed. Valuable time had been lost before she was under way again.

They reached Yarmouth in gusty rain, and so late that the swing bridge in the centre of town had closed for the night. Rather than suffer another twelve-hour hold-up, Elliot and Peter Beard leaped ashore, hired a taxi, and with the help of the harbour-master managed to lure four of the bridge crew from their firesides to open up. They also realised they lacked a signalling lamp to announce their presence to coastguard stations round the coast, as is customary on maiden voyages. Elliot solved that problem by buying a car spotlight from an all-night garage. Meanwhile the workmen set about patching the float. It was late evening before they finally (with some relief) could drive back home. John Elliot, Peter Beard and Donald Crowhurst stayed behind as *Teignmouth Electron*'s first sea crew. Just after 2.00 a.m. they set sail and ventured off into the squally night.

A swell was running, and after rounding the harbour buoys and setting course southwards for the Goodwins, the three men soon felt queasy. Crowhurst in particular was repeatedly and violently seasick. His crew both admiringly testify that he did not let this interfere: for twelve hours he sat at the helm or at his chart table with a bucket beside him, retching every few minutes, but each time returning instantly to work. John Elliot says: "Donald was in a filthy temper. But oddly enough it was watching him then that really convinced me he was a man to sail round the world. He revealed his incredible determination and stubbornness. Once he had decided to do something, neither disaster nor persuasion could deflect him."

After daybreak, with a favourable wind, *Teignmouth Electron* sprinted down the North Sea towards the Thames estuary. Everyone was well pleased with her. Crowhurst, once his seasickness had subsided, was in an ecstatic mood. But then, at five that evening, the wind shifted, and the boat faced her first big test. She did not come out of it very well.

*   *   *

Trimarans, with no keel to dig into the water and prevent sideways movement, are notoriously poor to windward. It was immediately apparent that *Teignmouth Electron* was even worse than most. The sails did not balance well, and without stores aboard the hulls were more than usually shallow in the water.

The change of wind had occurred just past the South Goodwin lightship, and from that moment the boat virtually ceased to make progress. It took more than five hours to sail the next ten miles along the coast to Dover. Bewildered, Crowhurst started to experiment with sails: he took down the large jib and staysail and replaced them with a yankee and a running staysail; this reduced the sail area at the bows heading her off the wind. But two hours later they were still off Dover. "Fighting tide—no headway", the log records. Two hours later, the tide had swept them back to the South Goodwin light once more.

Under such circumstances, the most sensible solution would have been simply to look for an anchorage in contrary tides, and surge forward when the tide turned. But either out of stubbornness or because he wanted to test out the boat, Crowhurst decided to make a series of long tacks almost to the French coast and back. At the end of the first tack, with France only three miles away, the wind suddenly dropped. They hoisted the vast "ghoster" jib, but the boat was moving so slowly that they were able to plunge over the side for a short Channel swim.

Finally Crowhurst decided he must use the outboard motor again. Here at last was a useful trial. The outboard weighed nearly a hundredweight. Crowhurst could discover whether he was able, single-handed, to lift it out of its stowage (in the generator compartment beneath the cockpit) and fix it on its bracket on the port float. There was a block and tackle on the main boom to help him, but it was a tricky job. He struggled with it for almost an hour, rapidly losing patience. In the end, with a vicious burst of temper, he almost threw the engine at its bracket, and it slotted into place. Peter Beard thought that hanging half overboard in an angry, violent mood was dangerous practice for a single-handed sailor; it was an obvious way to lose both balance and boat.

With the outboard working they puttered down the French coast to Boulogne. At this point, Crowhurst burnt his left hand on the generator exhaust pipe. A large patch of skin came off, but he concealed the injury and carried on. To Elliot this was proof of his stubborn will. To Beard it was proof both of his courage and his secretiveness. To his wife, Clare, when she saw the injury later, it was a portent. The burn, she said, had obliterated the lifeline on his palm. "I am superstitious and it worried me a lot," she said. "I also think it worried Donald."

For three days they tacked back and forth from France to England, and with each landfall they found they had made only a few miles of headway. For some reason, says Peter Beard, Crowhurst was stubbornly reluctant to make the pre-arranged signals to the coastguard stations. At one point this created so much alarm that the coastguards were preparing a special sea search. Why Crowhurst did not make the signals is not clear. It could have been his natural secretiveness; or it could, thinks Beard, have been due to his new enthusiasm for newspaper publicity. In the end, Clare Crowhurst so confidently reassured the coastguards that her husband could not possibly have come to any harm that there was no sea search—and no headlines.

It was during one of those three nights battling against the frustrating winds and tides of the Channel that Crowhurst and Beard started to talk seriously about the boat's failings. They were drinking coffee while John Elliot slept below. Suddenly Beard faced Crowhurst with the possibility that on this form he would not be capable of forcing his boat down the Atlantic into the Southern Ocean, let alone sail round the world. What would he do in such circumstances, he asked. Crowhurst smiled. The question didn't arise, he said. The prevailing winds would always be helping him on.

But what if they didn't? "Well, one could always shuttle around in the South Atlantic for a few months," said Crowhurst. "There are places out of the shipping lanes where no one would ever spot a boat like this." Then he took Beard's logbook to show him how it could be done. He drew Africa, and South America. He placed two small triangles between them to represent the Falkland Islands and Tristan da Cunha. With his pencil he lightly traced a lozenge-shaped course, round and round, between the two. It would be simple, he said, no one would ever find out. Crowhurst laughed : it was obviously a joke. The diagram is still in Peter Beard's logbook.

*　　　*　　　*

After four days, Beard and Elliot told their skipper they could stay aboard no longer. They had commitments, they said. With the outboard motor fixed once more, they motored into New-haven on the Sussex coast. Elliot telephoned his wife to say they were safe, somewhat to the fury of Crowhurst who perhaps still wanted to remain "missing" and induce a great headline-creating search. Then the three men sat moodily in a dockside pub, waiting for a reserve crew—Colin Wright and Dick Ralliston, both boat-builders summoned from Eastwood's yard—to turn up.

For hour after hour Crowhurst grumbled himself into a black rage. This was, in many ways, the worst moment of all. Days were passing swiftly—where was the time for his sea trials, his vaunted electronic assemblies, his modifications and repairs, his seduction of rich sponsors, his meticulous checking of supplies and equipment?—and he could do absolutely nothing. His rivals in the *Sunday Times* race—apart from Ridgway and Blyth who had dropped out—were at sea, doing well. Knox-Johnston was ploughing busily through the Indian Ocean, now approaching Australia; Moitessier, Tetley and King were in swift pursuit down the Atlantic. And what was he, Crowhurst, the cleverest of all, doing? He was stuck in a grubby Channel port while his friend chattered uxoriously on the telephone and two boat-builders drove the long journey down from Norfolk. He could still be the fastest in the race. But could he start at all? October 31st was now only three weeks away.

Crowhurst leaped up and strode out on to the quayside to look at *Teignmouth Electron*. He knew only too well by now she was not what he had hoped. Meanwhile that contrary south-westerly wind was building up to gale force, huge waves crashing against the harbour breakwater. He raised his arms and screamed against vile circumstance. He could contend with normal difficulties. Indeed, he was brilliant at it. But here the elements, the race rules, the change of crew, the vagaries of trimaran design—all were conspiring, as if in some monstrous hostile system, against him. Damn them all! If he was brave enough to set off round the world, he was brave enough to sail out of Newhaven harbour, single-handed, here and now! Beard and Elliot came out of the pub, and led him back into the warm. Crowhurst went and sulked in the bar corner. Finally he found something to occupy his mind. He wrote out an elaborate letter of apology to the Wiltshire Constabulary. He was sorry, he wrote, but it would not be possible for him to appear in court to answer the speeding charge they had booked him on. Unfortunately he would be unavoidably engaged at the time appointed for the hearing. He would be winning a round-the-world race.

*   *   *

Even after the fresh crew arrived in Newhaven, they had to spend two further infuriating days before the gale dropped and they could restart the voyage. Two even more infuriating days fighting wind and tide got them as far as Wootton Creek in the Isle of Wight. The two boatyard men left the trimaran and telephoned their yard. Please, they asked, could they come home? They hadn't enjoyed their trip.

Crowhurst sailed single-handed the few further miles to Cowes.

73

There he met a late and formidable entrant in the round-the-world race: Alex Carozzo, whose sailing exploits had already won him a reputation as the "Chichester of Italy". After an unsuccessful experience with a multihull boat in the *Observer* Transatlantic Race, Carozzo had opted for a monohull again. He had just had a huge 66-foot ketch of unusual design specially built for him by the Medina Yacht Company in Cowes. Building had begun even later than Crowhurst's, on August 19th, and was completed in just seven weeks. As Crowhurst became engrossed in his rival's problems—which so closely resembled his own—he suddenly lost all sense of frustration and urgency. He spent a day in Cowes harbour chatting to Carozzo, twice falling overboard while pottering around the boats anchored there. He seems to have been somewhat awed by the Italian's reputation, and impressed by his boat. He regarded him as the one, amongst all his rivals, most difficult to beat, which is perhaps why he subsequently arranged to send him a Navicator—so that, whoever won, Crowhurst's equipment would be on board.

Crowhurst discovered that Carozzo had written to the *Sunday Times* race judges asking if the deadline could be relaxed to allow him time for more leisurely preparations, but had been refused. This is probably why neither Crowhurst nor his sponsors asked for an extension, even in his most hectic last-minute rush, though the judges might just conceivably have relented on the grounds of safety.

On Sunday, October 13th, an experienced local sailor, Lieutenant-Commander Peter Eden, volunteered to accompany Crowhurst on the last leg of his voyage. As the pair climbed aboard *Teignmouth Electron* in Cowes harbour from a rubber dinghy, Crowhurst slipped on the outboard motor bracket, and fell into the water once again. Eden's description of his two days aboard *Teignmouth Electron* provides the most expert independent assessment we have of the performance of both boat and sailor, before the start of the race. He recalls that the trimaran sailed immensely swiftly, but could get no closer to the wind than 60°. The speed often reached 12 knots, he says, and the vibration in the bunk at the bow was so violent it gave him a toothache while trying to sleep. The Hasler self-steering worked superbly, but screws kept unfastening from it because of the vibrations caused by high speeds. "We had to keep leaning over the counter to do up the screws," he says. "It was a tricky and time-consuming business. I told Crowhurst he should get the fixings welded if he wanted it to survive a longer trip. Otherwise the boat seemed to be going well. She was certainly nippy."

During the trip Crowhurst seemed reluctant to talk in great detail about his race plans. He did tell Eden that his main fear was the danger of "pitch-poling" in the heavy following seas of the Southern Ocean. This is a particular danger in trimarans and catamarans. Because they can travel faster than waves, their bows are liable to bury themselves in a wave trough when the swell is coming from behind. A strong wind can then flip the entire boat head-over-heels.

"Crowhurst's sailing techniques were good," says Eden, "but I felt his navigation was a mite slapdash. I prefer, even in the Channel, to know exactly where I am. He didn't take too much bother with it, merely jotting down some figures on a few sheets of paper from time to time." [Crowhurst's log of this voyage accompanied him on the round-the-world race, and still survives. It consists, as Eden says, of a few scraps of paper covered in casual scribblings, in marked contrast to the rigorously presented navigational log of his longer voyage.] This last section of the voyage from Yarmouth was relatively easy. The first thirty-six hours were again spent struggling against westerlies. They tacked twice across the Channel and back again. Then, at long last, the wind changed and swept them swiftly towards Teignmouth. It was 2.30 p.m. on October 15th as they crossed the harbour bar. Crowhurst had spent thirteen days getting round the coast. There were now sixteen days until the October 31st deadline.

Five

Teignmouth

Teignmouth, with its sister village of Shaldon across the river estuary, is a small early nineteenth-century resort. It boasts a pier, a cinema, an aquarium, a hilly promontory called the Ness, two dozen hotels, and countless boarding houses. There are some fishing boats, a boat-building yard and a china clay industry, but basically the 13,000 inhabitants all depend on summer visitors.

Like any small town, Teignmouth can become deeply divided on parochial matters, and usually does. It divides by class, by occupation, by temperament, and above all by pubs. For the past two years, the major topic of contention has been Donald Crowhurst.

From the start, Crowhurst's supporters mustered at the Ship Inn, a rather racy, saloon-bar type of house with red-plush cushions and keg beer, which attracts the cosmopolitans, the hoteliers, the progressives and publicists. They regarded the voyage as one of Rodney Hallworth's greatest promotional coups. Not since the time when the Council Chamber was being redecorated and Hallworth organised a council meeting in full regalia, on the beach, had the little town received so much free mention in the newspapers.

Crowhurst's antagonists gathered at The Lifeboat, where fishermen, dock workers and local rustics congregate to drink the cheapest bitter in town. They would talk about Crowhurst in sceptical tones, combining a native suspicion of strangers with a nautical distaste for multihulled boats and electronic wizardry. There had, so far, been little popular support for Hallworth's "Name-it-Teignmouth" fund; only £250 of the hoped-for £1,500 had been collected.

His supporters greeted Crowhurst's long-awaited arrival enthusiastically. They wanted him to spend his first evening wandering round town, meeting the people, and persuading them to take their new, stranger-hero to their hearts. Crowhurst was too preoccupied. The supporting committee had to go on a Teignmouth pub-crawl without him.

The antagonists, on the other hand, saw much to confirm their deepest suspicions during the last two weeks before *Teignmouth Electron* set sail. The final preparations were made in an atmosphere of total confusion and rush. Crowhurst's helpers scurried round town buying supplies at random. For long periods, Crowhurst himself would disappear on mysterious assignments. Modifications were still being done to the boat that one might have expected to have been completed long ago.

The first day of the boat's arrival was typical. Even as the trimaran was dragged up the slipway of Morgan Giles's boatyard, four men from Eastwoods swarmed aboard and started to saw and hammer, while the BBC filmed heroic shots of Peter Eden under the impression he was Crowhurst. Meanwhile Crowhurst examined, appalled, the small pile of stores that had so far arrived, while Hallworth told him that he had garnered, amongst other things, huge supplies of Exeter cheese and local sherry for him. For John Eastwood there were numerous new problems. In particular, his vital "watertight" hatch on the cockpit floor had not been successful, and it was letting in gallons of water. Back at his drawing board he decided to add a low rubber-edged coaming. This time the hatch would *have* to work; there would be no more time for full-scale trials.

The list of tasks facing Crowhurst personally was forbidding. It was not just a matter of starting work on all his splendid electronic safety gadgets; the boat, as yet, did not even have ordinary radio equipment. He had intended to use a set he had built himself, but this was vetoed by the Post Office. He therefore had to buy Marconi Kestrel equipment, and to persuade Marconi to instal it at speed.

*   *   *

In the midst of all this disarray, Crowhurst found time after his arrival to record a long interview for the BBC. It was all fine, confident, heroic stuff.

He began by allowing the interviewers, Donald Kerr and John Norman to draw from him the admission that he was an "incurable romantic". Then—freely plagiarising from Chichester—he launched into a series of conventional wisdoms about single-handed sailing, almost as if he had already completed the voyage:

> I have felt a community with long dead seamen on many occasions. This probably reverts to the incurable romanticism that I was talking about. One does feel that one is doing the same things . . . that seamen who have come this way centuries before you would understand your feelings, and you understand theirs . . .

> Talking to yourself is very important. When one has been awake for a couple of days, soaking wet and perhaps hadn't had enough to eat . . . you can restore a sense of urgency by telling yourself what the consequences of your lack of attention to detail are . . . This is a tremendous help because the very process of speaking, forming the words, helps to crystallise one's thoughts in a way that no mere process of thought can ever do.

Crowhurst then neatly worked in a reference to Electron Utilisation by disarmingly admitting that "I do it because I want to do it . . . of course, having said that, it's also true that if I couldn't justify it commercially I wouldn't be doing it." And he described his buoyancy bag and self-righting mechanism in terms that implied not only that they were already fully working, but that his firm was about to start marketing the equipment.

He went on to assure the interviewer that he had never had any second thoughts or doubts about the trip:

> I don't operate like that. If I decide to do it, then I do not decide until I have satisfied myself that on the whole it's a worthwhile thing to do . . . Having decided you forget the

decision and take it as a matter of course that that is what is going to happen.

But the most intriguing part of the interview ran as follows:

KERR: Can you describe any situation at sea you've ever been in when you thought you were going to drown? What happened? What was it like?

CROWHURST: Well there have been situations . . .

KERR: Can you think of a day, a particular day?

CROWHURST: There was an occasion once when I was sailing on the South Coast. I was sailing with a following wind . . . blowing about force seven. The boat was set up for self-steering and I must have been about twenty miles from shore. There were no guard rails, and I didn't have a safety harness — and I fell overboard. I thought, as the boat sailed on that I was either going to drown or else I was in for a very long swim. I realised of course that it was entirely my own fault and I didn't waste any time blaming myself. I just made a mental note that this sort of practice had to be avoided in the future and got on with thinking about what one had to do about it. I was very lucky on that occasion because my boat, in point of fact came up into the wind. My self-steering arrangements had in fact relied on a little manual assistance from myself from time to time . . . But she did sail on something like a quarter of a mile before coming up into the wind and it was quite long enough to give me a fright.

This remarkable adventure was quite unknown to his wife and friends. Nobody can recall his even having mentioned it in conversation, though it was eminently the kind of self-dramatising, self-deprecating story he would have enjoyed telling. If the story were true, it would be further proof of Crowhurst's accident-proneness, though it should have put him on his guard against future troubles. But the most likely explanation is that he had made it up on the spur of the moment, prompted by Kerr's insistent question.

The interview over, Crowhurst shook Peter Eden by the hand and thanked him, left Hallworth to organise the painting of "Teignmouth Electron" on the hull of the boat then leaped into John Norman's car to race back to his Bridgwater workshop.

*   *   *

At Morgan Giles's boatyard, work began on the boat. A strut was added to strengthen the Hasler, though there was not time to follow Eden's suggestion of replacing the screws with welded joints. Work began on modifying the cockpit hatch. The Marconi men laboured through several nights to fix the radio transmitter. The mechanical hardware of Crowhurst's safety gear had to be completed (though the electrical components were never assembled to make it work). And there were countless small, vital jobs to be finished on the rigging and fittings.

The Morgan Giles workers gave the Eastwoods men what help they could, but raised a chorus of disapproval at the state of the boat and at Crowhurst himself. A year later, their descriptions of the chaos were still enlivening the gossip at The Lifeboat:

All hell broke out during those two weeks he was here. Everyone was trying to help, but nobody rightly knew what to do. As for Crowhurst, he didn't look the man to go at all. He hadn't an inkling where anything was, or what was happening. He didn't test nothing. He didn't stay with his boat, as a skipper ought to. He'd suddenly clear off for something, and we'd be wandering around trying to find him. If it wasn't some mysterious drive up to London it was a wine-and-cheese publicity party up the Royal. That's no way to start off round the world.

You couldn't tell what was going on inside of him. He just wasn't integrated with us, if you know what that means. He was in a daze. We'd have admired him much more if he'd simply said "I've lost me nerve. Let's drop the whole business." Obviously he was in a blind panic and didn't have the guts to call it off. So what if it made him bankrupt and penniless? Life is very sweet, brother, even without money, and even looking a fool.

And that boat of his! It was just bloody ridiculous. A right load of plywood it was. The attitude here was he couldn't get further than Brixham.

The nearest thing to a systematic plan for preparing the boat was a bundle of loose sheets on which Crowhurst scribbled down thoughts as they occurred to him. They still survive: list upon list of missing items and unfinished jobs, jumbled with diagrams, addresses, telephone numbers, workmen's hours, half-drafted letters and personal reminders.

The Crowhurst family, a week before he set sail. From left: Simon, Rachel, Clare, Donald, Roger, James

BELOW: A publicity picture posed in church on departure day. Hallworth urged him to pray. Crowhurst would only meditate

The departure, hours before deadline on October 31st. Helpers had fouled the halyards a attached the headsails in the reverse order. Crowhurst gestures angrily at them

"Chase flags from *Sunday Times*" records one jotting, referring to the M, I and K flags—meaning "report my position to Lloyd's of London"—which the race organisers were issuing to each competitor. It is an indication, if such were needed, that no premeditated plan for faking a circumnavigation was in Crowhurst's mind.

Another sheet presents one of the major mysteries of the voyage. It is a list of things he had to buy in Teignmouth—socks, blowlamp, brass strip, gloves, hacksaw blades, pencils, and so on. Most of the items are crossed out in red ink, presumably to indicate that the purchase had been successfully made. One of these items says "Log books—4". Aboard the boat after the voyage were only *three* log books.

*　　*　　*

As the preparations stumbled on, Crowhurst's friends began assembling in Teignmouth, eager to assist. Stanley Best had installed some of his caravans in a parking lot, where he stayed with the Beards, the Eastwoods and the Elliots. Ron Winspear and Clare's sister Helen were staying at the Royal Hotel, where the proprietor had provided rooms for the Crowhursts. They can now recall ominous premonitions that assailed them at the time, but each—according to his temperament—remembers differently.

To Stanley Best, still reluctantly paying out increasingly large sums for stores and equipment, Crowhurst seemed determined, confident and eager, if a bit disorganised. They had suffered an unpleasant showdown over money, Best insisting that all the cost of radios and other internal equipment must be borne by Electron Utilisation, Crowhurst reluctantly conceding. But abandonment of the voyage wasn't raised. "If Donald had frankly told me at that moment that it was unsafe to go," he says, "I would have been angry, but I would, of course, not have insisted that he did so. But he never hinted at any doubt." To Rodney Hallworth, Crowhurst was optimism itself. "He was cheery and raring to go," he says. To Ron Winspear, on the other hand, Crowhurst was "strange, not all there. He had gone peculiarly quiet. It worried me. It was a mood I had never seen before. I knew Donald's explosive fits of temper, and would have welcomed a familiar outburst or two; that would have meant he was trying to get things done. But in those last few days he seemed absolutely subdued, as if his mind was paralysed." John Elliot remembers saying to Crowhurst, time and again: "You mustn't go. You won't be ready in time." But his warnings ceased after he realised they were useless; Crowhurst would always reply: "It's too late. I can't turn back now."

The general impression that Crowhurst gave was that he had been numbed into inefficiency by the overwhelming number of things to be done, and the appalling lack of time. He would get obsessed with tiny irrelevant points, and spent hours driving furiously around on minor tasks. His letters soliciting equipment continued until a few days before his departure. There were civic functions to attend and interviews to be given. His mind raced from thought to thought. As the need for some essential — or inessential — bit of equipment occurred to him, a helper would be dispatched to buy or beg it from a local shop.

John Eastwood remembers lighting a cigarette in front of Crowhurst with his Ronson Variflame lighter. "All at once Donald thought it would be better to have one of those instead of a pile of matches. So I had to buy one for him at the local tobacconist, plus fuel and a set of flints." Stanley Best was sent scurrying off to an Exeter second-hand car dealer to buy two dozen small electrical petrol pumps. "I had no idea what they were for. Something to do with the buoyancy bag I think." Clare visited Gordon Yelland, the local baker, to enquire about a recipe for baking bread at sea. Yelland experimented for a couple of days with flour, yeast, a chemical preservative and Teignmouth sea-water. (One of his experimental loaves was still edible a year after Crowhurst's departure.) The Beards remember meeting Crowhurst on the Bridgwater–Exeter road. "He was haring along in his little mini-van. We honked him and he stopped. Among other things, he was looking for a barometer. We had one in our front hall and offered it to him. Luckily it was a properly calibrated one."

The weather at Teignmouth in those last few days was continuously grey and drizzly. Everyone was growing increasingly tense and bewildered. Crowhurst, in his preoccupied state, became clumsy. Clambering out of his dinghy one night he tripped and fell across Clare. One of her ribs was cracked. He also became intolerant. When Clare pointed out that one of the trimaran's floats, temporarily raised from the water, was dripping, he shrugged it angrily aside. Those drips possibly meant that the float was leaking — a serious potential danger. Crowhurst either did not realise this, or was so bemused by his problems that he wanted to hear no more warnings.

*   *   *

Five days before departure, Crowhurst took *Teignmouth Electron* out of the harbour for one day's final sailing trials. With him went John Elliot, John Norman of the BBC, and a cameraman. The trip lasted from mid-day until darkness, and was not reassuring. The trimaran's performance to windward was no better than before; on two occasions she simply refused to go about until two men at the bows had backed the jib to force her round.

Crowhurst was in a particularly bad mood. He kept complaining about the fittings on the boat, though Eastwoods had everywhere installed them one size heavier than the normal "Victress" specification. The fittings, Crowhurst declared angrily, were just not good enough for a trip round the world.

The trials were officially to test the twin foresails and other sails used for running before the wind, most of which Crowhurst had not taken out of their sailmaker's bags. He opened them all up on deck and tried to discover which was which, and how they were hoisted. He spent hours stumbling around the piled sailcloth on the decks as he tried out the sails one by one. John Norman noticed that part of a length of special deck tracking to which the ropes from the running foresails were attached was lifting from the deck. A screw at the end of the tracking was loose; so he tried to tighten it with a screwdriver. But it turned round and round, refusing to bite home. He was afraid the tracking would rip out completely in a high wind, and pointed it out. Crowhurst just shook his head. Just one more thing to try to put right. Norman also noticed a similar fault in one of the float hatches. While screwing and unscrewing the twelve wingbolts around this hatch someone had tried to tighten them too fiercely. Some threads had stripped. When they lifted the crucial hatch in the cockpit floor—newly remodelled and rebuilt—the rubber sealing came away from its seating. "How the hell is that going to stand up to the Southern Ocean?" cried Crowhurst in vexation.

He was so busy trying to sort out his sails and sailbags that he stayed on the foredeck until dusk fell. He even asked John Norman to take the helm back into harbour.

Two days later the other BBC man, Donald Kerr, returned to Teignmouth. As he surveyed the scene, the boatyard in chaos, supplies piled indiscriminately on the trimaran's decks, and Clare, despite her cracked rib, bravely varnishing eggs in a nearby shed, he at once sensed catastrophe. He quietly ordered his camera crew to change the emphasis of their filming. They should shoot in the awareness that they were no longer publicising a potential triumph, but a potential tragedy. One interview they shot, with two local fishermen, was a classic of Devonian scorn.

*　　　*　　　*

About this time, it was suddenly realised that the extra Heliflex piping—which it had been known from the start would be needed for pumping out water from the boat—had not been acquired. An urgent telephone call was made to the pump-makers, Henderson's of the Isle of Wight. The piping was vital, and so eloquent were the appeals that one of Henderson's directors, John Lewis, actually put the piping aboard his own private aeroplane, a Cessna 172, and flew with it to Exeter. June Elliot volunteered to drive over to Exeter to collect it, and suggested that she took the Crowhurst children, James, Simon, Roger and Rachel, for an outing. It would help Clare to work unhindered on the food stores.

They spent five hours wandering round the airport looking for the pipe. It was never found. "The children were little angels," recalls June. "Imagine traipsing around a place like that, asking people to search through piles of parcels just for a length of pipe! I still remember James telling his brothers they shouldn't eat any more crisps because it was bad manners and too expensive." She telephoned Teignmouth to say there was no pipe at Exeter; Teignmouth telephoned Hendersons at Cowes. Unluckily, John Lewis was still in the air on his way back. All Hendersons could say was the pipe had definitely been delivered, but they didn't know where in the airport it had been left. June Elliot returned to Exeter again the following day. Once more, no pipe. They telephoned Hendersons again but still John Lewis couldn't be contacted. "I can only think someone pinched it, for their garden or something," Mrs Elliot says.

The accounts of what happened next differ. According to Clare Crowhurst, the Elliots never properly told Donald that the pipe was missing, and he sailed thinking it was aboard. Furthermore, she maintains, John Elliot said to her: "Never mind, I'll attend to it", which meant, she presumed, that he was going to buy a length of ordinary hose from a local shop as an emergency replacement.

Donald Crowhurst was certainly aware of the problem after June Elliot's first visit to Exeter airport. One of the lists of unfinished jobs contains the annotation in Crowhurst's handwriting: "TUESDAY . . . Mr Elliot—Exeter say not on plane—(Pilot rang up) Company says loaded before take-off to Exeter". The lists, however, contain no subsequent reference to the matter.

John Elliot declares he told Crowhurst very clearly before he set off that there was no pipe on board for bailing. He says that he never told anyone that he would arrange to get replacement piping, and ordinary hose would in any case have been no good as the Henderson pumps were so powerful they would have closed up unreinforced pipe with their suction. (Hendersons, in turn, say that unreinforced hose of the right dimensions—$1\frac{1}{2}$ inches in diameter—would have been better than nothing.)

Crowhurst certainly had *some* knowledge of the problem, though it may not have fully registered on his mind. The truth probably is that he may either have subconsciously suppressed it, unable to cope with yet more difficulties, or he may have simply expected that one of his many helpers would have had the good sense to put things right without worrying him further.

John Elliot is also a witness to another disputed matter: did someone unload a vital pile of spare parts from the deck of *Teignmouth Electron* before she sailed? These supplies—ready-cut pieces of plywood for hull replacements, odd bits of rigging, nuts, screws and various oddments—could have been mistaken for rubbish. After Crowhurst had sailed, Elliot saw all the spare parts innocently piled on the Morgan Giles slipway, and he declares he personally put them aboard the boat. Everyone agrees the spares were left ashore, but Morgan Giles workmen say they were never put aboard.

However, here Clare Crowhurst's testimony tends to back up John Elliot. She borrowed a carrier bag from the Royal Hotel and filled it with a hotel meal of buns, ham and salad. She added her own special Christmas present for Donald, a soft cuddly ventriloquist's doll with blonde woollen hair for him to talk to on the voyage, plus a small book on Yoga exercises, a china spoon for him to eat his favourite curry, and a box of cherry nougat, which he specially enjoyed. She also included a long, personal letter. She took the carrier bag and carefully placed it on Donald's bunk, in the front of the cabin. Her recollection of doing this is very distinct. Two days later, Stanley Best arrived at Bridgwater, and handed her back the carrier bag. It had also been found, he said, on the slipway..

* * *

On the eve of Crowhurst's departure, October 30th, things were even more hectic and disorganised than they had been throughout the five months of preparation. There was such chaos that Donald Kerr actually called off his BBC camera crew. He told them to stop filming and help the preparations instead. They rushed off to buy flares, a life-jacket, and other fundamentals that were still lacking. "Donald had no lunch that day, there wasn't time," says Kerr. "He stood on the boat trying to organise the stuff as it piled on board. Round about teatime we dragged him off to a local tea shop with Clare to have a snack of some sort. He was in a terrible state, quivering from lack of sleep and food. There was no doubt he clearly didn't want to go. He kept murmuring 'It's no good. It's no good.' He knew it could kill him, but he could never quite bring himself to say so."

It may be difficult to understand, in retrospect, why no one was able to halt this nightmare progress. But it was not as extra-ordinary as it might seem. Everyone was so eager for the great project to succeed. Donald Crowhurst himself set the tone. His intentions were genuine, and heroic; but as had happened so many times before, he managed to persuade himself that his intentions had become established fact. There was no one to persuade him that these intentions could not change the reality of the situation.

In Teignmouth during those last two weeks they re-enacted a nautical version of the oldest of all stories of publicity acting upon vanity, The Emperor's New Clothes. First everyone read of the riches and glories of emperors. Then they learnt they were to have their own emperor. Then the Town Crier told them how splendid he would be. Then he arrived. He was not only late, he was naked, but there was no one who pointed out what his eyes should have told him, in a loud enough voice. The splendour of the idea had grown so much more powerful than the naked reality.

This familiar process of hypnotism by self-perpetuating myths was best described by Daniel Boorstin, the American historian, in another classic of publicity acting upon vanity, The Image:

In the last half-century we have misled ourselves, not only about how much novelty the world contains, but about men themselves, and how much greatness can be found among them ... Two centuries ago when a great man appeared, people looked for God's purpose in him; today we look for his press agent.

The root of the problem, the social source of these exaggerated expectations, is in our novel power to make men famous ... We do not like to believe that our admiration is focussed on a largely synthetic product. Having manufactured our celebrities, having willy-nilly made them our cynosures — the guiding stars of our interest — we are tempted to believe that they are not synthetic at all, that they are somehow still God-made heroes who now abound with a marvellous modern prodigality.

In many ways it was the combination of small town endeavour and national publicity that was to blame. Like many clever but unsophisticated people, Donald Crowhurst was both seduced by the glamour of publicity, and scornful of it. He believed newspaper stories, yet thought he could play-act a part in them for an exaggerated fee. With half his mind he thought the magical tales of heroism and scandal were more real than they could ever be; with the other half he thought them such a facile pretence they could be artificially duplicated with little more than good intentions, a bravura manner, and a skilful press agent. And, of course, he was bemused by the aura of big men and big money which, to provincial aspirants, always seems to surround all London-based activity. Fame was a game: a bonanza of easy money and flattering headlines which came as an automatic reward for a proclaimed enterprise which — in Crowhurst's mind — was heroic largely because millions of newspaper readers would be cajoled into thinking it so. If Fleet Street has to take any blame for pushing Donald Crowhurst out to sea, it is because it sometimes seems willing to encourage self-delusions like these, since they sell newspapers.

*   *   *

All the rest of that afternoon, and much of the evening, was spent shovelling equipment aboard. After nightfall, Crowhurst came ashore, walked up to the Royal Hotel, and sat down to a last dinner-party with Clare, her sister Helen, and Ron Winspear. The rest had been invited but had been caught up with other plans. The hotel owner sent in a celebration bottle of champagne. It did not enliven the meal, which was subdued. For the first time in his friendship with Crowhurst, Ron Winspear found himself having to lead the conversation. He declared how wonderful it would be that by the time of Donald's return there would probably be a newly returned, and strengthened, Labour Government (Ron is a staunch Labour supporter). Crowhurst rose to the argument, but without much enthusiasm.

After dinner the Eastwoods, Elliots, Beards, Stanley Best and Rodney Hallworth turned up for a last drink, which was less subdued. Hallworth was still bubbling with ideas. One Hallworth idea was that Miss Teignmouth 1968 should sail out with the lone mariner towards the starting line. She would kiss him just before the gun, then leap overboard. Another was that Donald and Clare Crowhurst should visit a waterside chapel for a few moments of silent, photographed, prayer just before the departure. (Donald, without Clare, was finally lured to the chapel. Hallworth still has pictures of him there, refusing to pray.)

After this drink Donald and Clare rowed out to the boat for a final inspection. It was still smothered with piled-up equipment. They sorted out as much as they could and then, at two in the morning, went back to the hotel. Once in bed, Donald lay silent beside Clare. After struggling for the right words, he finally said, in a very quiet voice: "Darling, I'm very disappointed in the boat. She's not right. I'm not prepared. If I leave with things in this hopeless state will you go out of your mind with worry?" Clare, in her turn, could only reply with another question. "If you give up now," she said, "will you be unhappy for the rest of your life?"

Donald did not answer, but started to cry. He wept until morning. During that last night he had less than five minutes' sleep. "I was such a fool!" says Clare Crowhurst now. "Such a stupid fool! With all the evidence in front of me, I still didn't realise Don was telling me he'd failed, and wanted me to stop him. He had always been so brilliant at making things come right in a crisis that I never imagined he couldn't do it again. It was inconceivable that he might let himself die. So I refused his appeal. I was such a fool!"

Six

The Last Letter

Before he set sail, Donald Crowhurst told his friends that he knew there was a small possibility he might die during his voyage. He said that, just in case, he had made out a will, and written special letters to his wife and four children. The will and the four letters to his children are still unlocated. It may well be that he finally did not have time to write them, or the letters might have been given to some friend to be concealed until the children are old enough to read them. His letter to his wife, or one version of it, was found. Four months after his departure, Clare Crowhurst was sorting out old business papers on his desk at Woodlands. Concealed between documents she found five sheets of paper on which Donald had written a first draft of a letter to be given her in the event of his death. The letter must have been written in his study, at some moment during the summer. Mrs Crowhurst has given us her permission to publish it.

*　　*　　*

Darling,
My most fervent hope is that you never see this writing. If you ever do, it will mean that by the pursuit of my own ends I have

placed an almost intolerable emotional burden on you, but *it is not* intolerable, and it is to give some last physical support that I am writing now. I am well aware that it will be of no immediate help, but in time may well prove to be so . . .

It is a task of the utmost difficulty, yet one in which I must put more of my utmost effort than any I have ever attempted. It is my last opportunity to express my overwhelming love for you and gratitude for the joy our marriage has brought me. The words are desperately inadequate—how can one talk of words like "gratitude" that carry an implication of polite thanks? But *you* will know what I mean, and will forgive my choice.

You have made my whole existence a great and powerful rapture for 12 years, you have turned what was grey into what has been full of colour, light and love and I would not have exchanged those times for anything. It seems that the book must be closed, not because the reader is tired but because there is no more to read. No more, that is, in terms *we* can foresee with certainty, but if intensity of spiritual feeling has any endurance my love will be with you always. If we can comfort those we love and cannot physically reach, in any way, then I shall comfort you.

Don't fall into the dreadful trap of looking for signs of my continued existence that is baited by mediums and their ilk— I mean no disrespect to the worthy ones but they are easily led by their own preconceptions and the less scrupulous are simply awful. Stick to everyday things. The full burden of family responsibility now rest on your shoulders, you will have no shortage of *practical* things to occupy you—let them. (You will have help from professional and legal advisers—remember they are *advisers*—listen to them and make your *own* mind up. I have tried to ensure that you will have no worries about money.)

More of this later. What I am trying to say now is that I will give you whatever is possible in the way of spiritual comfort—you must not seek it, for this path leads into areas the stricken mind cannot be trusted to cope with reasonably—you must keep out of them and retain a practical, everyday outlook.

If I take this possibility really seriously, why do I go? Because I am certain that our life is but the twinkling of a star and can only be characterised by beauty, which is eternal, and not by its duration which in eternity is so short as to be meaningless. You have given my life its beauty—the only great beauty I can see in it. If I had not taken up this challenge the future may not have held anything so joyful as our years together have been (would we necessarily have continued to be so happy together?)

Nothing is certain—least of all life, from day to day, minute to minute, or even second to second. This *was* the manner of my death. What does that matter? A car crash, a falling slate, thrombosis . . . ten thousand alternatives lie ready waiting to sever the tenuous links of circumstance that keep us alive. I do not expect to die. There is no awful pall of fear hanging over my soul and there will probably never be, because I am not afraid of the thing or its consequences to me—only deeply concerned with those to you and the children that I love only second to you. Whatever happens you can be certain I did not spend my last moments paralysed with fear, by striving to the last to keep myself alive for you and them. With you reading these words I will have failed, though I should have been *much* more likely to have succeeded. Do not fret about it, treat it as a matter of course. And settle down to routine as though my absence was longer than expected. Please don't let any of the complications bother you at first—they can easily be looked after by professionals. Later on, when you *can* cope . . .

Turning to the children. I have left letters for each of them on their 16th birthday. This birthday is much more important than one's 21st, in my view. At 21 there's little one can do about attitudes and behaviour but at 16 one shapes one's course to adult values, though there is still a long way to go to maturity.

A gentle reminder about Roger. Never let him exasperate you, he is so emotional that so long as he is a child he will never be able to cope under emotional stress, and may never be able to cope unless he has the affection to which he responds so well amply, if not lavishly, bestowed.

The rest will emerge. Don't take Rachel and Simon *too* much for granted, and don't let James become too dreamy. I know all this is terribly obvious, but it is nice to have a simple guidelines when things get very complicated and involved. When you have a difficult situation to cope with I hope you will be able to clear your own thinking a little by remembering these simple guides and that is why I put them down.

I hope the nursery is a great success and that you will decide to keep it on and that it will provide everything you need. [Mrs Crowhurst had planned to start a nursery school at Woodlands, but the scheme never got going.] It is a very suitable employment in a great many ways. Resist the temptation to close down for emotional reasons most strongly. Do try to write seriously if the nursery thing doesn't work. You will have to make a really concentrated effort at it if you are ever to get anything produced— I'm not just scheming again, darling, but trying to lay foundations for you to do something I know you can do, and do quite well. It takes discipline and effort, though, and you must realise my love that no one achieves much as a professional writer without both.

I am not talking, of course, of anything you may come to write as a hobby. The writers group is a good thing for you (they will be the first to scold you for lack of discipline, though!) and could be a stimulus to you if you do decide to write professionally.

So much for what is practical—Now I must take my leave of you and it breaks my heart. You are working in the kitchen and singing. I am, but for the subject I am dealing with now, an immensely happy man, and the root of my happiness has been your constant love. It is not to throw it all away, nor to lay claim to the rewards that I am going, though I will try to give you them. I am going because it is worthwhile, it is my particular challenge, it will most likely bring benefits, but that is not why—I am going because I would have no peace if I stayed. Peace within myself, for no matter how happy a man is made by his wife and family life, if he turns down the one major challenge of his life he can never be the same, especially when the challenge is of his own devising! I am going because I must. I cannot turn away, nor do I wish to. I would certainly not go if I thought there was a very little chance of success, but I must go because I know I have a very, very good chance of success. We have said all this to each other from time to time—not in these words perhaps, but with this meaning. I go over it here so that there will be no recriminations in the event that you should be reading these words, and to remind you that this was not a blind and foolish venture, but one in which the risk was understood and which we accepted. When one has considered the consequences of an action as we have done together, there is no need for reproaches of any sort if our enterprises fail. We knew they might, we accept the risks in order to claim the rewards, and we do both together. I have no feeling of regret, and hope you will not have any either, but I am deeply concerned by the consequences of the sort of failure that will lead to you seeing this letter.

The burden falling on you is going to be heavy. Father and mother to the children and financial manager to the household.

Do the job well for me, and it will tax you enough without the strain of pointless grief. Nothing can touch or tarnish our happiness —not time nor brief future misery nor anything that lies ahead. The joys we have shared, always simple ones, always intense, are past—behind us and established forever as a fact of our partnership.

What lies ahead is pure conjecture. Do not lament the fact that joy and happiness could not endure longer. The end must come to all human experience and that alone is certain. So, my love, though I do not know if it is for all eternity or just the twinkling of that feeble star that is mortality, I take my leave of you. May pain be spared you. May you find joy in life and in your children. May they grow to reflect credit on you, to testify our love, to give you the love I will not now be able to, to comfort and console and to give purpose to your future life as they have to the years, those immortal, happy, happy years you and I spent with one another.

Bless you, my love.

Seven

The First Two Weeks at Sea

At three o'clock on Thursday, October 31st—with only nine hours in hand—Donald Crowhurst was towed over the bar of Teignmouth Harbour to start his voyage. The weather was cold and drizzly. Three motor boats, with forty friends and the BBC aboard, accompanied him, and a further forty or so spectators watched from the shore. The last of the last-minute supplies, a parcel of torch batteries, was tossed aboard as he prepared to raise his sails. Then, instantly, things went wrong. Crowhurst had found that his rubber buoyancy bag, which had been hurriedly lashed round the top of the mainmast the day before, had also been lashed around two halyards; he could not hoist his foresails. Furthermore, John Elliot had accidentally attached the jib and staysail to the wrong stays; they were in reverse order. Crowhurst could, with reasonable ease, have climbed the mast and cleared the halyards, but he did not want to alarm his wife while she was still watching. He screamed: "I'll be glad when I'm on my own without help from you bloody lot!" and asked for a tow back into harbour. Then he gave Clare a heavy, reassuring wink. Things might be going badly, but he was happy to be on the move at last.

94

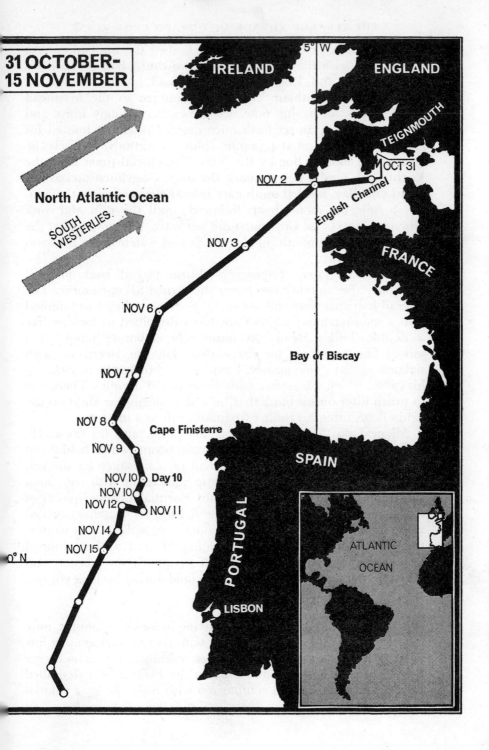

31 OCTOBER–15 NOVEMBER

IRELAND

ENGLAND

5° W

TEIGNMOUTH

OCT 31

NOV 2

English Channel

North Atlantic Ocean

SOUTH WESTERLIES

FRANCE

NOV 3

NOV 6

Bay of Biscay

NOV 7

NOV 8

Cape Finisterre

NOV 9

SPAIN

NOV 10   Day 10

NOV 10

NOV 12   NOV 11

PORTUGAL

NOV 14

NOV 15

0° N

ATLANTIC OCEAN

LISBON

After a Morgan Giles rigger had climbed the mast to correct the mistake with the buoyancy bag, Crowhurst had reversed his two foresails, and Rodney Hallworth had tactfully hoisted a Teignmouth Corinthian Yacht Club burgee to the masthead (local scepticism having now become embarrassingly frank and vocal), the trimaran set forth once more. Crowhurst hoisted his sails successfully, and at 4.52 p.m. (plus five seconds) precisely, he crossed the starting line by the Ness. The official timer from the Yacht Club fired a gun to mark the start. Crowhurst tacked out into Lyme Bay, headed south-east against a strongish south wind. For a mile the motor boats followed, until the rain and dusk obscured him. Clare Crowhurst did not wave, she just stood at the bow of the Teignmouth pilot's launch and watched her husband as he sailed away.

Four hours later, *Teignmouth Electron* tacked back towards Torquay, after another two hours she turned SE once more. The foresail halyards were still not right. Somehow they had jammed into a monster knot, which Crowhurst described as looking like a double Turk's Head — an immensely elaborate tangle that sailors like to weave for decoration. He was overcome with sickness again — "nervousness I suppose" — but began to clear up his cabin, which was strewn with disorganised supplies. There was so much litter on his bunk that he had to sleep that night on the cabin floor, using his rubber frogman's suit as a mattress.

All next day he spent clearing his cabin, and his bunk. He recorded that the lacing eyes of the main boom (which hold down the mainsail) had broken — "that will be a nuisance for the rest of the trip" — and decided to rig up something with rope as a substitute. He kept finding odd but essential bits-and-pieces of equipment (flints for his Variflame lighter, for instance) tucked away in unexpected Tupperware containers, as he sought to stow them away methodically. By evening he had at last stopped feeling sick, the Eddystone light off Plymouth was abeam, and his cabin was beginning to look as it would during his long voyage.

* * *

It was a tiny place to contemplate living in for eight months, only nine feet long and eight feet wide, with its roof deliberately low and curved to reduce wind and water resistance. It was no bigger then Robin Knox-Johnston's cabin in his tiny single-hulled *Suhaili*, and minuscule in comparison with Nigel Tetley's palatial quarters aboard his standard "Victress" trimaran. The gangway down the centre of the cabin was two feet wide. On the starboard side was a long chart table surmounted by the dials of the wind direction and speed indicator. On the table was a screw-on vice for repair work, and forward a smaller table designed to carry the Marconi Kestrel radio-telephone. On the port side the cabin was divided equally between a sink and cooking units, and a small built-in table with a red cushioned seat. This is where Donald Crowhurst sat to eat, think and write his logs.

Across the front end of the cabin was a bulkhead, where hung Peter Beard's barometer, a radio loudspeaker, and a festoon of tangled wiring for the Marconi, a Racal RA 6217 communications receiver, and a Shannon Mark 3 transmitter/receiver, along with their jumbled power units, aerial connections, and microphones, headsets, morse keys and switch panels. The equipment would not have disgraced a radio ham's attic. In fact the major impression for anyone entering *Teignmouth Electron*'s cabin was wiring — hanging everywhere. Down the port side, disappearing behind the red cushions of Crowhurst's seat, ran a thick cluster of neatly colour-coded wires. This was the spinal cord of the vaunted electrical and electronic system, which above deck fanned out to the masts and various parts of the rigging and floats. It all looked very impressive, seemingly justifying all the lyrical talk of "a miracle of electronic wizardry". But it seemed less impressive to Donald Crowhurst as he tidied up his cabin. Each time he lifted the bottom cushion of that seat he would reveal all the wires ending abruptly there, in an unruly tangle. There had simply not yet been time to design and build his magic "computer", though a gaping hole underneath the seat had been specially cut out to house it. (It was therefore not so remarkable that the other ends of these wires, arriving at their destinations around the boat, also hung virgin and unconnected.)

Forward of the main cabin, through a low arch where the two Henderson diaphragm pumps were installed, was the trimaran's single bunk. It was just over two feet wide, and hemmed in on either side by shelves holding double rows of Tupperware containers that Crowhurst was slowly filling up with an unsystematic mixture of stores and spares — dried vegetables, tools, boat fittings, the BBC's cine-camera and tapes, packaged curries, flour, batteries, powdered milk, and above all radio spares. Radio spares! Not by the dozen, but by the gross. Box upon box of transistors, condensers, resistors, reed switches, valves, cable, printed circuit board, heat sinks, plugs and sockets ... they filled at least ten Tupperware containers. Why so many? Perhaps because any man, faced by confusion, makes obsessively over-certain that the one thing he really knows about will never let him down.

Other oddments were stowed around the bunk and the cabin. Tucked behind the companionway ladder were two life-jackets, three safety harnesses for Crowhurst to attach to deck wires to prevent him falling overboard, and six unopened sets of the *Sunday Times* M, I and K signalling flags. These were jumbled with eight Plysu containers holding part of his water supply and immediately below was one of his large fixed water tanks.

Above the chart table was a bookshelf, on it the Admiralty *Pilots*, *Ocean Passages*, and three of the four radio manuals. There were also navigational and tide tables, Reed's *Nautical Almanacs* for 1968 and 1969, and instruction manuals for the generator, the self-steering and the radio gear. For his own reading, Crowhurst had brought only a few books: *Shanties from the Seven Seas*, an anthology by Stan Hugill; *Gipsy Moth Circles the World*, by Sir Francis Chichester; *Servomechanisms* by P. L. Taylor; *Mathematics of Engineering Systems*; and *Relativity, the Special and the General Theory* by Albert Einstein. He didn't want novels, he had told his wife. Mathematical text-books would engross him for long enough.

On an upper shelf was the neck of the champagne bottle used at the launching, wrapped in pink ribbon. Stowed in various drawers were plates, knives and forks, Crowhurst's own sextant, and Hohner chromatic mouth-organ, a pot of champagne mustard, his medical supplies, a hot water bottle, an enscribed scroll "from the hoteliers of Teignmouth" wishing him—of course—"bon voyage", a few tins of beer, and a bottle of methylated spirit to start the galley stove.

*　　　　*　　　　*

Even on his third day at sea, Crowhurst was already fretting about the methylated spirit. He had worked out the amounts he needed from Eric Hiscock's book *Voyaging Under Sail*. Hiscock had required half a gallon for two people for eighty-one days; Crowhurst had halved the amount, forgetting that one man cooks as often as two, and therefore needs as much. Crowhurst only had one and a half gallons on board. "It should be OK though, as on that reckoning it should last 81 × 3 = 243 days." (It was enough. By some macabre irony Donald Crowhurst's voyage lasted precisely 243 days. There was less than a pint left unused.)

On that same day he tried to work his radio equipment, but could not get through. He grumbled some more about the peculiar knot that had formed itself in the foresail halyards: "One of the sea's nastier practical jokes. It would take hours to tie, and it's going to take even more hours to untie up there."

It was at this point, still in sight of the Lizard Head, off Falmouth, that his real problems began. His Hasler self-steering gear was the first to give trouble.* Despite the modifications made in Teignmouth, he recorded in his log that it shed two screws. Crowhurst replaced them with others stolen from less essential parts of the gear, but he had virtually no spare screws or bolts. If the shedding continued he would lose control of *Teignmouth Electron* while not at the helm. While at work on this, he discovered his logline (which was streaming astern to measure the distance travelled) had caught on the rudder, and the rotator had jammed. He looked at his log reading: it recorded only seven miles travelled. He lashed the logline to his tiller to keep it clear of the other machinery, and prepared a fresh line to get accurate readings. It was getting dark; so he decided to hoist the metal radar reflector higher up the mast. It swung and cut the second finger of his left hand badly. "Blood everywhere—first aid kit out. Certainly well stocked in this department!!"

The problems with the Hasler had obviously depressed Crowhurst. To compensate, he promised himself a feast for breakfast the next day, and sat down to write a jaunty nautical passage in his narrative log. It was underlined as important, and obviously intended for publication:

Earlier today porpoises came out to greet me. There were about 30 of them playing round the boat, accompanied by a mass of gulls. Sometimes as many as 6 pairs in a line (they seemed to prefer swimming in pairs) would jump on the starboard side and swim across the bows to port. All round the boat

* In fairness to the Hasler design it must be remembered that it was designed for use on monohulled boats and not for the phenomenal speeds sometimes achieved by trimarans. In its conventional use the Hasler mechanism is highly effective and reliable. Crowhurst's type 1AQH vane gear was in fact identical with the gear which Dr. Guy Cappeliez used for his successful circumnavigation in *Procax*.

they were leaping around and inspecting me! I remembered the old saying: "When the sea hog . . ."

Crowhurst stayed up most of that third night reading the Admiralty book on recommended courses for steam and sailing boats known as *Ocean Passages*. This volume, the result of centuries of maritime experience, describes the most favourable courses to reach various destinations at different times of the year, and records the prevailing winds in any area. Because of these winds, *Ocean Passages* recommends any sailing boat travelling down the Atlantic to set a course along the old clipper route—getting well to the west before turning southwards past Portugal and Madeira, then following a wide arc to the west through the South Atlantic. Crowhurst must have known all about this from his extensive reading, but for some reason he felt bound to confirm the information that night. Unlike Chichester he had not carefully planned his course before setting off: he was seemingly making it up as he went along.*

On Sunday morning he ate the promised monster breakfast of "tea, porridge, scrambled egg on toast, toast and jam, more tea", and then slept. The wind, at least, was perfect: a 15-knot blow from the north-east. *Teignmouth Electron* ran swiftly out into the Atlantic before it. He discovered his radio receiver wasn't working: "no more use than a concrete mooring sinker to me now. Hope I can get it going again." Once more there was a lyrical passage-for-publication in the log to compensate:

> After reading *Ocean Passages* I decided to make a westing. The weather would delight a clipper captain . . . A voice keeps saying "Carozzo coming" and urges me to cut Ushant fine, but blow that, I'll sail this boat like a clipper. I may miss a few days, but it will be a lot safer, and anyway could just as easily save time if a West or South-West blow comes—as it very well may.

(As it happens, the voice telling him that Carozzo was coming was misinformed. Carozzo's start had also been rushed, but he had responded differently from Crowhurst. To comply with the race

---

* Knox-Johnston—who had passed this way four and a half months before—also left his detailed route plans until after he had set sail. "One *can* plan an exact route for a sailing vessel," he explained, "but one cannot expect to stick to it."

rules he had cast-off on October 31st, but had then anchored his boat just offshore to spend a whole week stowing his gear, working on his equipment and making sure everything was safe before braving the Atlantic.)

Crowhurst was now learning the problems of coping with initial snags two hundred miles out in the ocean. He began an elaborate investigation of his broken Racal radio receiver; after spending hours stripping it down he discovered, shamefacedly, that the only thing wrong was a blown fuse. The Hasler self-steering gear was giving trouble again. The wind had shifted to the south-east during the night, and when Crowhurst woke up *Teignmouth Electron* was sailing northwards. Crowhurst battled with the gear most of the morning, trying to make it work on the new tack. Eventually he had to lower the mainsail to slow the boat down, as he could only get the Hasler to hold him on course at between two and seven knots. He returned to his domestic tasks and cooked three days' supply of curry and rice. The boil on his forehead which had grown during his trip round the coast was swelling again, and beginning to close up his left eye. He resolved to find his vitamin pills, still stowed in one of the trimaran floats.

On Tuesday, November 5th, the second really serious trouble showed itself:

Rachel's birthday. Happy birthday Rachel. Hell of a morning for me though. After putting up the main and making a course of SW, I was feeling pleased with myself when I noticed that bubbles were blowing out from the hatch when *Teignmouth Electron* rolled! To confirm my fears, the port bow float was shipping an awful lot more water than it should, as we were on the port tack. All the evidence was that the compartment was full of water.

I eased the ship to a course of West, and undid the butterfly nuts. The whole compartment WAS flooded, to deck level. I bailed out with a bucket, mopped up, and screwed down on a Sylglas fibreglass gasket. That should avoid further trouble. It was a long, exhausting job that took 3 hours, as I was shipping a good bit of water. The seas were 15 feet high, and the wind was about Force 7, so that as fast as I bailed, it came pouring back in!

Then came Crowhurst's first burst of despair, momentary, but real:

I cursed the people who'd been kind enough to help me stow ship, and I cursed myself for a fool. I swore the boat was a toy fit only for the Broads or the pool at Earl's Court. But when I'd got the job done, eaten some curry and rice with an apple and some tea, I experienced the great satisfaction that something I'd been fearing had happened and had been dealt with. Now I must do all the other hatches. I looked into the port main hatch, and things seemed OK. I got out my vitamin pills. A whaler, French or Spanish, said hullo.

The outburst against the people who helped to stow boat may have been provoked by the belief that they had not screwed the hatches down properly. But Crowhurst admitted that he had already been fearing leaks, presumably of a less easily curable nature. It seems odd, therefore, that he had not more carefully explored Clare's observation of the dripping float and double-checked his baling arrangements before leaving Teignmouth.

That evening, Crowhurst tried to lance his boil—which turned out to be bottomless—and decided that penicillin pills as well as vitamins might help to cure it. He charged his batteries and tried, unsuccessfully, to contact Portishead radio. This radio failure, relatively unimportant, apparently depressed him more than the earlier trials of the day. "Went to bed in disgust," he wrote.

*   *   *

At this stage Crowhurst took stock of his progress. He did a little calculation in his logbook. From November 2nd to 6th he had covered 538 miles, which meant an average of 134 miles a day. It seemed, on the face of it, Chichester-like progress. What Crowhurst did not record was that much of the distance had been logged while tacking back and forth into the wind, which for two days now had been blowing steadily from the south. The weakness of his trimaran to windward was again beginning to show. In those four days, he had, in fact, covered only 290 miles along his intended route.

He also, that Wednesday, began to fix his position by celestial navigation (up to this point he had not bothered about precise positions, except for one radio fix, with his Navicator). Crowhurst's navigation methods* remained as Peter Eden had described them,

* See Appendix 1.

"a mite slapdash". Most days, he would take a conventional sight of the sun at noon with his sextant and quite often another sight in the morning or evening, and, with the help of a nautical almanac, chronometer and "short method" tables, was able to establish a reasonably accurate position. He rarely took simultaneous sights of stars or of the planets, and when he did so (there were occasional attempts with Venus) he invariably got peculiar results.

On many occasions, however, he used a far cruder, though much simpler, method. By observing the time when the sun was at its maximum altitude and comparing it with the time of the maximum altitude of the sun at Greenwich he would calculate his latitude and longitude. Unfortunately, although latitude can be calculated accurately this way, longitude cannot. Because of the difficulty of establishing the exact moment of the sun's transit, errors of forty miles or so can occur – and with inaccurate chronometers, errors can be double even that.

His first attempt that Wednesday was not very auspicious. "Got a couple of sun-sights for a fix," he wrote in his log, "but later confirmed 3 mins error on chronometer – may not have noticed it except for Rotary!" His troubles, trying to synchronise his Hamilton chronometer, his Zenith deck watch, and his Rotary wrist watch were to involve him in hours of patient checking, and later became an obsession.

*   *   *

So far as he could tell, Crowhurst was now some eighty miles west of Brittany. The wind was veering to the west, and for the first time he was able to sail due south. He managed to contact both Rugby radio station to arrange a radio-telephone call, and Portishead to send a birthday telegram to his daughter Rachel. "Quite a field day," he wrote, euphoric again.

The next day – one week at sea – there was Hasler trouble once more. Two more screws had fallen out. With an abrupt switch of mood, he gave himself over to vivid complaints:

That's four [screws] gone now – can't keep cannibalising from other spots forever! The thing will soon fall to bits. More trouble with wire strop. While trying to cope with Hasler, log-line fouled rudder and servo blade! This stern board is all very well but it means shipping the logline at every tack!!! I suppose gybing is the answer.

103

Trying to do up the screws (which I have to do morning and evening) is like trying to repair the inside of a mincing machine while it's running. The power generated at speed by the servo blade is quite considerable and would make a nasty mess of a finger.

Crowhurst spent the rest of this day bringing in further stores from the floats—"cabin looking like Steptoe's living-room"—trying to fix his position, and estimating his day's run. His boil was recovering, but the cabin was starting to smell, and hygiene worried him. Once again, after a depressing day, there was an obligatory brave passage in the log:

I got out the bread and toaster and had toasted bread (4 slices) for supper—2 with the last of the curry and 2 with jam and butter. The toaster is remarkable—it was blowing 7 (gusting 8—right up to 39 knots, and I was running) and it was quite incredible how 4 slices of bread stay balanced on it. It reminded me very strongly of Clare, there was something very marvellous about the way it worked away under impossible conditions. I would have said it was doing all anyone could possibly ask of it. I'm a lucky man to have such a toaster!

*   *   *

"I'm a lucky man to have such a toaster!"—the tone of this pluckiness-for-publication passage, like some others, is oddly out of key with the rest of the logbook. In the popular literature of single-handed sailing there are various stock themes. One is the companionship of dolphins, sea-birds, porpoises, and other marine creatures; one is the evocation of the clippers on their epic voyages; one is the comfort given in solitude by the domestic routines of baking bread, flying fish breakfasts, and other ingenious masculine cookery. Within a week, Donald Crowhurst had already dealt with all three of these stock themes in his logbook narrative, and had written them in a way that was clearly in imitation of the sailing books he had read with such passionate attention. It was possible for Eric Hiscock, Sir Alec Rose, and even the more sophisticated Sir Francis Chichester to write of such salt-sprayed themes with a bluff directness that was entirely unselfconscious. For Donald Crowhurst, an intellectual with a penchant for role-playing, it was not.

The problem for anyone trying to interpret Crowhurst's voyage is to untangle this role-playing from genuine observation. Obviously, the two mingle frequently. But by close study one can distinguish the public tone of Crowhurst the Hero from the private tone of Donald Crowhurst the real, and suffering, man. It is the difference, for instance, between his posturing letters to Frank Carr or Stanley Best, and his posthumous letter to his wife Clare. He never absolutely ceased to pose (who does?), but the contrast is striking enough to be called the difference between sincerity and pretence. In the logbooks Donald Crowhurst is sometimes—as in the three "public" passages we have quoted— writing as a Hero, and imitatively; at other times, usually when frankly depressed, he is much closer to his genuine self.

When he was making tape recordings for the BBC, he was almost always playing a self-conscious and disingenuous role. His wife noticed this, and subsequently would always say how much she disliked the recordings. "They're not the real Donald," she said. "They're so trite." This imitative element in Crowhurst's record of his trip is difficult to demonstrate conclusively; it only emerges as a cumulative impression. At one point, however, it becomes obvious, and although it occurred later in the voyage it is worth quoting here. Crowhurst was recording a highly amusing session on tape. In the middle of it all, conscious that perhaps the BBC needed heroism rather than amusement, he pulled himself together to perform. "Now then, how about some timeless prose, eh? Bit of the old Hemingway . . ." he said, and pitching his voice in a deep and portentous tone, began to orate:

. . . an involuntary gybe had hurtled my head against the cockpit side, and now I was conscious that my head hurt and my back hurt. I wondered if any serious damage had been done. Very tentatively I moved one foot and one leg, and then the others. I lay there for a minute, thinking how careless I'd been, and then, very slowly sat up. I sat very quietly for about three minutes, and then very gingerly got up. Everything seemed to be all right. I didn't know then that it was going to be three days before I was going to be able to move again. I gathered myself together, got to my feet, and finished making the attachment of the trisail to the boom, and continued my way eastwards . . .

This is dramatic stuff, but his inspiration came not from Hemingway, but from Chichester's book *Gipsy Moth Circles the World*, which he had with him. On page 195 Sir Francis had written:

> ... I was flung in a heap to the bottom of the far side of the cockpit. I stayed motionless where I landed, wondering if my leg was broken. I relaxed everything while I wondered. For about a minute I made no motion at all, and then slowly uncurled myself. To my astonishment—and infinite relief—nothing seemed broken ... Picking myself up and collecting my wits, I carried on with my radio work ... During the night I had some difficulty in moving my ribs and ankle, and feared a bad stiffening ... I sailed out of the Forties that evening ... I tried to celebrate the event with a bottle of Veuve Cliquot,* but it was a flop drinking by myself ...

* * *

After nine days at sea, Crowhurst worked out his rough position from the navigational Consol radio beacon at Lugo, in northern Spain, and discovered he was well to the west of dangerous Cape Finisterre. As his course was south-west, he decided to enjoy a long sleep, and did not wake until eleven in the morning. This was not entirely wise, as he was in the shipping lanes and in some danger of being run down. On waking he thrust his head out of the cabin hatch and saw a large liner astern, roughly following him on a WSW course. He ate another monster breakfast and hoisted the mainsail. When he went to hoist the mizzen as well he found one of the halyard shackles used to attach the sail had disappeared during the night, and the halyard rope itself was half-way up the mast. He needed to climb the mast to retrieve it. The first action he recorded in his log is the streaming of a one and a half-inch plaited rope astern so that if he fell off the mast he could swim to the rope and get back aboard. Such a tumble is a constant terror of single-handed sailors, and this log entry is clear evidence that, at this time at least, he was taking the most scrupulous precautions not to

---

* Just before orating his pastiche, Crowhurst had also taken a drink from a bottle of champagne he carried aboard. Chichester had completed his journey through the Roaring Forties; Crowhurst wanted to have sailed the Roaring Forties. Chichester won glory by his feat, and celebrated with Veuve Cliquot; Crowhurst wanted similar glory, and drank Moët et Chandon. As he drank, did he imagine himself into the same situation as Chichester, so there was no conscious pretence in his role-playing? This is one of the central questions of his voyage.

lose his boat. He climbed the mast successfully, and retrieved the halyard, noticing as he did so that his buoyancy bag was still so inefficiently lashed to the masthead that the whole lower half of the bag was hanging loose. The hose intended to inflate it was not attached, and the masthead green light was about to fall off. He spent the evening trying to sort out the radio transmissions from Portishead, but, instead of navigational warnings, heard a news bulletin about Yoko Ono, who had suffered a miscarriage.

He also heard the Admiralty issue a warning that a "drifting bow section" had been spotted in the sea area he had just left. Lucky he had not run into it! Or could the so-called bow-section be *Teignmouth Electron* sailing under jib, nearly run down, and mis-identified? There had, after all, been that liner astern in the morning. "Perhaps I'd had a narrow squeak without knowing? If it was *Teignmouth Electron* I didn't take kindly to the use of the word 'adrift' to describe her movements."

There followed a period of slow progress. The wind kept shifting, and the boat kept gybing and heading in the wrong direction. Each night he would take down the mainsail; this kept him more on course but slowed him down disastrously. For three days he grew increasingly depressed, and sluggardly. He confessed himself sleepy and fuzzy-headed, and decided the lack of oxygen in the cabin must be affecting him.

On Saturday he noticed that a screw had fallen from the cross-tree spar on the mizzen mast: "This bloody boat is just falling to pieces due to lack of attention to engineering detail!!!"*

Meanwhile his navigation was perplexing. Each day, when he took a sight, it placed him in virtually the same position. Either he was sailing round in circles, he wrote, or there was something wrong with the sights he was taking on the sun. In fact both seem to have been the case. His navigation was certainly erratic at this stage, but it took him, in contrary winds, a whole week to sail only 210 miles from Cape Finisterre down the coast of Spain and Portugal. Tuesday was typical. At two in the morning the wind

---

* In his desperation, Crowhurst was now beginning to respond excessively even to trivial defects. The screw missing from the mizzen cross-trees was the kind of routine snag that any long-distance yachtsman might regularly expect. He did nothing about it, and the screw was still missing at the end of the voyage, though he had managed to sail many thousands of miles in the meantime. The problems of the self-steering gear and the leaks were, on the other hand, genuinely serious, and were borne out by an inspection of the boat afterwards. But it would perhaps have been fairer for Crowhurst to have been blaming not the engineering, but the conditions provoked by his rushed start—which indeed he does a little further in his log.

shifted, and *Teignmouth Electron* started to sail due north. "Too tired to care," he wrote, but in the morning came remorse:

> Got up late again, having sailed 7 hours due north. This is not good enough. I must not allow myself to get so lazy. True it was blowing hard all yesterday and I was tired, but I am not here for a rest or to catch up sleep. It will take me 4 hours to make up the lost distance, a total waste of 11 hours—half a day. If I did that every day it would take over a year to finish. I MUST NOT ALLOW MYSELF TO BE LAZY.

His Hamilton chronometer mainspring was bent, his Racal receiver out of action again, and he had brought the wrong book of radio signals:

> I had believed Hiscock when he said time signals were in *Admiralty List of Radio Signals* Volume II. They are in IV!* I haven't got it! I hadn't fussed overmuch, as with the Racal receiver I could always pull in WWV time signals, but now I did not have that either.
>
> Damn this rushed start, the number of things that should have been carefully checked that have not makes an almost endless list. Then there's the damage to the offcourse alarm. That could have been avoided by a couple of days' delay; the ghastly state of tune etc. etc. 14 days would have made such a difference; but of course impossible.

His next day at sea, Wednesday, November 13th, brought the third major disaster. He had already suffered his steering gear trouble and his leaking float. Now his Onan electricity generator was in peril:

> Wed 13. I disposed of an uneasy feeling about the date in the morning— I told myself 13 had never had an especially sinister significance for me. Today has had a sinister significance all right. Plugging away to westward in a southerly gale the cockpit hatch has been leaking and has flooded the engine compartment, electrics and Onan. Unless I can get the Onan to work I will have to think very seriously about the continuation of the project. With so much wrong with the boat in so

---

* Crowhurst was wrong too. Time signals are in Volume V.

many respects—it would perhaps be foolish or at any rate a subjective decision to continue. I will try to get the generator working, and think about the alternatives open to me.

This was a real catastrophe. To have the steering or even the buoyancy of his boat threatened was to Crowhurst a danger far more remote than to have the source of his electricity (albeit for largely non-existent safety devices) cut off. The leaky cockpit hatch should have been no more a surprise to him than his other disasters. John Eastwood had warned him, right at the start when they were discussing the design, that it was vulnerable; it had failed him on the trip round the coast; and on the trial sail it had shown how inadequate it was. But the fact that he should have been prepared for it made the blow more, not less, shattering.

"I will think about the alternatives open to me."—For the first time he had allowed himself to think he might have to give up. Donald Crowhurst was still being entirely frank at this point; whenever he felt terrified, or in despair, or ready to surrender, he wrote it down immediately and without guile.

Eight

Two Conflicting Testimonies

One might have expected that at this moment of total despair Donald Crowhurst's psychological make-up would force him to write into his log yet another jaunty passage of mariner's chit-chat. There is none; in fact we are about to come to his longest, frankest, and most logically devastating assessment of the hopeless position. The lack, however, is remedied by his first tape recording on the BBC equipment he had on board. This was the moment Crowhurst chose to record tape number one, and his choice was clearly deliberate. He had decided from then on to use public performance over the tape recorder as his optimistic therapy.

This chapter is largely composed of these two, long, contrasting declarations by Crowhurst. They are both informative, and sum up his position well. The first (from the tape recording) demonstrates in its bluff optimism Crowhurst the Hero, as he would like to appear. The second (from the log) reveals him as he really was. Anyone tempted to underestimate Donald Crowhurst should note how much more impressive is the second text.

Donald Crowhurst speaking on the tape recorder:

This small boat is the *Teignmouth Electron*. I've been at sea now

for very nearly fourteen days and I'm on my way to a rendezvous with Cape Horn. The reason, if one needs a reason, is that
nobody has ever before attempted the voyage ... I may not
have any chance at all of winning the Golden Globe, but I
think I have a chance of winning the prize, that explains why
I'm here in the middle of November in the North Atlantic
making tape recordings in a small boat. So much for the
reason.

What's it like? Well, if you know anything about small boats
you can imagine what it's like. If you don't, I don't think you
can. I think the thing that most people associate with small boats
is glorious afternoons in the Solent and pretty girls in bikinis
lounging about on the deck of some vast schooner while men in
natty yachting clothes stand with rugged determined looks on
their faces, grasping the wheel with a pipe clenched firmly
between their teeth, as some beautiful bird of a boat skims
across blue waters. Well, there may be circumstances when
that's a reasonable picture, unhappily I have never encountered
them. Conditions in a small boat are so peculiarly devastating
that it's amazing that people go to sea in small boats at all.
Everything in this boat is wet, I mean wet not damp. Wet.
Condensation is on the roof, it drips in your ear when you're
trying to sleep, every hole is a potential leak, and the noise, as
you've heard, is continuous and often deafening. You seldom
get a chance to have a good wash, bathing except in sea salt
water is out of the question, and the food of course is — well,
what you make it. I'll admit, of course, that conditions in a
single-handed race are not quite the same as when you go
cruising with your family or with a crew when things are a lot
more relaxed.

Of course single-handing has its compensations. No matter
how schizophrenic you are, it's difficult to fall out with the crew,
they're excellent people from the captain to the cabin boy.
However, it does mean that the cabin boy has to do the navigation while the captain has to wash out the socks. But so long as
you can keep a sense of proportion this doesn't matter too much.
The thing about single-handing is it puts a great deal of pressure
on the man, it explores his weaknesses with a penetration that
very few other occupations can manage. If he's lazy he'll be
twice as lazy when he's on his own, if he's easily dispirited it'll
knock the stuffing out of him in no time at all, if he's easily

frightened he's best staying at home—I wouldn't mind a dose of it myself right now.

Well now then, this race, particularly my participation in it: as a matter of records, I started on Thursday, October 31st, the last permissible day according to the race regulations, and I started in a flat spin. I've never put to sea in such a completely unprepared state in my life. I started without even hoisting the sails that I intended to use; on a voyage of this sort this is very close to foolishness. Nevertheless stipulations were that competitors would leave by the 31st, and leave by the 31st I did. I said to myself if I really can't sort this lot out in the first few weeks then at least I can turn back and come back home. It would have been a terrible and hard decision but I believe I would have made it had it been necessary. I've got problems still but I think they . . . they can be surmounted and I've got a fairly long spell in trade winds and doldrums in which to get the boat really ready for its ordeal in the great Southern Ocean and the Roaring Forties, and Cape Horn itself.

I'm a little bit worried about my arrival at the Horn because time is passing and I've been delayed a week already with head winds and the expected weather, according to the Admiralty Routeing Charts, just hasn't materialised. I'm persisting though in my determination to pass west of Madeira because I feel that a boat with the handling characteristics that my boat has, this is really the only safe course, and this will continue to be my criterion throughout the trip. I will sail this boat as though she were a clipper ship and I will stick to the traditional clipper ship routes if it takes me a month longer, that's what I'll do. At the moment of course there's a tremendous temptation to cut the corner, pass to the east of Madeira and close to the African coast, but I shall resist it.

The thing I don't understand is where these south-westerly winds are coming from, winds blow from the south-western quadrant day after day and they're not supposed to, it's most discouraging. And they're hard winds, too, 7, 8, and 9 most of the time except when they're so light as to be unusable. One thing, though, that has surprised me is the way this trimaran stands up to her canvas, she really is phenomenally stable and she seems to be able to keep sailing when I'm sure a conventional boat of the same water-line length wouldn't be able to.

Considering the problems Crowhurst was encountering with his Hasler steering gear, and his general trim of sails, it is extraordinary that he should have praised his trimaran in such extravagant terms.

Here, for comparison, is how he assessed his position at this time in his logbook. The account, written by torchlight in his cabin, covers nine closely written pages and is impressive in its logical coherence:

Friday 15: . . . Racked by the growing awareness that I must soon decide whether or not I can go on in the face of the actual situation. What a bloody awful decision—to chuck it in at this stage—what a bloody awful decision! But if I go on I am doing [two] things:

1: I am breaking my promise to Clare that I would only continue if I was happy that everything was as it should be to ensure the safe conclusion of the project. Unless I can get the electrics sorted out I cannot honestly say the condition is met. Furthermore I am placing Clare in the terrible position of having no news of me for 7 to 9 months as the radio would not be functioning.

2: As the boat stands I could not drive her much above 4 knots in the 40s. The Hasler performs wild broaches that would be fatal in big—really big—seas, when running. I would have to depend on the twin foresails, spread out at the bows, and they are virtually untried. At any event I cannot reasonably see a fast passage in the 40s in safety without self-righting gear, the buoyancy bag device, in operation. Particularly bearing in mind that I started late —October 31st—this is of special significance, as it means arriving at the Horn far later than I anticipated, in six or seven months' time—April/May. With the boat in its present state my chances of survival would not, I think, be better than 50–50, which I would not regard as acceptable.

"The boat in its present state"—what does that mean? I'll make a list:

1: No electrics:—
    (a) no radio communications
    (b) no masthead buoyancy
    (c) no time signals, and my chronometer is useless
    (d) no light—not essential I suppose

(a and d are endurable. b precludes the Horn in April/May—
if not the 40s altogether. I could arrange a manual release and
hope I had time to reach it. I could put something on deck to
actuate the buoyancy bag, as well as below. It would help if I
knew how much time I would have. c is fairly, no very, serious.
I could try to adapt a Navicator to 10 and 15 megacycles for
WWV but cannot use the soldering iron—have blowlamps
however.)

2: Leaky hatches:—
   (a) The port forward float hatch let in something like 120
       gallons in 5 days, though I think I've cured that.
   (b) The cockpit hatch has leaked 75 gallons overnight. I
       see no way out but to screw it down permanently and
       seal off the electrics. If I do that, of course, I am unable
       to clear it of any leaks, which would be a most dan-
       gerous situation.

(Let us assume the hatches could be cured. The cockpit hatch
screwed down on Sylglas after sawing off the edge. They could
not be pumped then.)

3: Incorrectly cut sails:—
   The main and mizzen sails set so full that in any condition
   except close-hauled they chafe on the shrouds.

4: Shroud placing and chafe prevention unsatisfactory.

(These are a nuisance, and make a really fast time impossible.
But endurable, and not in themselves dangerous.)

5: No method of pumping out forward and aft float hatches,
   forward main hatch, or aft main hatch without lifting
   hatches, which is potentially highly dangerous, and balnig.

6: No method of pumping out main saloon, which must be
   baled out. This inability to pump out is due to the fact
   that piping I asked for is not on board, and the pump
   provided is ludicrously inadequate.

(Vitally important. If I had a pipe on board maybe I could. I
don't see a way out. It would be crazy to go into the 40s with
present pumping arrangements.)

7: The concept of a hatch in the cockpit floor is wrong, I am
   more than ever convinced. I will only be happy when that
   cockpit floor is solid bottomed, but I could do that, I think,
   even if it involved cutting an access hole in saloon or aft
   bulkhead.

(Dealt with in 2 above)

8: The after collision bulkhead is leaking. The evidence of this is in the brown water in the saloon. It is obviously discoloured in the same way as the water in the engine compartment. I do not see how one could find the leak at sea.
(A worry, but endurable—with some risk in the event of damage to stern.)

9: The masthead buoyancy and sheet release mechanisms are not functioning. That's my own fault. The masthead bag stowage is very badly arranged, also my fault.
(Dealt with in 1 above. Masthead stowage could be improvised at sea however.)

10: The stowage arrangements could be improved. I do not see the perishable stuff surviving mould attack. Rice and flour are what I have in mind.
(No comment really needed. This certainly would not stop me, but could be a nuisance.)

11: The Hasler gear needs attention to screws every few hours, and they still drop out.
(Much more serious. I have tried varnish and Bostic. Neither seems to work. I could drill and tap each screwhead with a 4BA hole and put in small locking screws. Would take a day or two, but providing I did not break the tap due to the boat's motion, a reasonably feasible proposition. The gear is not, all the same, a reliable method of running in big seas even when working correctly. For that purpose twins would have to be used. My smallest twins are the working jibs, there is no twin storm jib. This means that when the wind was really strong there would be no alternative but trailing warps.* The system is untried and I have doubts about
    (a) the strength of the cleats
    (b) the possibility of forming a bight around the Hasler without fouling it.
Definitely need some sort of trial, but I could do that at sea, now.)

In its clarity, its self-awareness, and brave acceptance of the situation as it genuinely was, this analysis would do credit to any sailor. For once, Donald Crowhurst spared neither the boat nor

---

* This refers not to the normal method of trailing ropes to slow the boat down and keep the stern into the wind, but to a more sophisticated plan of Crowhurst's for self-steering, described in Appendix 2.

himself, and made no attempt to avoid the present challenge by casting himself forward into some future one. If there was any distortion, it was in his apparent unwillingness to admit that faults like the leaky hatch over the generator, on the floor of the cockpit, were partly his own fault. His analysis also mentioned, for the first time, the lack of the Heliflex pipe for pumping, which he appeared to think he had arranged to be on board.

Having analysed the problems, and whether they can be solved, Crowhurst then went on:

> This may look like a load of excuses for stopping. That's not what I *want* to do. If I stop I'll disappoint a lot of people. Stanley Best, most important, then fringe people, Rodney Hallworth, the folks at Teignmouth who've supported the scheme, and my own family. There would be a certain amount of derision, but that is irrelevant. I would be really no worse off starting again next August, because my only chance now is everyone else dropping out of the race. Then I'd only have a 50–50 chance of survival—many folks would put it lower. If I can persuade Stanley to hang on to the project till then I'd certainly have a go at breaking the record—if anyone does it this time, or at the Golden Globe, which would still be available, and probably the prize too, if it's not awarded to the one who gets furthest.

Already Crowhurst was beginning to take refuge in two of his pet obsessions: the paramountcy of logic, and the lure of a bigger, later challenge—trying the circumnavigation next year—to obliterate present failure. He argued round every possibility, finding each one unacceptable. And the problem of money, even in the middle of the North Atlantic, grew more and more important:

> But if Mr Best abandons the idea of this circumnavigation and Electron Utilisation Ltd then things would be black, as his option requiring E.U. to purchase could be invoked. Would getting to Australia materially affect this decision? This would depend on how correct the decision to abandon the race seemed to him, and without radio I cannot have any indication except the logical conclusions I draw myself. If they *are* logical they will carry weight. So: what do I do? Go on to Australia to "put up a show" and waste a year? Would it be a waste? It boils

down to evaluating whether a non-stop voyage next year would appeal as much as a stopping voyage this year. I do not think I can make the trip this year in reasonable safety.

This means: which is likely to yield most profit or produce less loss? What would I do in [Stanley Best's] place? I suppose it would depend on how much of the cost I could recover. If 80% or more I'd be tempted. Electron Utilisation could not find it. But is it only a cash transaction or something more? Has the challenge of the thing crept into it? More than a little, I think. It's impossible to analyse whether he will lose all interest. I will have to depend on logic, and if there is a more personal involvement, well that's a "bonus". But I do believe, in fact I almost certainly know it's there. Logic, then, for that's the vital thing, and in the end carries weight.

What courses are open? Either I abandon the non-stop attempt or I go on with it. If I go on I have an equal chance of making the trip or drowning. I may win either the £5,000 or even the Golden Globe as well if others all drop out. It's very doubtful otherwise. Assuming everyone has already dropped out, would a 50–50 chance be one that should be acceptable? The balance lies between the gain if I won and the suffering if the gamble failed. Clare would think the risk was unacceptable, and my first duty is to her. Though I think the benefits derived in various ways tempting, on the whole it must be regarded as unacceptable for a married man with a moderately large family. The strain on poor Clare would be terrible—she may not be able to take it.

Here Crowhurst was unable—as at Teignmouth—to admit that *his* emotions might be responsible for his giving up. He tried to load that responsibility on to his wife.

The weight of this argument lies in the assessment of the 50–50 chance. How accurate is it? The truth is, I do not know. It may be high or low—but from everything I've read I think it's not overstating the risk. Bardiaux capsized twice off the Horn, so did the Smeatons. In a keel boat you can survive with luck. In a tri—not likely at all. No, to have any sort of chance worth taking you must be self-righting—or rightable. Then there's the pumping situation. No, it's not feasible.

He had now argued himself—with characteristic self-convincing dialectic—to the final and inescapable conclusion that he must give up his round-the-world attempt. Subsequently, in places, his old tendency not to recognise failure when it confronted him reasserted itself, but such hopes never carried great conviction. This argument, and its conclusion, remained inviolable.

Then Crowhurst started to work through the possibilities open to him, and whether frank failure was possible. His hope was to make a publicity stunt, and marketing trip, even out of failure:

So: some form of salvage is necessary. But what's most effective?

1) Go on to Australia or
2) save face by going to Capetown?

[Capetown] is further than Ridgway got, and as far as King and Blyth; so involves no disgrace. But what a waste of precious time! There's no market for Navicators or Trimarans there; so Australia is the logical next step. It has the merit that it ranks as quite an achievement—but no more than at least two other men have already done, and several of the *Sunday Times* fleet may also do. Knox-Johnston and Tetley (if he gets that far) and Fougeron are all likely stoppers in my view. Moitessier may go on—if he does he'll probably see the thing through, but there's a *good* chance no one will make the whole trip, and Australia will be a posting place for retired *S.T.* entrants. There would be no *great* publicity for the firm or the boat, but it could be a useful sort of exercise if I could sell the boat and a few Navicators . . .

At this point Crowhurst obviously stopped writing for some time and thought, hard. Would it really be any use to go to Australia? When he started again, it was with a new, sharper pencil, and he had obviously decided against Australia. He completed the sentence with a second "but":

. . . but hardly justifies the expenditure of so much time and money.

Time and Money. If one considers time only, the thing to do is turn back now, not sail south another day. Where does this leave the money side? The fact is that the boat is a very expensive entrant in a race; but the race cannot be won—that is, I believe it cannot be won short of everyone else retiring and myself with a *great deal* of luck completing the course. The assessment *is* reasonable: apart from luck I cannot win the race. Nevertheless, the disappointment resulting from immediate withdrawal is bound to be acute—to all involved, myself included, but especially to Mr Best. To turn up at a UK port and say "I'm back folks" is not feasible, because

a) it involves Clare in 14 days or so of unnecessary worry.
b) it restricts the choice of further action to some extent—to a large extent.

So it seems I should put in locally, where

1) I can communicate with Mr Best.
2) I can go on to America, Australia, South Africa, or back to UK.
3) I can get the necessary work done if going on.

Money. This area is the most worrying. The costs will be increased, and the chance of large returns apparently reduced. If I can get Mr Best's support for having a go next year most problems could disappear—or at all events the major ones would become soluble.

In these passages Crowhurst seemed to be retreating once more into a fantasy of trying again: a future challenge. Each of the alternatives presented by giving up appears unbearable. He clearly paused in his writing once more, and by the time he started again he has decided to delay the decision:

I will continue south and try to get the generator working so that I can talk to Mr Best before committing myself to any particular course or retiring from the race. I suppose I'm just putting off the decision? No. It's far better that he should know before I commit the project to withdrawal, and that I should have his views. If he doesn't want anything further to do with the non-stop project (as distinct from the *S.T.* race) things would be really black—but at least I'd know where he stood. In the final analysis—if the whole thing goes quite sour: Electron Utilisation bankrupt and Woodlands sold, ten years of work and worry down the drain, I would have Clare and the children still and:

If you can make a heap of all your worries
And risk it on one turn of pitch and toss,
And lose, and start again at your beginnings,
And never breathe a word about your loss—

Failure? Only if the project cannot be attempted again next year. 4½ months from sawing the first plank is quite an achievement in itself, but not quite good enough. The concept is OK, the execution fails to meet the high requirements of such an arduous trip.

Superficial assessments of success or failure are worthless. What Nazi party member would have thought Hitler a failure in '41? What Pharisee would have considered the carpenter a success as he hung dying between the two thieves? Success lies in the satisfaction of having done one's utmost, I think, more than anything else. Having honestly tried to see the best course and then pursuing it.

Philosophising is irrelevant, however, and must stop. I have things to do! It is also wasting the torch battery.

Nine

The Fraudulent Record

From this point Donald Crowhurst's own account of his voyage ceases to be reliable. He is no longer absolutely frank, and often deliberately fails to record his most important thoughts. From now on, therefore, the story is not a simple narrative based on Crowhurst's own testimony; it becomes a detective story, and all his records become evidence (some of it accurate, some not) from which to deduce what really happened. The most important evidence remains the logbooks found aboard *Teignmouth Electron*. The BBC tapes are informative but—as we have seen—seldom honest. In addition, there are all the many papers, charts, odd notes, and objects found in the trimaran's cabin. These we have examined at length. They show that by the time he had sailed for three more weeks Donald Crowhurst had already become—in one aspect at least—consciously fraudulent.

After the long analysis of his dilemma on November 15th Crowhurst continued for nearly a month to make regular entries in the same logbook that he had kept from the start of the voyage. This we shall call Logbook One. It is (like his others) a large, ruled exercise book containing 192 foolscap pages,* with a stiff dark-blue cover.

The right-hand pages of Logbook One are devoted to navigation—his sun-sights and calculated positions, with two outside columns for log mileages and course. The left-hand pages give a corresponding narrative account of the events of each day, such as those we have been quoting. When there is a particularly long entry—as on November 15th—the narrative spills over to the right-hand pages, but the original pattern is then restored as soon as possible. Compared with his previous attempts at log-keeping it is all surprisingly methodical. As pages were filled he would neatly clip off the top right-hand corner so that his place could easily be found. He wrote always in pencil. An occasional word was rubbed out, but at this stage he had not succumbed to his usual habit of covering his writings with deletions and insertions. However his erratic spelling, plus his frequent use of a very hard pencil which dug fiercely through the paper, makes his log entries, even at this early stage, difficult to decipher.

A similar book—decorated with distinctive white tape on the binding—was used for a daily Radio Log. It records, in careful capitals, the text of the radio-telegrams which he tapped out in morse. These seem to have been documented with complete accuracy throughout the voyage: they correspond precisely with what was received in England. At intervals there are mentions of conversations on the radio-telephone—sometimes accompanied by notes on their content. But since the notes are always sketchy we can be less sure of exactly what information was exchanged. There are also a large number of apparently irrelevant messages passing between transmitting stations and ships in various parts of the world. These seem mostly to have been scribbled down just for morse practice; but as we shall see some have greater relevance.

*   *   *

For the moment, however, Crowhurst was still grappling with immediate practical problems. By November 15th—beginning his sixteenth day at sea—he had logged some 1,300 miles, but his route had been so tortuous that he had travelled barely 800 miles along his intended path (and the full course was 30,000 miles). By either reckoning he was doing badly—worse than any other

---

* These are sewn in six sections of 32, and it can be seen that no pages have been torn out.

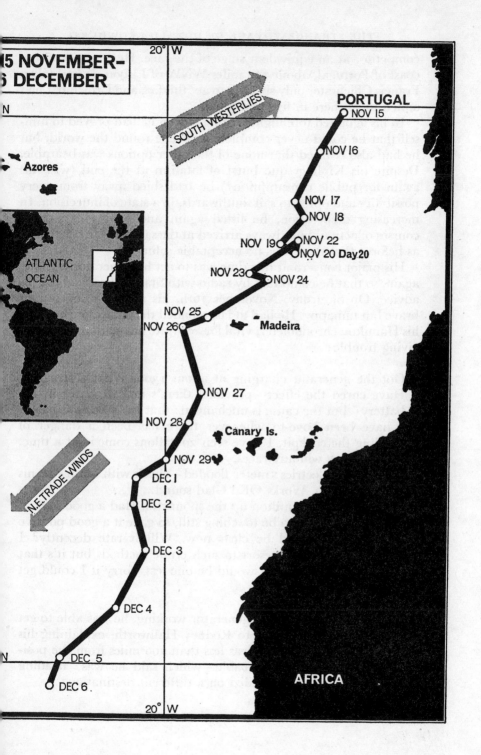

**15 NOVEMBER–
6 DECEMBER**

N

SOUTH WESTERLIES

20° W

PORTUGAL
NOV 15

Azores

NOV 16

NOV 17
NOV 18

ATLANTIC
OCEAN

NOV 19   NOV 22
NOV 20 Day 20
NOV 23
NOV 24

NOV 25
NOV 26   Madeira

NOV 27

NOV 28
Canary Is.

NOV 29
DEC 1

N.E. TRADE WINDS

DEC 2

DEC 3

DEC 4

DEC 5

N   DEC 6

AFRICA

20° W

competitor at an equivalent stage of the race. He was still off the coast of Portugal, about 120 miles WNW of Lisbon. It had taken Francis Chichester only six days to get this far, and Crowhurst had aimed to get here in five and a half.

In his agonised torchlight writing session he had proved to himself that he could never complete a voyage round the world, but he had also realised that none of the other options was bearable. Despite his Kiplingesque burst of fatalism at the end (was this again for public consumption?) he had shied away from every possibility and opted to sail southwards, in a state of indecision. In increasing desperation, he listed again and again his various courses of action, but always arrived at the same, bleak conclusion as before: that there was no acceptable solution.

His major concern at this time was to get his generator working again, so that he could talk by radio with Stanley Best and ask his advice. On Saturday, November 16th, his narrative log sounds brave but unhappy. He had at last mended the generator; but now his Hamilton chronometer, vital for accurate navigation was again giving trouble:

> Got the generator charging at about 1300. What a struggle! Have cured the effect—provided there's no salt water in the battery—but the cause is unchanged: that leaky cockpit hatch. I have been hove-to whenever there has been a danger of flooding the cockpit. I have seen 20 gallons come in at a time. That will *not* win any races.
>
> To check electrics: meter flooded—check with lamp—seems OK. Radio on. Works OK! Glad sound.
>
> Time check. Hamilton up the spout still. Had a good look at hairspring. Seems to be touching still, so gave it a good positive bend and it should be clear now. Will it rate decently? I would not normally resort to such crude methods but it's that or nothing out here! It would be one less worry if I could get a decent rate out of it.

Late that night, with his generator working, he was able to get off a delayed Press report to Rodney Hallworth, explaining his radio silence. Although he was less than 200 miles from the position of his previous Press cable—which said he was "heading Azores"—he had now decided on a different destination:

SILENCE DUE ENGINE COMPARTMENT FLOODED SEVERE GALE
STOP   STRIPPED MAGNETO REPLACED COILS STRIP DRY OUT
GENERATOR OVERHAULED BRUSHGEAR STOP   GOING ON TOWARDS
MADEIRA

The message, like most that Crowhurst sent for publication, gave no position and just named a destination. In fact both the Azores and Madeira were still several hundred miles away. Hallworth, in his turn, put the best possible gloss on the situation before passing it on to television and the newspapers. The resultant Press reports duly put Crowhurst's position as "near Madeira". Hallworth's local paper in Exeter said that severe head winds had cut Crowhurst's speed to "less than 100 miles a day" (less than 50 would have been closer) but immediately added that his boat was "capable of twice that". This was to become increasingly the pattern of the reporting of Crowhurst's voyage. The combination of secretive (and, later, misleading) telegrams plus Hallworth's optimistic interpretations in the end produced some ludicruous results.

After tapping out the Press telegram, Crowhurst wrote his final log entry of the day, in which the seriousness of the missing length of Heliflex baling pipe (mentioned only in passing in his list of defects of the previous day) seems suddenly to have occurred to him:

Good supper—Paella Electron. Radio playing, generator running, weather mild. Holiday conditions, but it does not change my pessimism I'm afraid. I'll search the boat from stem to stern tomorrow. If that pipe's aboard I'll find it, though it has not come to light so far, nor is it on the stowage lists. I thought it was on the drum with the spare rigging wire. What a blow—though I didn't realise its full significance at the time.

The following day, he searched his boat thoroughly and tersely recorded: "Definitely no hose on board". He was soon to regret its absence even more; on Monday he opened up the forward compartment of the starboard float and found that it too—like the port forward compartment at the beginning of the voyage—was badly flooded. And this despite the Sylglas seal. To make matters worse, it was the hatch in which his instant coffee had been stowed:

Two-thirds full of coffee. Ages to mop up. Oilskins or bareskins? Chose bareskins. Emerged covered in brown specks and mashed-up carton — something terrible from the deep. Baling out when lumpy seas gave a good shower bath. Sealed up again. Then took 70 gallons out of forward hatch. [So his centre hull was leaking too.]

There is a vivid account of this coffee-baling incident in a tape recording made much later in the voyage:

I'm restricted to cocoa because I've drunk all the coffee. I lost half my coffee in the flooding . . . in the early days. Half my coffee supply was in sachets and a packet containing it was immersed with a rather comical result. The water in the float was in fact salt coffee — cold salt coffee — and in the process of getting it out I got more than a fair share over myself . . . I took the task on in bare skin and of course the coffee coloured water gave me a premature sun-tan. I looked pretty horrible actually, with blotches of this brown all over me. When I finished the job I looked as though I had some terrible disease. However it washed off.

Crowhurst had booked two radio-telephone calls for Monday, November 18th — one to his wife and one to Stanley Best. In preparation, he spent two days on yet another analysis of the options open to him. He began by drawing up a neat table showing where he would have to retire on various assumptions of speed. This he realistically calculated as low as ninety and even sixty miles per day: an ironic contrast to his original 220 miles a day forecast on the Woodlands grand piano . . .

Miles per week	Miles per day	Av. speed	Cape of Good Hope	Australia	Horn	UK	Retire	UK
420	60	2·5	Feb '69	May (5)	Sep '69	Feb '70	C of GH	May
630	90	3·5	Jan	March(7)	July	Oct	Aust.	Feb '70
840	120	5	Dec	Feb (8)	May	Aug	Aust.	Feb '70
1050	150	6·25	Dec	Jan (9)	April	June (?)	Aust.	Feb '70
1400	200	8·3	Early Dec	Jan	Feb	April		

The purpose of the table was to see if he could get past the Horn or to Australia before the southern winter clamped down in April or May. At realistic speeds, it was clear that he couldn't. Crowhurst entered the table into his log on November 17th, and on the following day continued:

Phone call this evening. To sum up:

1) The hatches all leak badly and my efforts to seal them have failed to stand up to the boat being driven at speed. 150 gallons [leaked in] overnight.

2) There is no method of pumping with the hatches on. This means that if the boat encountered several days of heavy weather she would be in danger of foundering. As it is, I keep her afloat by avoiding sailing to windward in rough conditions.*

I would be prepared to take the risk of getting to Capetown. If somehow I solved the problem of getting the water out of the hatches, I could conceivably get to Australia but *certainly no further*, as that would mean the Horn in winter. If I got to Cape-town I would be able to get back to UK in May '69. If Australia, February '70 at the earliest.

Summing up:

1) Go on. Arrive Horn June or April. 50/50 chance. (6/10 chance of capsize?)

2) Put up show—retire Capetown (UK May).

3) Sail to America where I could sell boat at best price.

4) Return to UK for record-breaking attempt.

It is a pretty hopeless picture. And yet, when he talked to Clare Crowhurst over the radio-telephone, he completely concealed his hopelessness. He summarised the points he wanted to make during the call in an entry in his Radio Log:

---

* This paragraph is interesting evidence that Crowhurst was thinking progressively about his plight. He had now realised that his pumping problem was even more radical than he had at first appreciated. Even if the missing length of hose had been aboard, he would still have had to open up the hatches to bale the floats. Therefore the hose would not have entirely solved his basic difficulty, even though it obviously would have made baling in heavy seas somewhat less dangerous. Tetley had anticipated the problem by putting permanent piping into the forward compartments of his "Victress". But *Teignmouth Electron* would never have been able to cope with leaks in the continuous rough weather of the Roaring Forties.

1) How are you?
2) Everything OK.
3) Having trouble with mechanical component ordering —
   Dave Baker will be able to sort out. [This was a reference
   to some problem at home with the Navicator construc-
   tion].

That, Clare Crowhurst confirms, was all the call amounted to.
Nor did Crowhurst mention his dilemma (about continuing the
voyage) to Stanley Best, though this had been the original reason
for the call. It is clear that Crowhurst had changed his mind.
The call is not described at all in Crowhurst's Radio Log, but
Best has written down his recollection of it. Crowhurst said he was
in good health, but disappointed by progress so far. He gave his
position (optimistically) as some hundred miles north of Madeira.
But most of the conversation was about the pumping problem. Best
was asked to check if any hose had been put on board, and to ask
around for ideas on what to do about it,* ready for another
radio-telephone call in three days' time.

*   *   *

The following weekend, a long article by Murray Sayle in the
Sunday Times described this stage of the race as "The Week it All
Happened". Alex Carozzo was limping towards Lisbon and out
of the competition. For him, the strain of a rushed start had
shown not on his boat but on his health — he had been struck down
with a stomach ulcer. Bill King's *Galway Blazer* had just been
towed into Capetown with a smashed mast, having turned turtle
in a South Atlantic storm. Knox-Johnston had broken Chichester's
distance record for a non-stop voyage. He was off New Zealand,
his boat battered, his self-steering gear shattered in a capsize, and
his rudder in disrepair; but he had spiritedly patched things up
and was battling on. Tetley had exceeded the record for the longest
voyage in a multihull and was nearing the Cape of Good Hope.
Moitessier, though he had no radio (he had resisted all attempts to
provide him with one arguing that they were both irritating and
dangerous because they distracted one from serious sailing), was

* John Elliot suggested using Seelastic around the hatches, or possibly drilling
through the bulkheads into the centre float compartments where the permanent
pumping arrangements existed as part of the self-righting mechanism. Best himself
thought of various ideas, such as filling the floats with empty Tupperware containers
to provide permanent buoyancy.

known to have closed the gap on Knox-Johnston. He was, meanwhile, filling his logbook with gentle abuse against civilisation and
thoroughly enjoying the Roaring Forties. His countryman,
Fougeron, by contrast, had not at all enjoyed the Roaring
Forties, which had knocked his boat over and wrecked most of its
contents. He had decided that civilisation was not so bad after all
and was heading gratefully for dry land.

The only competitor that Sayle could find little of interest to
write about was Crowhurst. In fact, for him more than anyone
else, it was "the week it all happened". He just had not told
anyone.

*　　　*　　　*

The news of other competitors, as it filtered bit by bit over
Crowhurst's radio, must have both frightened and encouraged
him. It emphasised the dangers of being in mid-ocean in a small
boat. But as his opponents reduced in number it raised again the
glimmer of hope that if, somehow, he could finish the course he
might be the only one to do so. Even Knox-Johnston seemed, in his
battered boat, unlikely to get back to England, though when
Crowhurst heard that he had passed New Zealand—on the One
o'clock News of November 19th—he wrote admiringly in his log:
'He is certainly doing well. Good luck to him, the swine."

Paralysed by indecision, Crowhurst had come to an almost dead
halt. He spent the next three days going round in a slow circle in
filthy weather north of Madeira, and in the entire week made only
180 miles southwards.

There is evidence that at this stage he came very close to putting
in at the nearest port, Funchal (the capital of Madeira), and giving
up immediately. In addition to his logbooks, Crowhurst had with
him a pad of foolscap paper for odd notes. Several of these notes
were preserved, and on one of them he had drawn a detailed map
of Funchal with all the necessary information for putting in there,
including tides, landmarks and moorings. Also on board were all
the volumes relevant to his voyage of the Admiralty *Pilot*, which
describes the coastlines of the world and their attendant shipping
hazards. When Crowhurst set out, his *Pilot* books were all new and
unopened; after the voyage, the pages covering the ports of
Madeira were heavily thumbed and annotated.

On Thursday, November 21st he made his second radio-
telephone call to Stanley Best. Here Crowhurst's behaviour

became really mysterious. We know he wanted to pour out all his time-and-money difficulties to his sponsor. A sufficiently pathetic recital of problems might even have moved Best himself to suggest abandonment of the voyage, thus diverting blame from Crowhurst. Before this second telephone call, he even transcribed all the various retirement possibilities from Logbook One into his Radio Log ready to list them one by one.

But again, says Stanley Best, the subject of retirement was not raised. The conversation lasted seven or eight minutes and was devoted, Best says, to technical discussion of the baling problem. Crowhurst also warned that, because of troubles with the generator, there might be radio silence in future.

This last point is the first clue to Crowhurst's real intentions. One explanation for his lack of frankness could be that—as with Clare in Teignmouth—he could not finally bring himself to a humiliating confession of failure. There is, however, another possibility. Between planning the call, and actually speaking to Best a quite different solution to his problems—one that would obliterate present failure—might have started to take shape in his mind, and that was a solution that could not be discussed with Best.

If this *was* the first clue to future fraud, we only have Crowhurst's physical actions for corroboration, because from now on his narrative log becomes uncommunicative. For the two days of November 20th and 21st there is only one brief, secretive, entry: 'Foul weather, had to heave-to. Fairly depressed about hatches." However, he certainly seemed to have come to a decision of some sort, because there is at once new heart in his approach to the voyage and discussion of his dilemma in the logbooks abruptly stops.

The following morning he got straight down to the task of replacing his Hasler servo blade, which had broken in the gale of November 20th. It was a tricky job because a fixing pin and clip had been lost with the broken blade, and he had to improvise. Then, in improving weather, he began to head determinedly south-westwards.

On Saturday he even decided to climb the mast to deal with the double Turk's Head knot in the jib halyard—a job that he had been putting off ever since Teignmouth. The experience at once restored him to his jaunty best, writing about clipper ships and combining with it some highly individual Crowhurst popular mathematics:

Up the mast one has to hang on pretty damn well, for even with the comparative small seas now running (7 feet) there's quite a lot of rapid acceleration up there! I wondered how it compared with being aloft on a clipper. Lower but probably quite as ferocious I suppose due to the easier motion of a larger ship. The actual distance moved would be far greater on a clipper but the acceleration would be about the same, even in the worst weather. Interesting problem in dynamics. Anyway this mast climbing is good exercise—I feel exhausted. "I'll take my constitutional now," says he, disappearing up the mast twice daily!

Now averaging well over a hundred miles per day, he made an unnecessarily wide arc to the west to avoid hitting Madeira (his navigation, with his suspect chronometer, couldn't be trusted too far). "Obviously will not sight Madeira," he wrote wistfully. "Just as well. Funchal sounds delightful." And he drafted several cheerful Press telegrams to Rodney Hallworth, which he could not send because of radio conditions. They each harped on the problems he had been having with the boat (to explain his week of slow progress) but worked round to the new message: "TUNING TRIALS OVER RACE BEGINS".

He had, by now, at last come to the end of the prevailing westerlies. Ahead of him lay the North-East Trades, with more than a thousand miles of straight sailing with following winds. There, at least, his trimaran should come into her own. For his voyage to regain any level of credibility, her performance through the Trades would need to be dramatic.

*   *   *

The second clue to Crowhurst's new intentions appears on November 26th. For no apparent reason, he suddenly wrote, "I am obviously going to run out of logbook space", and announced that he was going to double up his writing, two lines to each space. The remaining entries in Logbook One are written in such tiny script that more than a thousand words would fit on a page. It was a strange decision: there were still 150 empty pages in Logbook One, and as we know, there were (apart from the Radio Log) two empty logbooks in reserve. Crowhurst was obviously not going to run out of logbook space—unless, that is, he needed his reserve logbooks for some other purpose.

At the same time, Crowhurst gave up his format of navigation-on-the-right and narrative-on-the-left. Instead he started merely to intersperse brief comments through his navigational calculations. The comments themselves suddenly seem forced, stilted, and inconsequential:

Chicken Capri is quite nice with a fresh onion, extra dried peas and cheese added.
Tried hoisting Yankee jib on boom. Problem to control boom & sail during hoist.
During sight: spherical object, rusty, 2/3 submerged. 4 cables distant. Sewage scraps alongside boat. Possibly gash bin? Diameter apparently 3 ft.

Also the pages now have a quite unnatural neatness. His navigational results are underscored fussily with double lines. There are regular disclaimers against navigational inconsistencies: "The Venus sight is worrying"; "Hamilton stopped . . ."; "Rework Morning Sight"; "So THAT's where we are!" At one point—on the turn of page—the series of log readings suddenly falls by a hundred miles. Of course, the log could simply have been misread—but then the error would not have been maintained on later readings. These pages all give the strong impression of having been copied out from a preliminary draft.

However we believe that up to December 5th the main navigational record in Logbook One remains broadly accurate. After that date it is certainly fraudulent.

The evidence for thinking the earlier information is accurate is circumstantial but persuasive. First, Crowhurst had no reason to fake his navigational record before December 5th, though, as we shall see, he had a very specific reason for doing so afterwards. Second, all Crowhurst's calculations have been checked through by our navigational adviser,* and there are no significant internal inconsistencies before December 5th. There is also a third piece of contributory evidence, based not on his logbooks but on the papers found on his boat.

Before Crowhurst set sail, he was given a pile of forms on Teignmouth Urban District Council notepaper. They read:

* Captain Craig A. Rich, instructor at the School of Navigation, London.

FROM DONALD CROWHURST, SAILING
ALONE, NON-STOP AROUND THE WORLD
The bottle containing this message was placed
in the sea at . . . . . . hours on . . . . 196 . .
my position being . . . . and my log reading
. . . . miles
Signed . . . .

The finder of this message will be
rewarded if he sends it to Mr D. H. Sharpe.
Bitton House, Teignmouth, England

The idea was, of course, that Crowhurst should scatter these in bottles around the oceans of the world—one every few days—as a publicity stunt. Crowhurst, it will be remembered, used a very hard pencil, so whenever he filled in a form at the top of the pile, its indentation showed through to the blank form below. In fact, when we examined the blank forms after the voyage, the indentations from two entries could be seen on the top paper of the pile. One was for November 24th; the later one was for December 1st.

We know from his subsequent actions that during the fraudulent part of his voyage, Crowhurst was extremely loath to give *precise* information, true or false, about his whereabouts; certainly he would not voluntarily have scattered around bottles with exact times, latitudes and longitudes. This all suggests that up to December 1st and maybe for a few days afterwards, he was recording correct positions in his log. It is also significant that after early December his bottle-scattering abruptly ceased.

The reason for changing the logbook on November 26th was probably to experiment with a new, less informative, logbook style in which subsequent faking would be easier. He gave himself ten days to get the new style established. Then, in the second week of December, beginning on Friday the 6th, Crowhurst embarked on deliberate and constructive faking of his navigational record. The evidence for this is quite conclusive. It is even probable that he deliberately preserved it, knowing that it would be found.

*　　　　*　　　　*

On December 10th, as Crowhurst approached the end of the

133

Trade winds, the following declamatory telegram, giving his mileages of the previous five days, arrived for Rodney Hallworth in Exeter:

```
PRESSE — DEVONNEWS EXETER
HURTLED SOUTH    FRIDAY 172 BROKE JIB POLE
SATURDAY 109    SUNDAY 243    NEW RECORD
SINGLE HANDER    MONDAY 174    TUESDAY 145
NORTH EAST TRADE FINISHED
```

Hallworth must have been delighted. The cables over the previous two weeks had, it is true, been cheerful — recording satisfactory progress and the inevitable "flying fish breakfast" approaching the Cape Verde Islands. But now his boy was at last fulfilling all his record-breaking promises. On December 11th, Hallworth received a radio-telephone call from Crowhurst giving further details. He then eagerly set about informing the newspapers about the triumphant record run. The *Daily Mirror*'s story was typical:

LONE SAILOR CLAIMS A NEW RECORD
Round the world yachtsman Donald Crowhurst yesterday claimed a new record for a lone sailor.

He covered 243 miles last Sunday — and he believes this is the most a single-handed sailor has logged in twenty-four hours.

Captain Terence Shaw, sailing secretary of the Royal Western Yacht Club said yesterday: "I doubt if anyone has ever done better."

Donald, from Bridgwater in Somerset, is one of the four remaining yachtsmen in a race — organised by the Sunday Times — to sail around the world.

He is now south of the Equator and heading towards Cape Town.

The claimed distance was almost certainly a record: the best run previously publicised was by Geoffrey Williams, who had logged about 220 miles six months earlier in the *Observer* Trans-atlantic Race. Crowhurst's euphoric radio-telephone comments to Hallworth were lengthily quoted in the *Sunday Times* story three days later. For the first time Crowhurst was not just a condescending last paragraph in the race round-up. His name led all the rest:

CROWHURST SPEED WORLD RECORD?

Donald Crowhurst, last man out in the Sunday Times round-the-world lone-man yacht race, covered a breathtaking and possibly record-breaking 243 miles in his 41 foot trimaran Teignmouth Electron last Sunday. The achievement is even more remarkable in the light of the very poor speeds in the first three weeks of his voyage; he took longer to reach the Cape Verdes than any other competitor.

In his last radio message Crowhurst said he was on watch for the full 24 hours. "It took a pretty strong nerve. I have never sailed so fast in my life and I could only manage speeds of up to 15 knots because the sea was never higher than 10 feet. If I get the chance again and the seas run any higher I doubt if I will take it because it might prove too dangerous . . .

As a piece of public relations, the record run was triumphantly successful. It re-awakened possibilities that, even at this late stage, a commercial sponsor might be found. With only three other contestants left — Knox-Johnston, Moitessier and Tetley — some people even saw Crowhurst as a possible race winner. Hallworth ingeniously managed to keep the story running for yet another week in the *Sunday Times* by releasing the actual, historic, unpublished text.

Among non-journalists there were, it should be admitted, one or two sceptics. Sir Francis Chichester rang up the *Sunday Times* saying that Crowhurst was "a bit of a joker", and needed careful examination. His suggestion was dismissed as obviously impractical. And Captain Craig Rich who was advising the race organisers on navigation, expressed some considerable surprise. He had been keeping a "performance index" which expressed competitors' speeds as a proportion of Chichester's speed at an equivalent stage of the voyage. For all the others, this index had remained remarkably constant; Crowhurst's had been moving like a yo-yo. But the *Sunday Times* reflected Rich's scepticism only by the rather surprised tone of the first paragraph of its report. Otherwise, only the *Observer* yachting correspondent, Frank Page, even hinted at doubt by describing it as "a typically forthright claim from Donald Crowhurst, currently lying a poor fourth in the race". For the most part, Fleet Street and the yachting world had swallowed Crowhurst's story.

*　　*　　*

We can now return to *Teignmouth Electron* to discover what really happened. The trimaran, in her first week of running before the Trade Winds, had performed adequately but not spectacularly. Crowhurst may have made genuine attempts to set up twenty-four hour records but his best distances had been around 160 miles. He knew the Trade Winds would soon be finished, and that if he was to put up a dramatic credit-restoring performance, it would have to be now.

Then, from December 7th to 11th he began to write down his genuine log details on the top left-hand corner of a large blank plotting sheet—one of a pile he kept on his chart table. The calculations were written in neat columns, just as he would in his normal log, but recording an unusually large number of sun-sights. The reason for this extra navigational care was not directly to assist faking, but because he was about to pass within a few miles of the Cape Verde Islands, and he dare not rely on his normal erratic methods. It would have been an acutely embarrassing moment to be spotted from land, or even worse to run aground. He judged this nicely, as it happened, passing just fourteen miles from the tip of Sto Antão island. This genuine log shows Crowhurst in fact to have been making excellent progress along a very straight course of SSW—but not breaking any records.

Crowhurst then opened up another of the large plotting sheets and—with the two sheets side by side—started to invent a complementary set of fraudulent navigational details. His forgery is, in many ways, the most impressive bit of technical expertise of the entire voyage. To calculate backwards from an imagined distance to a series of daily positions, and from them via declination and other tables to the correct sun-sightings is a formidable and unfamiliar job, far harder than honest navigation.

He knew well the target which was to be beaten—Williams's 220 plus miles—and chose a figure safely (but not too extravagantly) above this: 243 miles. He hypothesised plausible conditions for record-breaking (ENE wind, force 6, gusting to 25 knots, but only a moderate swell). And he devised a way of getting an accurate-seeming running fix on the sun. He then wrote down on the first sheet yet another of his meticulous little tables. It had two columns. In the right-hand column he wrote his actual noon-to-noon distances. In the left, repeatedly rubbed out until they were in the most convincing form, were his "claimed" distances:

		Claimed	Actual
Thursday	5		
		172	60
Friday	6		
		109	110
Saturday	7		
		243	170
Sunday	8		
		174	170
Monday	9		
		145	177
Tuesday	10		
		843	687

Here his talent for plausible pastiche was being stretched to its limit. It was necessary to have some small, convincing, little disaster to make it all sound real. So he pencilled into the table, by the Thursday-Friday run, the little comment: "Broke pole". This he later embellished in the log.

In translating these distances to positions and sun-sights he covered both sheets with calculations, navigational diagrams, and elaborate cross-checks. There were two pitfalls to be avoided. At this stage of his voyage, while still likely to be seen by ships, he did not want his fake course to get too distant from his actual course. For this he found an elegant mathematical solution. He plotted his fake course out to the west and then back again—the two sides of the imagined triangle giving him most of the extra mileage for his record. Also he took great care to ensure that his fake course, like his actual course, did not run in sight of any of the Cape Verde Islands. To make quite sure, he hatched in the danger area on the fake plotting sheet. The end result was a neat column of sun-sights, calculated positions and log distances running down the right-hand side of the second sheet, ready for transcription into the logbook.

We discovered the two plotting sheets on board *Teignmouth Electron* after the voyage, and they are now in our possession. Of all the papers and charts we found, these were the most yellowed, dog-eared and worked over. They were lying prominently in the cabin, and no attempt had been made to conceal them.

* * *

137

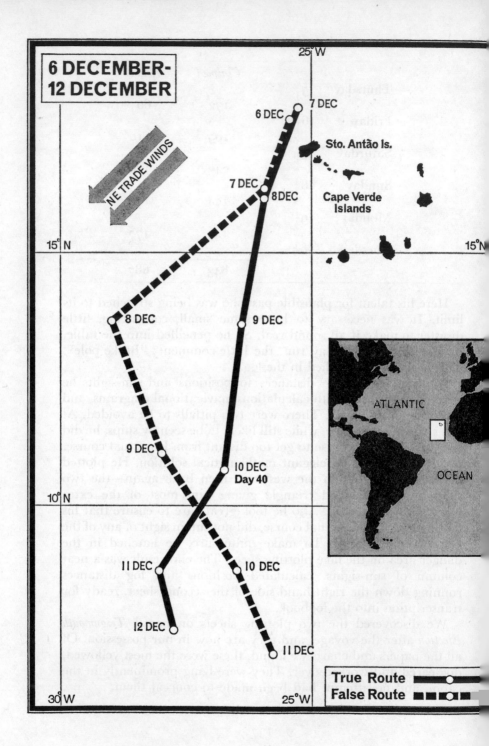

6 DECEMBER–12 DECEMBER

7 DEC

6 DEC

Sto. Antão Is.

NE TRADE WINDS

7 DEC

8 DEC

Cape Verde
Islands

15° N   15° N

8 DEC   9 DEC

ATLANTIC

9 DEC   10 DEC
                         Day 40

OCEAN

10° N

11 DEC   10 DEC

12 DEC

                         11 DEC

True Route
False Route

30° W   25° W

We have no means of knowing exactly when the fake record was copied into the logbook. It was probably still being worked on by December 20th, because there is a note on one of the sheets about St Paul's Rock, near the Equator, which was not passed until then. But at some date after this Crowhurst entered it up. Before doing so, he had to rub out some details that he had already entered for December 6th, which presumably did not link up with the faking. An indication of his meticulous approach was that, having done so, he wrote in explanation: "Inaccurate sun-sight. Probably knocked worm release climbing back to cabin." He ignored some small problems with inconsistent log distances, but this was perhaps not too important because his mileages are everywhere recorded erratically.

When he transcribed the details into the logs he could not resist adding some narrative to give them extra verisimilitude. This narrative makes a useful study; it has the vivid tone of Crowhurst when we know for certain he is lying:

Friday, 6th December.
Set course further Southward. Have sailed 69 miles in about 24 hours, not really pushing but snug and safe at night — more or less. Should be worth trying for 240 noon to noon. Must think about methods of establishing noon positions with minimum error. Will tell Rodney we are past Verde, by 1800 we will be, more or less. Boom guy parted, and jib pole folded up on shrouds — DAMN!

The word "DAMN!" is written in as an afterthought, in most unblasphemously neat pencil. There is evidence that Crowhurst's jib pole did break at some point. It is interesting, however, that one of the most memorable incidents in Chichester's *Gipsy Moth Circles the World* is a breaking jib pole.

Saturday, 7th December.
1337 These sights seem good. Sun dead ahead.
1340 Alter course. Hoisted second large jib.
1400 Going very well. Wind ENE 6 gusting over 25 kt.
1600 Excellent conditions, steady fresh wind. Seas never more [than] 10 ft. 10.5 knots. [here a small calculation to appear as if he was working out speed from log readings] If this holds we'll do it for sure — there is a tide and westing time

bonus. Tremendous sailing but saw a curious raft about 4 ft square, just submerged with two spherical floats either side forming what seemed to be handles. It hurtled past 20ft away — just to remind me of the fact that the sea surface is not ALL water! Wind seems to be holding and set fair. Williams' run was 232,* I think. I must clock up 3210 to be sure of equalling his run (13.40 hrs + 12 = 01.40 hrs — 2994 miles). Spectacular sunset watched from the bows. Noticed the water take on a distinctly purple hue as the red from the sky was reflected with blue water. The sky cleared towards evening but the wind is holding.

Sunday, 8th December.
0110   If this wind holds I will do it! It seems as though it will blow forever!
1335   Done it! Sun still climbing.
[here follow navigational calculations to "prove" his record run]
1638   I'll get an early night tonight. Cooked a huge curried beef vindaloo, and paella cooked in beer. The effect was good but led to extra large helpings. Now I am stuffed too full to move but should sleep well I reckon. The Prior is still around — I'll call him Peter the Prior. I wonder what he lives on normally. It *is* the same one I suppose? It must be because I only ever see one. If they swapped stations I would see others, surely? What a life! He doesn't seem keen on the water but I suppose must swim?

MONDAY, 9th December.
174 miles run today by the log, without any real effort!

*   *   *

If Crowhurst had returned triumphantly from his voyage and presented his logbooks for examination, would his fake record have been believed? We can, fortuitously, answer this. When we studied the documentation from Crowhurst's boat, we did not at first realise the significance of the two plotting sheets. We therefore asked Captain Rich to examine the logbooks for navigational inconsistencies, without warning him of the evidence of faking: indeed, at the time, we thought Logbook One to be entirely honest.

* Crowhurst's figure was a little high.

In the entries surrounding the record run, Captain Rich noticed one or two slight oddities, but nothing that forced him to the conclusion that the sun-sights must have been faked.

He did, however, have doubts on textual grounds. He noticed that the entire week had apparently been entered up with the same pencil, with no variation of pencil sharpness, and had none of the changes in writing style and speed that one might have expected during such hectic sailing. Also the comments in the log just did not ring true.

This logbook entry would not have made a sceptic believe Crowhurst's claim. If suspicion existed, there would have been much for it to feed on. On the other hand, given the risks of libel, there would have been insufficient evidence for anyone to denounce Crowhurst publicly. It is more than possible that he would have got away with it.

Ten

The Plan

Faking a speed record is a very different thing from faking an entire round-the-world voyage, and the evidence up to Thursday, December 12th, does not show conclusively that Crowhurst had yet committed himself to the bigger fraud. However, on that date, there is a much more certain clue to what Crowhurst had in mind. He took out a second of his large blue exercise books and started to use it as his log.

The inference is clear. Every mariner needs to keep a genuine daily record of his voyage for navigation. This Crowhurst decided to do in the new book—Logbook Two. Meanwhile Logbook One was put on one side so that he would later be able to continue it with a fictitious account of a voyage past the Cape of Good Hope, Australia, Cape Horn and back to the Atlantic—providing, of course, that he decided to go through with the deception.

It is important to note the proviso. Every sign is that he was uneasy about this plan. He may not yet have thought through all the problems, but he knew that even the most straightforward part—the invention of a convincing written account—was not going to be simple. Just one fraudulent page establishing his "record run" was at that time costing hours of patient effort.

12 DECEMBER – 26 DECEMBER

ATLANTIC

OCEAN

30°N

11 DEC

New York–Capetown

12 DEC

11 DEC

13 DEC

N.E. TRADE WINDS

14 DEC

16 DEC

15 DEC

17 DEC

Panama–Liberia

18 DEC

St. Paul's Rock

19 DEC

0°

EQUATOR

0°

Day 50
20 DEC

22 DEC

21 DEC

18 DEC

S. Fernando Naronha

23 DEC

23 DEC

24 DEC

25 DEC

BRAZIL

26 DEC

10°S

30°W

10°S

Rio de Janiero–Europe

22 DEC

Shipping Lanes - - - - -
True Route ━━◯━━
False Route ■■◯■■

The faking of navigational details might become less difficult when they did not have to tally with precise log distances, but there would be countless other pitfalls. What if weather reports were checked? How could he describe sailing conditions he had never encountered? Would his pastiche of Chichester, Rose, Slocum and Dumas be detected? And more directly: what if he were sighted and reported, or got into difficulties and needed help? The discovery would be humiliating. Then—most difficult of all—there would be the hero's welcome, the press conference and television interviews, the meetings with other mariners, the prize-giving dinner reminiscing with Chichester . . . Could even Crowhurst's capacity for role-playing carry it off? The very fact that he thought it possible shows that in his tortured, hopeless situation, his perception of reality was beginning to go.

For some time after the switch of logbooks, he had still not finally decided what he would do. His radio messages went no further than absolutely necessary to remain consistent with a round-the-world voyage. It was as if he wanted to preserve the option of faking the voyage without irrevocably committing himself to it. But options do not remain open for ever: even his secretive, ambiguous telegrams needed to contain some indication of progress. As the days went by, it became steadily less plausible simply to arrive at some unexpected port and retire honourably from the race. In the end, time made the decision for him.

Logbook Two we can presume to be a totally honest account of Crowhurst's genuine voyage—first because there was no reason for it to be otherwise (he no doubt intended to destroy it before his return) and second because at all points where it can be checked it is entirely accurate. It contains a full navigational record, very like the later entries in Logbook One, but no longer with the air of having been copied from a draft. The accompanying comments, however, become sparse and later non-existent. They seem mostly to have been written as private reminders, with little explanation and little literary development. Logbook Two, after all, was not written for public examination.

However by taking it together with the Radio Log, Crowhurst's other writings (soon to become very prolific), the documentation from the boat, the BBC tapes and our investigations after the voyage, we can continue to reconstruct the sequence of events in great detail.

The early hours of Thursday, 12th December, found Crowhurst

the start of the voyage: Crowhurst sets sail in a choppy sea

Stills from Crowhurst's own tele-films. Above, tightening screws on the self-steering

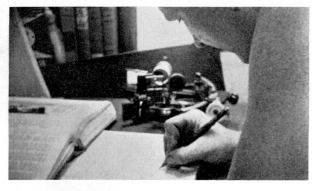

ABOVE:
**Filling in
the logbook**

LEFT:
**Timing a
sextant
sunsight**

RIGHT:
**Eating his
own 'bisque
bread'**

becalmed seven degrees north of the Equator and 3,300 miles
from the Lizard. The north-east Trades were behind him, and the
Admiralty South Atlantic Routeing Chart (which he had begun to
study) showed him that the calms and fitful squalls of the Doldrums and the South-East Trades lay ahead. They were conditions
in which he knew his trimaran would not perform well—yet he
had to press on, because he did not dare allow his imaginary route
get too far ahead of his actual position—the risks of being spotted
were too great. He was being delayed just where he did not want
to be—in the busy steamer lanes. His Routeing Chart showed him
to be in the middle of a nautical Clapham Junction, where the
North America to Capetown route, the South America to Europe
route and the West Africa to Panama Canal route all cross. He
decided, for the time being, to postpone claims of further dramatic
progress.

As the morning lightened, a 20-knot squall freshened from the
east. It produced yet another disaster, and further delay. Crowhurst tersely recorded: "Hasler side plate gave way. Helm lashed
to sail westward."

The following evening, with his Hasler still out of action, the
squalls got stronger; he could make only two knots under jib, and
he had to spend some hours hove-to. But his new plan required
some publicised optimism. That night he cabled Hallworth:

HASLER WINDVANE AND MAIN SERVO ASSEMBLY PLATES SMASHED
DURING 45 KNOT LINE SQUALL YESTERDAY   THINK REPAIR
POSSIBLE

On Saturday, he saw three steamers within four hours, and the
excitement caused him to lapse into the only example of jaunty
"public-voice" writing in the whole of Logbook Two:

2205: Steamer on course SW across stern. Flashed MZUW
MIK. No response. Answered · − · − · − with · − · − · − Doubtful
prospect.
0130 (Sunday): TWO steamers passed each other about 1½
miles astern of me! Both on opposite E–W headings. This makes
about one steamer per 1,000 miles when no land in sight.
Daresay it not like this at Cape Horn though.

His reference to flashing his signalling lamp is interesting.

MZUW was *Teignmouth Electron*'s morse code call-sign, and he followed it with MIK — "report my position to Lloyds of London". If he in fact did this, it was almost certainly for the last time of the voyage. Throughout his trip he was reported only once to Lloyds — in November, a few days out from Teignmouth. The six sets of MIK flags he took with him for use by daytime (sufficient to fly permanently) were almost totally unused. After the voyage, five sets were quite virgin; the sixth set still had packing creases, though slight traces of rust on the metal clips indicated a brief exposure of sea air. From now on, the flags would be kept stowed and steamers avoided as far as possible.

* * *

The next part of Crowhurst's route — south-westwards towards the Equator and thence to the coast of Brazil — still involved some chance of sightings from South America shipping, but he now decided to take a calculated risk to press his fake course ahead. At first his lies need only be small.

He started to make a plan of his fake voyage on the Admiralty Routeing Chart. He began by making a little calculation on the left of the map: 24 hours times 4 knots equals 96 miles a day; 96 miles times 7 days equals 672 miles a week. Evidently he decided that this fairly realistic estimate was not enough, because when he started to plot the false positions, they indicated much faster progress:

	False position	*(Actual position)*
December 18th	3 degrees South of equator	(2 degrees North)
December 22nd	10 degrees South; off north-eastern Brazil	(2 degrees South)
December 24th	15 degrees South; north-east of Rio de Janeiro	(6 degrees South)
January 5th	35 degrees South; between Buenos Aires and Capetown	(17 degrees South)
January 15th	42 degrees S, 12 deg W; south-east of Gough Island in the Roaring Forties	(22 deg S, 33 deg W)

His false progress calculated, he transmitted on the late afternoon of December 17th his first deliberately misleading telegram
to Rodney Hallworth:

THROUGH DOLDRUMS   OVER EQUATOR   SAILING FAST AGAIN

The telegram contained three lies. Crowhurst was still some 180
miles north of the Equator. In four days he had made only 150
miles to the south. And he appeared to claim the quickest ever
passage through the Doldrums. However, after all Crowhurst's
previous record-breaking, it was no more than Hallworth and the
world had come to expect. The message was scarcely noticed in the
Press.

On December 20th, Crowhurst sent a more dramatic progress
report. Before doing so, he pencilled in the latitude and longitude
of the December 22nd position from his fake Routeing Chart into
the Radio Log. His cables were thus getting slightly ahead even of
his own plan:

OFF BRAZIL   AVERAGING 170 MILES DAILY   STRONG SOUTHWEST
TRADEWIND STOP   BEST WISHES CHRISTMAS NEWYEAR TEIGNMOUTH

This contained the only give-away slip of all his phoney Press
telegrams. He described the South-East Trades, which blow off the
coast of Brazil, as south-*west*—a mistake he would scarcely have
made if he had actually been there. This, however, remained
unnoticed and would in any case have seemed a niggling point to
the delighted fans back home. They had, by now, only the vaguest
notion of where he actually was. "Off Brazil" is a classic of
ambiguity—virtually anywhere in the central or southern Atlantic
would fit the description. As for the claim of "170 miles daily" it
is ironic that Crowhurst had just begun the slowest day of his
voyage so far, making only 13 miles from noon to noon. (Perhaps
he was working on his Hasler? He does not say.) Afterwards, the
Portishead radio operators made their routine check: "Confirm
170 miles daily." Yes, 170 was correct, tapped out Crowhurst.

But despite his display of deceitful self-confidence, Crowhurst
was still consumed by doubt. The alternatives of pressing on
honestly or retiring honourably were still present in his mind.
There are two pieces of evidence to support this.

The first shows that even at this late stage he had not totally rejected the hope of putting his boat in shape to continue round the world, even though his logic had told him it was impossible. At the back of Logbook One is a list of jobs he had to finish. It is undated, but it seems to belong to between December 12th and 21st.* It reads:

1) Check sealing of hatches. Connect up immersion plates
2) Make aerial insulation shield
3) Prepare emergency pack and list immediate actions
4) Arrange to get sea water up
5) Stow buoyancy bag. Connect green masthead light. Connect bag to hose
6) Sort out leads to immersion plates
7) Make up control panel and cards
8) Modify Shannon a.f. and Tx
9) Stow stuff in cabin
10) Repair boom for jib
11) Make up sheet release mechanism
12) Make up bag inflation mechanism
13) Reassemble generator
14) Rebuild control box for generator
15) Rearrange mizzen sheeting
16) Repair Hasler gear

As can be seen, the list includes all the original plans for self-righting, which Crowhurst regarded as essential for the Southern Ocean, connecting the immersion plates, the control panel (which, in grander days, he had called the "computer"), the carbon dioxide inflation mechanism, the hose to the buoyancy bag, and the bag fixings. On top of this he was even thinking of completing the automatic sheet release mechanism, which would slacken the sails if the boat was in danger of capsize. Other items, such as the aerial insulation shield (to guard against spray from large seas) and the preparation of an emergency pack (for use if the boat foundered), all indicate that Crowhurst was contemplating some serious, heavy-weather sailing.

* The back of Logbook One remained in regular use for various notes, a chronometer rating table, and creative writing. December 12th is the earliest date consistent with a list of faults which includes the broken jib boom and the broken Hasler. December 21st is the date when another major fault (which will be mentioned shortly) developed on the boat, but was not listed. This dating is supported also by the surrounding writing in the logbook.

On December 21st, soon after the list was compiled Crowhurst tersely recorded a new problem in Logbook Two: "Discovered split skin of starboard float. Hove-to." The fault was to occupy his mind increasingly, and could have been what finally killed all hope of a genuine round-the-world voyage. In any event, we know that work on the list of jobs was scarcely started. Examination of the boat afterwards revealed various crude repairs on the Hasler, signs of work on the generator, and extensive modifications to the Shannon radio-telephone. But nothing else had been even attempted.

The other piece of evidence is a large piece of brown packing paper, which was found neatly folded in a briefcase which Crowhurst used for storing documents. On it were jotted notes, electrical calculations, and a circuit diagram for a new switching mechanism for the radio transmitters. It can be precisely dated from a number of morse messages he had been copying down, mostly Christmas greeting telegrams being received by other ships in the vicinity.

On one part of the brown paper, Crowhurst had been taking stock of the race. He wrote down the names of King, Ridgway, Blyth and Fougeron, then crossed them out. He put a question mark next to Tetley's name, and a box round Moitessier and Knox-Johnston, the two race leaders. He then did a table headed "Australia" and "Duration Horn and back" which also included previous circumnavigators, Dumas, Chichester and Rose. Then he abandoned the task and drew next to it a detailed sketch map of Rio de Janeiro harbour—similar to the one he had drawn six weeks before of Funchal, Madeira. It collated all the information from his charts and pilot book, with a list of lights, distances, landmarks and navigational hazards in the harbour approaches.

To have put into such a large port as Rio de Janeiro would have led to inevitable discovery, and retirement from the race. The only possible explanation for the map is that Crowhurst, in the two days before Christmas, was thinking seriously of giving up.

*　　　*　　　*

After fretting over his decision—which was worse: failure and bankruptcy, deceit and possible exposure, or risking his life by continuing?—Crowhurst took refuge again in nautical heroics.

He began by sending another ecstatic telegram to Rodney Hallworth. This time, he did give some suggestion of his position —naming his destination as the island of Trinidade, 350 miles south of the point he had plotted on his Routeing Chart for December 24th. Unfortunately, by the time the telegram had arrived at Devon News, the name of the island had shed its final letter during transmission.

ENJOYED ROUND THE HORN SAILING TOWARDS TRINIDAD WITH LAST SOUTHEAST TRADE AND BRAZIL CURRENT

Hallworth rightly worked out that "round the Horn sailing" meant round-the-Horn-*type* sailing. And he realised that Crowhurst could not mean he was en route to Trinidad in the West Indies. But somehow in the exegesis that appeared in various newspapers over the following week, Crowhurst was said to be approaching (and soon afterwards passing) Tristan da Cunha. Crowhurst had never mentioned Tristan in his telegrams, and it can only be assumed that out of a mixture of euphoria, optimism and innocence, Hallworth had selected it as the most likely correction for "Trinidad".

Tristan, it should be explained, *is* on the clipper route but 1,800 miles further on than Trinidade, the island to which Crowhurst meant he was heading. Trinidade, in turn, was 350 miles beyond the position marked on Crowhurst's fake route. And that, in its turn was 550 miles ahead of where Crowhurst actually was.

From this point, the Press coverage of the voyage became absurd. The only journalist to emerge with credit was the *Observer*'s yachting correspondent, Frank Page, who, perhaps puzzled by the reports, "presumed" Crowhurst to be somewhere in the South Atlantic. (He was just right: *Teignmouth Electron* had crossed the Equator into the South Atlantic only five days previously.)

Crowhurst also, that Christmas Eve, got out his BBC tape recorder, as he had done in previous moments of crisis, and began talking into the microphone.

Eleven

Christmas

Here we are in the good ship *Teignmouth Electron*, my calendar watch says it is the 24th, and that it is eleven minutes to midnight, the month is December. In other words, this is Christmas Eve, and I'm positive that this is the most solitary Christmas Eve I've ever spent. I've been alone now for very nearly two months, during which time I have not caught a glimpse of land, although I did spot the light on the Island of Fernando de Noronha which is just off the coast of Brazil just south of the Equator. I see from my pilot book that it is the location of a penal settlement—I hope the convicts are enjoying their Christmas.

As it comes up to Christmas Day, what have I been doing? Well, it's amazing how much work there is to do on a project like this. This list of things that have to be done is continually growing, and every day brings its fresh crop of failures, or a new circumstance that requires attention arises. There's wear and tear, chafe on the sails and the lines used for trimming the sails. They all have to be looked at and often renewed.

It's no good trying to put out enormous bursts of energy in the tropics in the middle of the afternoon because after a couple of hours of that sort of thing you're not going to be able to do very much else for the rest of the day. It's far better to leave whatever you have to do until the late evening, and — if necessary — carry on doing it through the night. You do a lot more that way, and your energy will be used a lot more effectively.

The progress of the boat, of course, is of paramount importance, and one's whole routine and programme is geared to the minimum of delays. Now, for instance, there are many occasions when the slacking off of effort for an hour or so can put you behind half a day.

These words come from Donald Crowhurst's Christmas tape recording. Once again he felt he needed a public performance to boost his morale, and turned to his BBC microphone for therapy. Although he took care to mention the pressures of speeding onwards, he was no longer over-worried about delays. The only real pressures that assailed him were psychological, as he tried to decide whether he should give up, or go through with his fake voyage. Even in the recording, this stress can be detected, for instance after a performance of "Silent Night" on his mouth-organ:

Oh, it's a beautiful and melancholy carol, and although it's not terribly well played, there is something in that very amateurishness ... the badly played mouth-organ is evocative of the situation of loneliness and peril in many ways that is undoubtedly associated with the instrument in the minds of a good many people. It's the sort of instrument that in the blitz somebody would play, or in a dug-out during a bombardment — or in a thousand and one situations where the human spirit is stressed. So it's not entirely inappropriate.

Not that I'm under any great stress, but there is something rather melancholy and desolate about this part of the Atlantic Ocean, and it's fitting somehow that I should be playing the mouth-organ on Christmas Eve.

Not that I'm depressed or feeling sorry for myself by any means, but there is a spirituality about this place and about the time — Christmas — that does tend to make one a little bit melancholy. And one thinks of one's friends and family, and one knows that they're thinking of one, and the sense of separation is somehow increased by the — by the loneliness of this spot, and, well, the sound that I've just made is representative in many ways of the ethos of the occasion. Anyway, enough of it — let us have something merry.

Whereupon Crowhurst picked up his mouth-organ again, and jigged his way through "God Rest Ye Merry, Gentlemen".

Already the relationship between the Public Hero and the private man was growing more tense. Crowhurst was still playing the role of a brave man under natural stress, but was beginning to lose control. His voice veered from mood to mood almost with every sentence, simultaneously asking for pity and denying that he needed any. The attitudes he was striking, both true and false, were growing increasingly personal.

Because he was not hurrying, he had time on his hands. The steady South-East Trades, which he had now reached, meant he could keep moving with little attention to the sails. As happens with many people in moments of unexpected leisure, Crowhurst took refuge in the dilettante pursuits of creative literature, and creative mathematics. He began to read the books he had taken aboard. It is probable that around this time he started to study *Relativity* by Albert Einstein, which attempts to explain the theory of relativity in popular terms. Perhaps he regretted having taken with him so few books, other than technical manuals and mathematical textbooks.

He wrote down snatches of Handel's *Messiah*, reminded of them by a radio broadcast: "Oh thou that tellest glad tidings to Zion . . ." "The glory, the glory of the Lord is upon thee . . ." "And they that dwelt in the land of the Shadow of Death . . ." He also took to writing poetry. He jotted each verse down, some surrounded with revised phrases, on the pages at the back of Logbook One.

His first poem, probably written somewhere near the Equator, was his most visionary, most heroic and — both in tone and geo-graphy — his most false. As he wrote it, he was more than 2,000 miles from the Southern Ocean:

LAWS

A Song of the Southern Ocean

There lies between Thirty and Sixty South
The wastes of the Southern Ocean.
And you who would learn what the sea's about
Should go there, you'll get a notion.
The rest of the world may go to the nick
But old Nature takes savage toll
On the slow, the unwary, sick or weak
Where those cold greybearders roll.

Look for no buoys nor beacons there
In the four thousand fathom deep
Nor for shipping lines to accept your fare
But wet comfort and little sleep.
For in all the years since the lightning flash
From whence all proteins come,
The peace of the deep, and the high seas crash
Are rewards enough, just the same.

There men may learn the Ways of the Seas,
The direct and immutable law,
Still standing, as it has stood, for centuries,
Long before Man returned from shore.
Unlike the muddled law of Man,
Sea law is simple and true.
She seldom strikes blindly, but destroys as she can
All things ill-conceived, not just new.

And you'll find time to think again
As you never find time ashore
Films of prejudice, expediency and strain
Wash from dusty eyes, once more
Revealing unwelcome detail and the lost horizon
Of that sharp-eyed childhood day
Before you learnt to blur the edges of your vision,
And trudge Man's compromising way.

Although the attitudinising in this poem is as dubious as its
metre, it contains two of Crowhurst's genuine obsessions: the

poetic-cum-scientific moment when proteins sprang to life in a lightning flash, and re-creation of childhood innocence by the sea's lonely integrity. These were ideas that had already fascinated him and would do so even more later. There was an attempt at a tender verse to a rose which, if it had any meaning, was probably also a love poem, evidence that he was thinking of one of his renounced loves, Enid perhaps. For the first time he described himself as a tormented soul:

ROSEBUD

Slender stem'd
Scarcely fragrant
Beautiful
Beyond shallow
Describing.

Why inclined
(Wonder of wonders)
Towards a
Tormented
Soul?

Softly, softly
Sadness and
Longing overmuch
Laughing
Seldom.

Stars would I give,
Shining suns.
All I can give
Are two
Small things.

So accept first
Secretly
My inner heart
My thoughts
Always.

Also I'll turn
Away sadly

Budding rose
Blossom
Perfectly.

Providence, constant
Protection,
Jealously guard your
Joys
Forever.

*   *   *

At this point it is interesting to compare Crowhurst's creative writing with that of the other meditative single-handed sailor in the race, Bernard Moitessier. Although his journey was far more arduous than Crowhurst's, there were some similarities in their reactions to solitude. Moitessier, too, could be driven to over-colourful attitudes:

A great Cape cannot simply be explained in terms of latitude and longitude. A great Cape has a soul with its shadows and colours, very soft and very violent. A soul as smooth as that of a child, and hard as a criminal's. That is why I go there. It isn't for the cash nor for the glory—it's for the love of life.

But on the other hand, Moitessier's words had a physical directness that proved there was nothing imitative, or imaginary, about his experience:

God, how good it is to live like an animal, to be caressed by a tepid and soft wind! How good it is to contemplate the Southern Cross, each night a little nearer the horizon. To sleep like a drunkard, to fill your stomach and belch with pleasure, to spread out in the sun till you are almost stupefied. I am no longer frightened of meeting men. I am at peace.

Even his highflown, more mystical passages, ring true:

When one has listened for months to the hum of the wind and the sea, to the language of infinity for so long—one is afraid of being brutally cast into company of people of having to listen to those empty vain conversations, that gossip. I don't mean I have become better than them, I have simply become more different in certain ways. What mattered before counts less now, even doesn't count at all. And there are things which were unimportant before which now count a lot. Time and material things do not have the same dimension they had when I left. When you have been rather deep into yourself, when you have hugged the wide horizons which reach further than the stars, you don't come back with the same eyes, you think more with the senses than with the brain. The brain deforms and falsifies. The brain is only useful for kissing your loved ones. While the senses give everything its dimension and its exact contour, its true shading and colour. That is how I see things now, through the skin and the stomach.

Robin Knox-Johnston—now beyond New Zealand—was inspired to some philosophical thoughts by Christmas too. No contrast could be stronger than that between him and the two single-handed intellectuals. He spoke naturally in the bluff mariner's voice which Crowhurst had been trying, so tortuously, to ape:

At 3 p.m. my time I drank a Loyal Toast, wishing that I had been up early enough to hear the Queen's Speech at 6 a.m. my time. Somehow, gathering together to listen to this speech adds to the charm of Christmas . . . In the evening I heard of *Apollo 8* and her crew, the first men actually to go round the moon, and it gave me food for thought. There they were, three men risking their lives to advance our knowledge, to expand the frontiers that have so far held us to this planet. The contrasts between their magnificent effort and my own trip were appalling . . . True, once Chichester and Rose had shown that this trip was possible, I could not accept that anyone but a Briton should be the first to do it, and I wanted to be that Briton. But nevertheless to my mind there was still an element of selfishness in it. My Mother when asked for her opinion of the voyage before I sailed, had replied that she considered it "totally irresponsible" and on this Christmas Day I began to think she was right. I was sailing round the world simply because I bloody well wanted to—and, I realised, I was thoroughly enjoying myself.*

*   *   *

The period around Christmas was a bad one for Crowhurst, full

* From *A World of My Own* by Robin Knox-Johnston (Cassell, 1969).

of introspection and self-doubt. He even allowed himself to write in his now almost exclusively navigational log: "This Christmas is powerful emotional stuff!" Most of his real concerns were being recorded in the large sheet of brown wrapping paper on which he had drawn his map of Rio de Janeiro. He was listening to the BBC Overseas Broadcasts, and tried to catch the words of some of the Top Twenty at that time (one tune was "Jennifer Eccles", another was "Lily the Pink" by the Scaffold). Like Knox-Johnston he noted the Apollo 8 splashdown in the Pacific.

On Christmas Eve he made a radio-telephone call to his wife which increased his melancholy. She immediately asked him for a precise navigational position, which Rodney Hallworth was demanding. In a clipped, strange voice he refused to give her one; he hadn't had a chance to take sun-sights, he told her. Then something must have made him panic. For the first time he told such a sensational lie it made nonsense of his carefully calculated false progress, and would have confounded anyone who was trying to make sense of his speeds. He was, he said, "somewhere off Cape-town". Even as he said it, Crowhurst must have realised that the lie trapped him even more inexorably. He could not with honour put in to Rio de Janeiro after giving such a distorted position, 3,000 miles to the east.

Both husband and wife were vividly aware that radio operators were monitoring the call, and even Christmas intimacies could not be private. None the less, he once again made a disguised appeal to Clare to force him to give up. "Are you all right at home?" he asked. "Are you sure you can cope with all the difficulties?" Clare Crowhurst, not realising the state he was in, felt it her duty to reassure him; everything was fine, she could certainly cope.

Crowhurst spent Christmas morning waiting for some reassuring personal messages over the radio. Although he had sent off his own greetings to Rodney Hallworth, Stanley Best, his family, and even the Town Councillors of Bridgwater, he had received nothing in return (all their replies arrived two days later). During the early morning transmission periods, he listed on his sheet of brown paper the various silent stations:

0430	Nil	GKL
0435	Nil	GKT4
0440	Nil	GKL
0450	Nil	GKH

and became so distressed that half-an-hour later he wrote:

0527 Sighs heard.

These sighs may have been wireless interference; but what is important is that Crowhurst, hungry for contact, thought they were sighs. Alone, monotonously sailing onwards day after day, he had so few things to stimulate his imagination; and he was in a mood — which became increasingly frequent as time went on — to inflate any speck of experience into an event of cosmic significance. Deprived of his Christmas messages, he elaborated the few materials he had — ship's provisions, mathematical knowledge and a radio transmission about Biafra on the 15·402 megHertz frequency — into an expression of his own misery. On the sheet of brown paper, he transformed them into a Christmas Day poem, a bitter mixture of electronics, mathematics and concern for Biafran babies:

> Keeping a sort of watch on sails by night,
> Alone,
> The rigging sighs a sigh of cosmic sorrow
> For weeping doves that die maybe tomorrow
> On 12.7×10^5 irradiated olive trees.
> A sigh to fill man's soul with melancholy.
> Waves! Sweep away my melancholy!
> My footstool's a 10lb case of rice
> To the North-east 2.5×10^3 miles,
> 250×10^3 babies will slowly die, too weak to fuss
> (Carbohydrate deficiency, they tell us
> on 15.402 mHz)
> Herrod, would you not solve overpopulation thus?
> Please, be informed, there is a Santa Claus!

Desperate feelings might not improve Crowhurst's metre or rhyme, but the contrast between this poem and "A Song of the Southern Ocean" is the immeasurable difference between sincere distress and posturing "courage".

Crowhurst's position on Christmas Day was less than 20 miles off the Brazilian coast. He could possibly see the land. After his radio-telephone call to his wife he had changed course towards the shore, impulsively needing at least some sign of solid land and independent life. Afterwards he turned away again, perhaps easier in his mind. Many pages later in Logbook One and — probably — many months later, Crowhurst wrote down the words:

Christmas off Rio de Janeiro. Lights, and strange things happening over Rio de Janeiro. Poetry is funny language.

This is an extraordinary passage, for as we now know he was nowhere near Rio de Janeiro, but off the coast a thousand miles to the north. Ashore there was only a small provincial capital called Joao Pessoa. If he saw lights at all, they came from there.

However, his pretended position *was* off Rio de Janeiro. He had carefully plotted himself there on the Admiralty Routeing Chart. When he later wrote those strange words, there would have been no point in faking such an observation; so they are probably the first evidence that, under great strain, delusion was beginning to replace conscious fraudulence. Crowhurst had thought so hard about his pretended positions and pretended course that he began to experience them completely. After the silent radio stations, the imagined sighs, the catharsis of writing "funny language" about dying babies, his illusions may momentarily have taken charge of him and become reality in his mind.

After daybreak he listened to Joan Sutherland sing "The Holly and the Ivy" on the radio, and looked to see if anyone had given him any Christmas presents or cards. The only thing he could find were cards from Peter and Pat Beard. On Peter Beard's card he read:

Happy Christmas, Don. Hope everything going ok. At a guess I would say you're off the Canary Islands. How far out am I? We all send our deepest regards to you. Do not worry about Clare and the kids. Pat and I will keep an eye their way. I expect by now you are well versed with the moods and ways of our old buddy "THE SEA" — even at this stage you must feel a great sense of achievement —
                              Best wishes Don,
                                    See you in about 7 months.

And on Pat Beard's card:

With all my love Don and very best wishes. Wish I were with you!!!!

ngland, January 1969: The wives meet aboard Cutty Sark. Standing behind Clare Crow-
st is Evelyn Tetley. Their husbands were later involved in a neck-and-neck duel

The Onan electricity generator (pictured after the voyage) rusted from seawater leak from the cockpit hatch. The damage was used to explain the 11-week radio silence

Two plywood patches screwed on during the secret stop at Rio Salado

LEFT: **The masthead buoyancy ba still not connected a: improperly lashed at the end of the voyage**

The troublesome port forward hatch attempt to fix a Sylglas seal is visible

Crowhurst described in Logbook Two his Christmas dinner of egg and corned-beef vindaloo, an orange (his last), brazil nuts, and some brown ale. He recorded a cheery description of cookery and gluttony on his tape recorder, and then wrote sadly in his log:

Peter and Pat were the only ones who gave me cards for Christmas. Is there any real conclusion to be drawn? Only that motivation is seldom judged with accuracy!

*   *   *

The Christmas gift that Clare Crowhurst had intended for her husband, that cuddly doll with long golden hair packed in the off-loaded carrier bag, was given, instead, to his daughter Rachel. After it had been mysteriously removed from *Teignmouth Electron*, Mrs Crowhurst decided it was too nice to waste. She removed the stuffing, sewed a zip-fastener on the front to make it into a little girl's nightdress case, and handed it over during Christmas lunch at Woodlands, together with presents for the other children.

Festivities in Bridgwater were scarcely more merry than in the South Atlantic. Crowhurst's third son Roger was having repeated nightmares in which his father stood, staring at him, in the door of his bedroom. His eldest son, James, was silent and subdued. Only Simon was in good spirits; he thought sailing round the world was easy, and intended to swim round when he was older. The Beards, true to their Christmas promise to "keep an eye" Clare's way, had brought a duck down to Woodlands. But Clare used her own turkey for the Christmas lunch. It gave the family a good rich meal, but it did little to cheer them up.

Two days before, the stable beside Woodlands had been badly damaged by fire. No one knew how it started, but it destroyed most of Crowhurst's workshop, and his sails and rigging for *Pot of Gold*. And there was trouble with Electron Utilisation. The problems of running the firm meant that Clare could not go out to earn money in any other job. It was not, however, producing the expected ten pounds a week income for her, and Stanley Best was growing increasingly disenchanted with it. Three months later Clare began living on "Supplementary Benefit"—the most recent euphemism for the dole.

Twelve

Silence and Loneliness

For the next month little notable happened to *Teignmouth Electron* at sea. Crowhurst was meandering southwards and eastwards without a clear destination, his course an aimless zig-zag designed primarily to take him far out into the empty ocean and away from the busy coast of South America. He needed only to expend time now, not cover distance, and these areas of the South Atlantic—normally devoid of shipping and violent storms—were not demanding.

He also had a damaged boat to nurse. On Boxing Day he opened up his starboard float hatch to make a thorough inspection of the split skin he had noticed six days before. He recorded that one of the internal wooden frames of the float had come away from the plywood skin. The skin had a largish split half-way along the float, beside the strips of metal which run under it to hold down the masthead shrouds. Where the glass fibre covering the float met the double plywood decking which Eastwoods had built, he found a three-foot split which seemed to justify all the doubts and fury of his first quarrel with the boatbuilders. Crowhurst's description of this damage in his log is entirely honest and accurate*(although the impression he gave of it in his cables to England was not).

* Our own inspection of the trimaran confirms this.

162

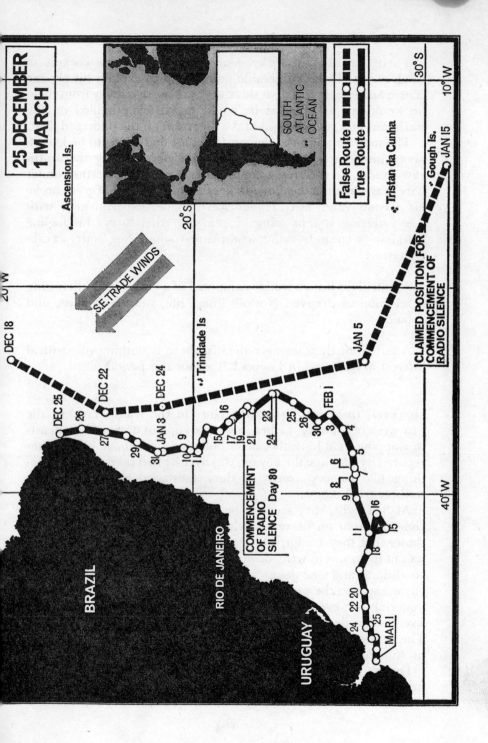

25 DECEMBER
1 MARCH

Ascension Is.

SOUTH
ATLANTIC
OCEAN

S.E. TRADE WINDS

False Route
True Route

Tristan da Cunha

Gough Is.

CLAIMED POSITION FOR
COMMENCEMENT OF
RADIO SILENCE

JAN 15

30° S

10° W

20° S

20° W

DEC 18

DEC 22

DEC 24

DEC 25

26

27

29

31

JAN 3

9

10

Trinidade Is

JAN 5

15

16

17

19

21

23

24

25

26

30

FEB 1

3

4

5

6

8

9

COMMENCEMENT
OF RADIO
SILENCE   Day 80

BRAZIL

RIO DE JANEIRO

URUGUAY

11

16

15

18

22 20

24

25

MAR 1

40° W

There was also the leaky generator hatch in the cockpit to think about. These vulnerable points help to explain his zig-zag course and erratic speeds at this time; to keep seas away from them he would try as often as he could to sail close-hauled on the starboard tack, which would take the strain off the damaged float.

The map on page 163 demonstrates all that needs to be known about his progress during this period. Before leaving the south-east Trades, he endured a couple of days of rough weather under bare masts, spent a day hove-to because of an attack of gout, broke his second (and last) Hasler servo blade, experimented with a self-steering system using his staysail, tried to get his logline working accurately, and complained that his water tanks contained:

A nutritious brown sludge composed of a varied and interesting selection of decayed Norfolk insect life, strands of glass, and paint.

Apart from these meagre details, there is nothing of nautical interest to be found in Logbook Two for this period.

*   *   *

However, there are fascinating clues in the Radio Log. In the first week of January, he began to take copious notes of broadcasts to shipping—cable traffic, news bulletins, and above all weather reports. By the time the voyage was over he had taken down something like 100,000 words of these messages, all in minuscule scribble from morse.

At first sight, they seem to be random jottings made to fill in time, or from an obsession with recording morse. Closer study shows that they conform to a rough pattern. What he evidently set out to do was to write down, as best he could, the local weather conditions and sea-going incidents corresponding to his fake voyage around the world. There is also a vast amount of extraneous material, but even with this the locations tend to move progressively across the South Atlantic then away into the Indian Ocean. The evidence from the met. reports is quite clear, and they were presumably the main purpose of this mammoth exercise.

During January and February, most of the messages originated from Capetown Radio, which puts out regular forecasts for the South-East Atlantic and the Southern Indian Ocean, and also rebroadcasts weather forecasts from Met. Mauritius. He took these all down indiscriminately; but when one of the forecasts coincided exactly with one of the meteorological areas along the clipper route—such as Tristan, Gough Forties, Meteor Forties, Marion Forties and Crozet Forties—it was neatly underlined. In March fewer weather reports were taken down, presumably because of the difficulty of picking up the Sydney and Wellington transmitters in Australia and New Zealand, where he was then supposed to be. But there were some successful contacts nevertheless, and again reports covering the relevant met. areas are neatly underlined. An indication of how systematically Crowhurst went about the task can be seen in a book found on board *Teignmouth Electron*: the Admiralty list of Radio Signals, Volume III, which documents weather broadcasts throughout the world. All the met. area maps covering bits of the clipper route were neatly marked off, and some of them annotated; the remainder of the book remained unused.

As well as embarking on this exhausting chore, Crowhurst was also worrying about his cables home; he was in an increasing quandary, with each succeeding cable giving a more and more false impression of his position. Every day made his coy refusal to broadcast precise positions more eccentric, and every day made the risk of being spotted in the wrong place more worrying. Although it is difficult for coastal radio stations to detect the direction from which a message is coming, his signals would shortly be so manifestly of the wrong strength, and coming from the wrong signalling area, that he would be in trouble. The logical solution was to contrive some reason for going off the air altogether, and this contrivance can be followed, as it develops on successive pages of the Radio Log.

He had already warned people back home that he might have to stop sending messages for a while because of generator trouble, and on December 29th he wrote out a message for Hallworth developing this theme. The message was to be the first sent via Capetown Radio, which would give the impression he was nearing Africa. First he wrote:

NEAR ILHA TRINIDADE HEADING FORTIES . . .

but crossed it out. This was too accurate, and would sabotage the blurrily optimistic impression given by previous cables. He recast it in breathtakingly vague terms, adding hints about a generator failure:

ALL WELL HEADING SOUTH TOWARDS FORTIES WHERE WORK BEGINS STOP MAY HAVE TO SEAL CHARGER COMPARTMENT

Caution, indecision, or inefficient radio operating held back this message, which he only sent—in a revised form—later.

On January 3rd he sent a short service message to Capetown Radio informing them he was moving into the long-range radio-telephone area 2a, which covers the south-western quarter of the Atlantic, down the coast of South America. This was consistent with the fake positions he had plotted on his Routeing Chart, but contrary to the impression at home that he was now past Tristan da Cunha on his way to the Cape of Good Hope. The point, however, was too sophisticated for anyone to notice. On January 8th another splendidly uncommunicative cable went off to Hallworth:

STRICKEN GOUT FOLLOWING NEWYEAR SHERRY PARTY NOW EQUAL FOOTING MERMAIDS STOP ALMOST INTO FORTIES

Two messages arrived back. One told him of the various dispositions in the race:

ROBIN LEADS BERNARD BEYOND TASMANIA TETLEY EASTERN INDIAN YOUR AVERAGE DAILY 30 MILES HIGHER SUNDAY TIMES RECKONS WINNER HOME APRIL NINE THIS YOUR TARGET

(To hit such a target Crowhurst would have had to travel 300 miles a day, more than twice as fast as the *Cutty Sark*.)

The second cable was an appeal from Hallworth for hard news, its yearning, plaintive text a tiny poem of journalistic frustration:

PLEASE GIVE WEEKLY POSITIONS AND MILEAGE CHEERS RODNEY

Crowhurst's really important messages, which ended his transmissions for eleven weeks, were written down on January 15th, and finally sent on January 19th. The first was a redrafted message to Hallworth:

100 SOUTHEAST GOUGH   1086 GENERATOR HATCH SEALED
TRANSMISSIONS WHEN POSSIBLE ESPECIALLY 80 EAST 140 WEST

In this cable Crowhurst had done three things. First, he had
taken pity on his publicist and given him a precise (but false)
position 100 miles southeast of Gough Island in the Roaring
Forties. (This is the same false position he had planned for that
day on his Admiralty Routeing Chart.) Second, he had given clear
warning that all messages were about to cease. Third, he had
dragged a red herring across his radio trail by asking coastal
stations in future to listen for him where he ought to have been,
between the longitudes 80° east (which runs down the centre of
the Indian Ocean) and 140° west (mid-way between New Zealand
and Cape Horn).

His other cable, to Stanley Best, had been even more carefully
composed. There are several drafts for this final text in the log,
which is primarily an exaggerated account of the damage to the
boat:

REGRET FLOAT FRAME SMASHED   SKIN SPLIT DECK JOINTS PARTING
REPAIRS   NOT HOLDING SPEED SO HORN AUTUMN   ILLFOUND
BOAT STOP   IF PREPARED DELETE CLAUSE UNCONDITIONAL
PURCHASE WILL TRY   OTHERWISE SUGGEST REVIEW NEWSPAPER
OFFERS   SOME DAYS IN HAND

This is an equivocal message to delight the sharpest of lawyers.
Nothing in it is literally untrue, but it gives an impression of
damage far worse than the boat had sustained. The reference to
parted deckjoints, for instance, conjured up images of the crossarms
and decking coming away from the floats. Whereas all that had
appeared were those small cracks between the glass fibre and the
plywood. Crowhurst's intention was to emphasise the heroism
to wring concessions out of Stanley Best, and to indicate how un-
fair was the contract clause forcing Electron Utilisation to buy
back a heap of disintegrating lumber should he decide to retire.
There was also, perhaps, a hope that Best would *order* him to
retire.

On this day Crowhurst wrote "Three Tels Off!" in Logbook
Two, which indicates how important to him the messages were.
The third telegram is something of a mystery. At the top of the
same page in the Radio Log where the two cables have been

written out, there is the text of another message to Stanley Best, which is manifestly an attempt to establish a code for secret messages. It reads:

XYZAB CDEFG HIJKH LMBNO PHQZG XYZRS TUVHW
NO TYPIST FOXED   CONFIRM DECODE SOONEST

This may, at first, appear incomprehensible, but it would not give any cryptologist a moment's pause. It obviously sets up a letter-substitution code. The "no typist foxed" phrase was a signal to write down the famous typewriter sentence which uses every letter of the alphabet—"The quick brown fox jumps over the lazy dog"—beside the groups of code letters, which also run straight through the alphabet, beginning at "x" rather than "a", and interrupted by the occasional duplicated letter. The code comes clear when this is done:

THEQU ICKBR OWNFO XJUMP SOVER THELA ZYDOG
XYZAB CDEFG HIJKH LMBNO PHQZG XYZRS TUVHW

Crowhurst himself had prepared decoding and encoding lists of these letters on the opposite page of his Radio Log. Armed with such a key, anyone could read the corresponding substituted letters instantly. Presumably if Best had replied that the code was deciphered, Crowhurst might have dared to explain his real predicament, and asked for the advice he desperately wanted; Best would have told him to give up.

Was this the third telegram Crowhurst sent? And did Best ever know of this code? The evidence shows that Crowhurst changed his mind, and never sent it off. He ruled lines round the other two texts and wrote "Sent 19th Jan" beside them, but he did not do so with the code cable. There is no sign of a response in the Radio Log, and Stanley Best confirms that he never received such a message. Furthermore, two pages back in the Radio Log there is a short acknowledgement message to one of Hallworth's cables, also with "Sent 19th Jan" written beside it, which would indicate that this was probably the mysterious third telegram sent off.

At all events, it had been a suitable last session. Ingenious, devious, begging others to make his decisions for him, it displayed, in cablese, Crowhurst's character under stress.

In the next few days Crowhurst toyed with some more public-voice heroic messages:

EXPECTANT NELSON UNHESITATING HORNBLOWER BOTH STICKY
ENDS HAVE REWORKED REPAIRS LOOKS PROMISING

He even started to draft a reassuring loving farewell to his family.
But he decided it would be wiser to close down. For nearly three
months he never once used his transmitter, even to respond to
incoming messages which he continued to receive perfectly.
Stanley Best's generous agreement to drop his contractual option:

CABLE RECEIVED DECISION YOURS STOP NO UNCONDITIONAL
PURCHASE REQUIRED GOOD LUCK

and a loving message from his sister-in-law Helen:

GOOD GOING STOP UPSPIRITS

were transmitted by Capetown radio again and again, apparently
into a void. Donald Crowhurst took them down each time, but
never dared to acknowledge them. They echo repeatedly through
the following pages of the Radio Log.

* * *

Meanwhile, back at Devon News, Rodney Hallworth had real
problems. To get headlines, he needed record bursts of speed,
backed by precise positions. We had left our hero, so far as newspaper readers were concerned, either just approaching Tristan da
Cunha, or just past it. Inspired by Mrs Crowhurst's Christmas
Eve report, Hallworth must have hoped for Capetown at the
very least. But all he had was the gnomic message:

STRICKEN GOUT FOLLOWING NEWYEAR SHERRY PARTY NOW
EQUAL FOOTING MERMAIDS STOP ALMOST INTO FORTIES

What on earth could he do with that? Editors were already
impatient of flying fish breakfasts devoid of latitudes and longitudes. Only to offer up a sherry party at this stage would invite
derision. After a couple of days, it no doubt seemed reasonable to
harden Crowhurst's prophecy into fact. "Almost into Forties" in
the cables therefore became "In Roaring Forties", and around this
achievement he spun a poetic web of extrapolated hopes and
expectations:

Donald Crowhurst has reached the Roaring Forties and is expected to round the Cape of Good Hope this week-end . . . Within another month he expects to be in sight of Australia . . . A cable received from Crowhurst shows him to be in good humour: "Stricken with gout after New Year Sherry Party. First [sic] footing mermaids. In Roaring Forties." Crowhurst was able to share his New Year with well-wishers. He received several cables of goodwill and broke open the sherry cask presented to him by Exeter landlord George Milford, just for the occasion . . .

The *Sunday Times* prudently did not print this story. Instead it went one better, recording Crowhurst's "latest known position" as 36° 30′ south, 15° east (which is on the clipper route, just before the Cape of Good Hope) and, extrapolating on the extrapolations, declared: "Donald Crowhurst should be in the Indian Ocean by now."

This further leap of the imagination carried Crowhurst another 300 miles away from himself.

In the following week, absurdity erupted into farce. Hallworth now had the two January 19th cables to contend with. They were to be his last for many months, and as the radio-telephone calls had ceased, those few words comprised his entire information. So he decided to amalgamate the sealing of the generator hatch with the exaggerated damage report into one artistically satisfying whole. Such damage required a cause; so Hallworth provided it:

The trimaran *Teignmouth Electron* being sailed round the world by Mr Donald Crowhurst is in trouble in the Indian Ocean. A huge wave smashed over the stern of the vessel damaging the cockpit and causing splits in the surrounding superstructure.

(Hallworth had here also invented an extra bit of boat. There was never any superstructure round the cockpit.)

Mr Crowhurst had to take down all his sail for about three days while he carried out emergency repairs. This involves completely sealing the rear cockpit compartment containing a generator. To prevent further damage he has also had to drastically cut down his speed, and he is now about 700 miles off the African coast . . .

Because his generator is now inaccessible Mr Crowhurst will have to conserve his batteries, and says that he will only radio home twice more.

We are now 4,000 miles from the truth, but of course Hallworth was unlucky with his cable. Crowhurst, remember, had transmitted a precise position and weekly mileage: "100 SOUTHEAST GOUGH, 1086". Alas, this was garbled in transmission to read "100 SOUTHEAST TOUGH, 1086" which Hallworth naturally presumed meant Crowhurst was having a tough time, but having it round Capetown. Had the correct wording come through it would have caused some embarrassment because – despite Crowhurst's own stretching of the truth – it would have thrust him backwards more than 1,500 miles. Even so, it might at least have cooled everyone's expectations.

From that moment onwards, with no messages from Crowhurst to guide them, the estimates of his position raced further and further away from reality into the Indian Ocean (as, of course, Crowhurst intended them to). As estimates based on his previous claimed times, they were reasonable enough. And they made Sir Francis Chichester's description of the lone hero, in a lecture to the Royal Institution (reprinted in the *Sunday Times* on February 2nd) look rather churlish. He was only willing to say:

> The last competitor, Donald Crowhurst . . . has claimed some fast bursts of speed, including a world record for the fastest day's run; but his average speed has not been fast – 101 miles per day – and at his last fix south of the Cape on January 10 he was about 8,800 miles behind Moitessier, so he does not seem a likely prize winner.

Later in Sir Francis's article, there was an even more sceptical passage:

> Recently there have been a number of loose claims for distances and speeds sailed, and I hope that a sporting club will check and recognise speed claims as the Royal Aero Club and the Federation Aeronautique Internationale have done for flying.

Not even Sir Francis knew, at that time, what a powerful

argument for such supervision was being mounted by Donald Crowhurst in the South Atlantic.

*   *   *

During this part of the voyage Crowhurst became fascinated by the birds and the fish he encountered. There are continual mentions of incidents in his logbook; he drew some of the stranger fish, and described each bird minutely. It was more than natural history to him, he needed living companionship badly. His writing about them, which is funny without being jaunty, precise without being stilted, and vivid without any pastiche of previous writers, shows how important they had become to him.

His first companion, which he had described to Rodney Hallworth, was Peter the Prior, a bird like a seagull, which had followed him, and eaten flying fish stranded on board. In the forged section of the first log he wrote that "he didn't seem keen on the water, but I supposed he must swim". On December 13th he noted that the bird was still with him. And in a page at the end of the first log he described him:

> Almost pure white below. Variegated light grey above. Darker "V" on the tops of the wings, swallow tail, long bill, the whole elegantly finished with black markings on the side of the head behind eyes.

Other sea creatures were also given personal names by Crowhurst. One of his favourites was Desmond the Doddery Dorado, who Crowhurst sadly recorded was eventually eaten by a shark.

On January 29th there was a momentary break in Crowhurst's reticence about his own emotional state. He wrote: "Last night, lying out on deck watching the moon and thinking about my . . ." followed by a word which is indistinct, and may be "fate", or "fortune", or "father". Whether he was contemplating his death, his present predicament, or his lost father, it was evidently an emotional moment for him.

This unhappy mood, plus his observations of birds and fish spurred him to write a descriptive fable expressing his state of mind. In it he used a bird (generalised from those he had seen), a pilot fish, and an albatross. The bird had ceased to be merely a useful bit of verisimilitude; he saw it, in its bedraggled doomed state, hopelessly out of its element, as a powerful symbol of his own mood, and his own possible self-destruction:

THE MISFIT

I must have disturbed him when I came up the companion. I was piddling over the stern to make my customary early morning contribution to the waters of the deep when I first became aware of the fluttering strenuous flight that so often characterises land birds. He landed on the dinghy—of all spots. A sort of owl, about eight inches from the tip of his beak to the tip of his tail. Brown, covered in buff speckles with two whitish patches on his wing tips (upper side). He was unapproachable, as a misfit should be. He flew away as soon as I made any effort to get near him, and on to the mizzen crosstrees, where he hung desperately to the shaky stays with claws useless for the task he had set himself: bedraggled, shivering, eyes closing with heavy fatigue, head withdrawn, his feathers fluffed up in scant protection against the icy wind, his wings twitching into a slight spread from time to time to take him instantly into the air if he should lose his grip.

There came a break in the dull greyness of the uniform horizon—a glimmering if distant light—and off he went. But the horizon closed, and he was back, on the mizzen boom, clinging desperately to the clew outhaul. I had set more sail, and he had a harder time reaching the boat at speed, and a harder time yet clinging to his selected perch.

Poor bloody misfit! A giant albatross, its great high-aspect wings sweeping like scimitars through the air with never a single beat slid effortlessly round the boat in mocking contrast to his ill-adapted efforts of survival.

I could not slow up to make the misfit's life easier. I had seen my own clearance on the distant horizon. At last the owl abandoned his insecure perch and gamely fought his way out of sight to windward. My heart turned to lead and my eyes filled. It was fitting that he left for the light of the sun to the east—to the east against the wind, where the nearest land was 4,000 miles away. Not for him the easy downwind flight of a few hundred miles to South America. He had left for the horizon that now was grey. He'd resolved to go east, and east he went.

Again I felt the temptation to ease up so that he could find some rest again if the struggles became too much, for I felt for him — but somehow I knew that he would not return. We were both victims of the one malaise. The victims of that malaise grow used to little quarter, and learn not to ask it, drawing only upon what is found by chance. Out of their own resources they delay as best they can the inevitable exhausted subsidence into the icy waters of death.

Was he the weakling of a migrating flight, or the strongest of the flock setting off alone to see what lay beyond the dangerous waters that the elders warned against? As far as I know owls don't migrate. I preferred to think he was one that had accepted that chance of finding new lands. Either way, he was a misfit, in all probability destined like the spirit of many of his human counterparts to die alone and anonymously, unseen by any of his species, yet accepting that one chance in a million of knowing things unknown.

I was reminded of the little pilot fish I had seen swim right up to a 10 foot shark and look him in the eye, shooting away as the shark rounded to make a snack of him. He could be the only pilot fish in the oceans that knows what the business end of a shark looks like at close quarters, even if he was lucky to be carrying the memory.

Beside this text, Crowhurst wrote a short poem on the same theme:

Save some pity for the Misfit, fighting on with bursting heart;
Not a trace of common sense, his is no common flight.
Save, save him some pity. But save the greater part
For him that sees no glimmer of the Misfit's guiding light.

"The Misfit" is the most powerful and well constructed piece Crowhurst wrote, but it shows him to be taking refuge from his predicament by playing yet another role. Previously he had seen himself as the hero lauded by society, now his guilt about the logbook forgeries and the potential fake voyage were too much for such straightforward display. Using the classic romantic device of the rebellious, the artistic, and the criminal, he had now cast himself as the hero rejected by society: The Misfit.

Thirteen

The Secret Landing

Donald Crowhurst knew that his most worrying immediate problem was the repair of his damaged starboard float. The split was getting larger, and trying to keep it out of the water meant it was impossible to steer any logical course. He also knew that thanks to the mix-up in Teignmouth he had none of the materials needed for such a repair; therefore he had to put ashore to get plywood and screws. However, by landing he would risk discovery, disqualification, and the revelation that he was nowhere near where he had said he was.

Towards the end of January, he seemed undecided on which direction to sail. For a week he meandered south-west, parallel with the coast of South America and then — after one inconsistent day heading south-east again — he started to sail slowly but steadily towards the mouth of the River Plate. A day of heavy weather seems to have finally decided him; he spent February 2nd riding it out with all sails down, and then headed firmly for land. His destination was not Buenos Aires, or Montevideo, or any of the larger towns there; a new plan was forming in his mind. He took down Volume One of the Admiralty *South America Pilot* (one of the eleven Pilot books he carried aboard) and searched through the coastline details for a suitable landing place. What he wanted was a small coastal settlement, large enough to provide wood and screws, but small enough for his arrival to remain secret.

Whatever his emotional state, he showed his usual detailed efficiency in the search. The fall of the pages in the *Pilot*, and grubby fingermarks, show very clearly which areas he surveyed, and pencil marks beside certain passages reveal what he was looking for. He studied the entries in the book from the River Plate to a bay called Golfo San Matias, some six hundred miles to the south. For some time he must have considered Golfo San Matias as a possible destination. He pencilled a line opposite an entry in the bay:

> Carros Dos Hermanas [hills] rise near this bay, and some houses stand on its shore. Vessels can anchor off Bahia Rosas in convenient depths.

Here was a good anchorage near a tiny settlement, which was ideal for his purposes. But it was a long way south, and he found another entry, even more to his taste, just inside the River Plate estuary:

> Bahia Samborombón: . . . the shore trends northwards for about 13½ miles to the mouth of Rio Salado (Lat 35° 41′ S, Long 57° 21′ W) and rises gradually . . . on the south bank of Rio Salado stands a group of sheds and buildings which form a good landmark. There are depths of 1 foot over the bar of Rio Salado, and greater depths within it . . . the best anchorages in Bahia Samborombón is about 5 miles offshore between the entrances to Canal 9 and Rio Salado, in a depth of 18 feet, firm clay and sand, with very good holding ground.

Rio Salado, in Samborombón Bay, had the great advantage that should his landing be discovered, and disqualify him, it was near enough to Buenos Aires and other large towns to seem a not too eccentric landing point.

So Crowhurst spent February dawdling back towards land. There was no particular rush, and his course was more than usually haphazard. The weather, to quote his log, was often "drizzly, muggy and 'orrible". For six days, two of them under bare poles in strong winds, he went round in a circle. By the end of the month, nearing the coast, he came almost to a halt, on

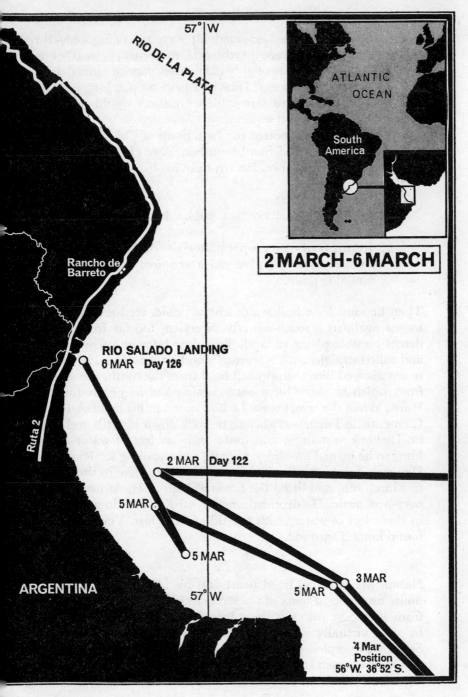

57° W

RIO DE LA PLATA

ATLANTIC OCEAN

South America

2 MARCH-6 MARCH

Rancho de Barreto

RIO SALADO LANDING
6 MAR   Day 126

Ruta 2

2 MAR   **Day 122**

5 MAR

5 MAR

3 MAR

ARGENTINA

57° W

5 MAR

4 Mar Position
56° W. 36°52′ S.

M

February 27th he was becalmed all day, travelling only three miles. These delays were partly due to contrary weather and indecision, but he had probably calculated that he must delay his landing in case of discovery. If he had to give up, a long haul back from Gough Island (his last cabled position) would seem more credible the later he put ashore.

On March 2nd he spotted the twin lights of Cabo San Antonio, at the southern end of Samborombón Bay. He turned towards them, searching the shore. He wrote in his log:

Immediate problems:
1: Establish visual contact (sighted coaster, San Antonio tower, Resort)
2: Repair float — no proper materials — large sheet ply — large timbers — screws — glue. Also require: oats, meths, rice, vindaloo paste.

Then he must have had a moment of panic. He headed right out to sea again in a south-easterly direction, too far from shore to detect possible places to land. Two days later he turned around, and sailed straight back towards Cabo San Antonio. His dash out to sea allowed him to approach land from the south, the direction from which he *should* have been coming had he just rounded the Horn. When the resort town he had noted in his logbook list, San Clemente de Tuyu, was abeam, he took down his sails and drifted in. He took soundings, and found only six feet of water beneath him; so he turned around yet again, now heading for Rio Salado. He worked out his estimated time of arrival as five in the morning of March 6th, and listed the times of high tides. As usual, he was over-optimistic. He dropped anchor off Rio Salado at 8.30 a.m., in three feet of water, with the tide falling fast. Very quickly, he found himself aground.

*   *   *

Nelson Messina had lived nearly all his fifty-five years in a little house on the right bank of the River Salado, only a hundred yards from the point where it flows into Samborombón Bay; he knew by sight virtually every vessel that used the River Plate estuary. So he was perplexed by the strange craft, with a wide flat deck, two stubby masts, and orange undersides, that he saw out in the bay that morning. He thought it might be one of the estuary dredgers. "But that was only a first impression," he said later. "I soon realised what it really was. I had seen a trimaran once before." He also realised that, despite the anchor chain hanging from the bows, it had run solidly aground, and needed help. He ran next door to ask his neighbour Santiago Franchessi what should be done. Franchessi was the right man to ask; he was Senior Petty Officer in charge of the local coastguard post, a few hundred yards up the river.

Crowhurst was unlucky in his choice of Rio Salado in that, unmentioned by the Admiralty *Pilot*, one of the "group of sheds and buildings which form a good landmark" was a four-room shack which was still a "Destacamento Prefectura Nacional Marítima", or small outpost of the Argentine coastguard. It had a staff of only three men (plus a brown and white collie dog), and its function was to observe the traffic coming in and out of the River Plate. Otherwise, the place could not have been more perfect. Rio Salado is less than a hundred miles from Buenos Aires, but has no telephone, no railway, no proper community, and only a narrow dirt road along the coast to link it to civilisation. The low-lying landscape abounds in trees and tall grass, which is too rough for the cattle that graze the more prosperous areas of the Argentine Pampa. The lagoons that lie along the coast are frequently replenished by floods. The population is sparse enough to encourage the ostriches, deer and wild hogs which have made the area popular with hunters. Tourists steer clear, the crabs have the beaches almost to themselves.

In such a setting, it is hardly surprising that the Rio Salado coastguard detachment went about its business in a relaxed manner. They did not even have a motorboat big enough to cope with *Teignmouth Electron*; so Nelson Messina, in his fishing launch *Favorito de Cambaceras*, took Franchessi and the young coastguard conscript, Rubén Dante Colli, out into Samborombón Bay.

They arrived at the trimaran at about 10.45 in the morning. To their surprise, there was only one person visible on deck. It was a man, extremely thin, with a soft, wispy beard, youngish, and dressed in khaki trousers with a wine-coloured shirt. From the launch Franchessi greeted the sailor in provincial Spanish, but got back only helpless smiles and probing phrases, first in English then in French. Finally the foreigner resorted to sign language, pointing at a hole in his starboard float, and vigorously miming the motions of a jockey flicking the haunch of his horse with a whip. Franchessi understood: the stranger was trying to say that he wanted to repair his yacht, because he was in some kind of race.

To tie Messina's tow rope to the damaged trimaran, Franchessi took a short step from the launch to one of the floats. It was, to paraphrase one of the newer catch-phrases of heroic endeavour, a small step for him, a giant one for Donald Crowhurst. The voyage up to that moment had been an unorthodox one, but until Senior Petty Officer Santiago Franchessi's boot touched the deck of *Teignmouth Electron*, it had not in fact broken any of the rules of the Round-the-World race.

Favorito de Cambaceras had no difficulty in pulling the yacht free of the sandbank, and towing it up the Rio Salado to the jetty of the coastguard station. Crowhurst wrote in his log: "11.00 Towed into Rio Salado by Prefectura Nacional Marítima de Argentina." When he finally arrived at the jetty, the third coastguard, Junior Petty Officer Cristobal Dupuy, recorded the incident in *his* log:

March 6. At 1430 hours there arrived at this port a yacht called by the name *Teignmouth Electron* flying the English flag and with damage in the hull, with one crewmember named Charles Alfred of English nationality, whose passport number corresponds to the number 842697.

A nice linguistic confusion had transformed Donald Charles Alfred Crowhurst into Mr Charles Alfred. Dupuy no doubt thought "Donald" some English title, corresponding to the Spanish "Don". His surname, Crowhurst, written on the next line of his passport, was ignored. But Dupuy took down the number of the passport accurately.

Crowhurst spent half-an-hour trying to convey to the coastguard that he wanted a sheet of plywood, screws and timbers to repair his float, but such elaborate mimings were beyond them. He also hoped for some electrical equipment, and drew in Logbook Two an armature for an electric engine or generator. He felt such an armature might be taken from a 12-volt toy car engine. The coastguards seem to have understood the drawing—and one of them wrote next to it the address of a shop in Buenos Aires. Finally they decided to drive him in their jeep seventeen miles northward along the coast road to find someone who spoke French. It would also be an opportunity to report the incident on the nearest telephone. Dupuy wrote in the log:

March 6. At 1500 hours the person in charge left for the Rancho Barreto in jip 415 to speak by telephone.

The Rancho Barreto, despite its grand name, is merely a converted hen-house standing beside the coastal road, Ruta 11, where Hector Salvati, his wife Rose, and daughter Marie live. They have a small trade in jams, honey, beer and pickles for motorists on the road, and occasionally serve meals. Hector Salvati is a sleepy ex-sergeant in the French Army, who has let his wife and daughter run his business for him since the family emigrated to Argentina in 1950.

The Salvatis were excited to be visited by the coastguard jeep, and even more interested in its strange passenger. Later, when shown a photograph of the clean-shaven, robust Crowhurst, taken before he set sail, Rose Salvati had difficulty believing it was the same man. "Although the person we met looked healthy enough, he was terribly thin. He was so wasted away that he had to keep hitching up his trousers. He told us they'd fitted him perfectly before he left England. And of course he hadn't shaved for a month."

Crowhurst, standing at the counter of the Rancho, told the Salvatis, in excellent French, that he had sailed from England four months before, to take part "in a regatta", that he had rounded Cape Horn, and that he expected to be back in England, the winner of the regatta, in a month's time—if only he could repair his yacht, and set sail again immediately. For that, he said, he needed plywood, nails, some screws, and timber.

Hector Salvati, translating this to Franchessi, asked Crowhurst —out of no more than idle curiosity—how he could prove he had indeed gone round Cape Horn. Crowhurst must have been startled, but replied, with much laughter and waving of his hands, that there was an apparatus fixed on one of the islands by the Horn which registered and identified passing vessels. He also mentioned some film he said he had taken off Cape Horn.

On grocery wrapping paper, Crowhurst then made three quick sketches. One showed the round-the-world route of the Golden Globe race, with a line curling out from the route near the southern tip of South America, and running in to Rio Salado. Another sketch was of a trimaran, showing it from the side and from above, giving measurements in metres. On it he wrote "Octobre 31–68", the date he set sail from Teignmouth.

The third sketch is the most interesting. It showed a totally different route, from England to Gough Island off the coast of South Africa, then across to South America and—in a much lighter line—back to England. It was a map reminiscent of the one he had jokingly drawn for Peter Beard, five months before, while sailing from Yarmouth to Teignmouth. Neither Franchessi nor the Salvatis could afterwards remember what was Crowhurst's explanation of this map. It certainly did not square with his initial explanations. He was "funny", they said, while drawing it. He spent much time talking loudly and disconnectedly.

Franchessi had brought Crowhurst a bottle of beer, and excused himself. He explained through the interpreters that he must call his superiors at the Prefectura in La Plata, sixty miles away, to ask for instructions. This, obviously was the reason for Crowhurst's agitation. "If it's found out that I'm here, I will be disqualified from the regatta!" he shouted at Hector Salvati. Then he calmed down, and seemed to take his predicament more philosophically. (They found him the most mercurial man they had ever met, with his swift changes.) "Oh well, if I am disqualified, I'll make my way on up to Buenos Aires and have a good time, and then on up to Rio de Janeiro." He did not explain how he would manage to do this, as he had also told them he was penniless.

The fear of exposure is one explanation for the Gough Island map. If unmasked in Rio Salado, he could always point to that sketch as the real map of his route, out to Gough Island and then back to South America because of the damaged float. Other awkward facts, such as the statement that he was "winning a race", he could explain away as misunderstandings caused by faulty translation. And the other map, he would say, was only a diagram of the general course of the race. He had with the third map ensured that he could still retire honourably, without his attempted fraud being discovered.

However, he was in luck. Senior Petty Officer Franchessi managed to get through from the public telephone booth at the Rancho Barreto to a junior midshipman on duty at the La Plata Prefectura. The midshipman was the lowest possible grade of officer who could receive such a report and make a decision. And he knew nothing of any race. After hearing Franchessi's description of his visitor, the midshipman told him to give the Englishman all he required, and allow him to set sail again at his own convenience. It was obvious to the midshipman that this was an entirely routine matter. He did not even advise his superiors at the Headquarters Prefectura of the River Plate zone, in Buenos Aires.

While waiting for the result of Franchessi's call, Crowhurst said to Rose Salvati "Il faut vivre la vie." He repeated it many times, excitedly, as though "Life should be lived" represented some profound truth. He was often so ebullient he seemed incoherent to his listeners. He mentioned what Rose remembered as "a transistor apparatus", which he said he was testing on the voyage. Later Rose Salvati was very emphatic about her exotic visitor. "He laughed a lot, as though he were making fun of us. We thought that something was wrong, that he might be a smuggler."

Crowhurst rode back to the coastguard post with Franchessi and Colli, and was promptly given the materials he wanted. He slept on his trimaran that night, and set about repairing the starboard float the next morning. By late afternoon, he had screwed on the patches, two of them, side by side, about eighteen inches square, and painted them white. Dupuy and Colli invited him to dine with them, on fried beefsteaks, that evening at the coastguard post where they — being unmarried — slept. So Crowhurst ceremonially shaved off his beard, and joined them in the kitchen of the destacamento. During the meal Crowhurst drank a glass of wine, mixed with soda water, and sat contentedly with them sipping coffee. But there could be no long, revealing conversation to enliven the meal. He made a few idle jokes in mime, but mostly ate and drank in silence. For a second night he slept on *Teignmouth Electron*, tied up at the jetty.

The next day, Messina the fisherman was summoned: the Englishman wanted to leave, and needed to be towed back down the short stretch of the Salado River and out into Samborombón Bay. There were some last minute attempts at communication between Crowhurst and Franchessi, who had enjoyed each other's company — despite the language difficulties. Both Franchessi and Rubén Dante Colli wrote their names in Logbook Two, and Franchessi added their address:

Destacamento Rio Salado
Las Pipina
Republica Argentina 1.

The Senior Petty Officer's impression of his visitor was markedly different from Rose Salvati's: "He liked it here. I would say that he was in excellent spirits and completely normal."

In the Rio Salado coastguard log, they wrote down a farewell mention of Crowhurst's trimaran:

March 8. At 1400 hours the yacht called *Teignmouth Electron* set sail.

Fourteen

"Heading Digger Ramrez"

Sir Francis Chichester has said that the period of greatest psychological strain during his voyage was just after he left Australia. The experience of meeting human beings again had served not to alleviate loneliness but to intensify it. There were, for many days, the problems of rehabilitating himself to the stern regime of the sea, and of knowing that the second half of the voyage would not only be as long as the first, but would contain even greater perils. Much later, Chichester and Robin Knox-Johnston speculated together on whether a long single-handed voyage was, in fact, made easier by stopping. They concluded that for wear and tear on the boat it obviously was: but for its wearing effect on the mind, perhaps it was not.

Chichester, as he set off from Australia already a hero and with his boat expertly repaired, found the problems real but manageable. Crowhurst, casting off from Rio Salado in a web of deception and in an ailing, patched-up boat, must have felt overwhelmed.

Even his nautical task was considerable. He was by now some 7,500 miles from home—and although this was only half the distance to Australia, it was still a long way to sail in any small boat. On top of this was the much greater strain of lying. Would the coastguard keep the landing secret—and if not how could his strange behaviour be explained? And there were the practical problems of deception too. For a few more weeks it would be largely a matter of waiting for his false route to circle the Southern Ocean and return to reality in the Atlantic. But where in the Atlantic? And how and when should he break radio silence? It all had to be managed with subtlety and skill; credibility had already been strained.

Before leaving Rio Salado, Crowhurst had already decided to sail further south. This was not just from force of habit; there were important reasons for his choice. He needed to be in the best place to monitor Wellington's Radio's New Zealand weather reports— and perhaps even to transmit a message to Wellington. To do this from the wrong side of South America would be risky, but by going further south he would reduce the chance of detection. He also needed a taste—however brief—of the Roaring Forties. His log demanded first-hand description, and he also knew that a few feet of film of the south's white-foamed seas would add conviction to his story. And there was the additional worry that his luck in avoiding contact with shipping could not be relied on for ever. He would be safer in the desolate south.

His course after leaving Rio Salado—carefully documented in Logbook Two—shows how his mind was working. After nosing into the River Plate estuary, he at once set his bows to the north-east, as if he were sailing back to England. That was what his cover story to the coastguard required, and with his careful attention to the detail of his deception he was taking no chances. Not until forty hours later, with the coastline well over the horizon did he turn abruptly towards the south.

His logbook for his first day at sea contained only one tiny incident: "Swam out for log plank". It seems that even after his trip ashore he was still so short of timber for repairs that it was worth taking the chance of going over the side for more. (Again he must have cursed the absence of the vital spares). Then, over the next few days, he had to begin the calculations for timing his "re-appearance".

From Gough Island—which he had supposedly passed on January 15th—the distance by normal sailing routes past the Cape of Good Hope, Australia and New Zealand to Cape Horn is nearly 13,000 miles. It is possible to reduce this distance slightly in January and February (the southern summer) by keeping

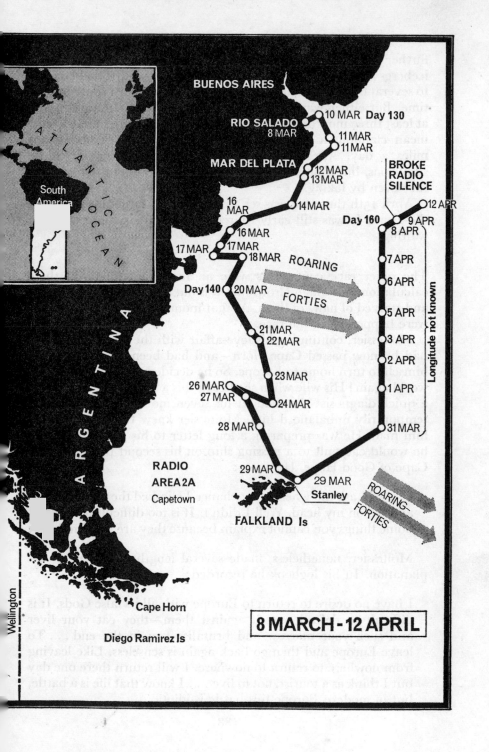

BUENOS AIRES

RIO SALADO
8 MAR

10 MAR Day 130

11 MAR
11 MAR

MAR DEL PLATA

12 MAR
13 MAR

14 MAR

16
MAR

16 MAR

17 MAR
17 MAR

18 MAR

ROARING

Day 140

20 MAR

FORTIES

21 MAR
22 MAR

23 MAR

26 MAR
27 MAR

24 MAR

28 MAR

29 MAR

RADIO
AREA 2A
Capetown

29 MAR
Stanley

ROARING-

FORTIES

FALKLAND Is

BROKE
RADIO
SILENCE

12 APR

Day 160

9 APR

8 APR

7 APR

6 APR

5 APR

3 APR

2 APR

1 APR

31 MAR

Longitude not known

ATLANTIC OCEAN

South
America

ARGENTINA

Wellington

Cape Horn

Diego Ramirez Is

8 MARCH - 12 APRIL

further to the south, though this involves greater danger from icebergs and storms. Before he had set out, Crowhurst had boasted to several friends that he might attempt the southern route to save time. But either way, Crowhurst now calculated, he must allow at least three months from Gough Island to the Horn. That would mean claiming a better-than-Chichester average of about 140 miles a day. After his slow start, people at home might be suspicious, but if he allowed a longer time, he might not win the race even by faking.

April 15th therefore was set as the notional target for rounding the Horn. It was still early March, which left six more weeks of waiting.

*   *   *

The other race contestants were an important factor in these calculations, although Crowhurst was out of contact with London and starved of news of them. At that moment some strange things were happening in the race.

Moitessier, continuing his love-affair with the Roaring Forties, had by now passed Cape Horn—and had been unable to bring himself to turn home to Europe. So he decided to set off round the world again! His wife when she heard this a short time later made a quick diagnosis: she thought his seven months of solitude had temporarily unbalanced him. Moitessier knew they would think him mad. He was preparing a long letter to his publisher which he would catapult to a passing ship on his second passage of the Cape of Good Hope. He wrote:

> You will ask me whether by chance I climbed the mast recently and fell on my head. Well I didn't. It is too difficult to explain. Some things you cannot explain because they are too simple . . .

Moitessier, nonetheless, made several lengthy attempts at explanation. In his logbook he recorded:

> I have no desire to return to Europe with all its false Gods. It is difficult to defend oneself against them—they eat your liver and suck your marrow and brutalise you in the end . . . To leave Europe and then go back again is senseless. Like leaving from nowhere to return to nowhere. I will return there one day but I think as a tourist, not to live . . . I know that life is a battle, but in modern Europe this battle is idiotic.

Make money, make money — to do what? To change your car when it is still going well, to dress 'decently' — this word makes me laugh — to pay an exorbitant rent, to pay for the right to moor one's boat in a port for almost the price of a servant's room in Paris, and perhaps one day to have a television; pushed, forced, ordered about by those false Gods ... I am going where you can tie up a boat where you want and the sun is free, and so is the air you breathe and the sea where you swim, and you can roast yourself on a coral reef ...

The letter Moitessier wrote to his publisher was even more lyrical:

Why am I playing a trick like this? Imagine yourself in the forest of the Amazon, looking for something new, because you wanted to feel the earth, trees, nature. You suddenly come across a small temple of an ancient, lost civilisation. You are not simply going to come back and say: "Well I found a temple, a civilisation nobody knows." You would stay there, try to understand it, try to decipher it ... And then you discover that 100 kilometres further on is another temple, only the main temple this time. Would you return?

Had Moitessier gone mad? Or had he found a peculiar form of sanity? If he was mad, it was very different from the sickness that was slowly overtaking Crowhurst. The words the two men used were often similar. ("At sea," Moitessier wrote a little later in his log, "time takes on a cosmic dimension ... where you had the feeling you could sail for a thousand years.") But the content was different, and so were the personalities and motivations that drove them. Moitessier himself had no doubt:

Don't think I'm mad, but I have the impression that there's something that resembles not the third dimension but the fourth. I repeat, don't think I'm crazy. I am in very good health.

Moitessier was now effectively out of the race, having seemed likely to win both prizes — to say nothing of the *Légion d'honneur* said to be awaiting him in France. This left Knox-Johnston, Tetley and (so the world thought) Crowhurst still battling on. For the moment, Tetley was the favourite, because Knox-Johnson with his battered boat and low-powered radio transmitter had been out of contact for over four months since last seen heading to Cape Horn from New Zealand. His sponsors, the *Sunday Mirror*, had already published a sombre article that read like a thinly-disguised obituary. But in fact he had struggled past the Horn and was now fluttering his lone British flag up the Atlantic. He had even reached flying fish latitudes again, as his logbook duly recorded:

March 11th: I made what I consider to be an excellent fish pie —from flying fish I found lying on the deck this morning (I've mastered cheese sauce at last).

Otherwise he was spending his time reading his *Golden Treasury of English Verse*, trying to imitate the Duke of Edinburgh's photograph of a leaping porpoise, writing angry rebukes of de Gaulle for daring to insult the British Ambassador, and reminiscing about the personal wartime experiences of Knox-Johnston (aged five):

Awoke for the news at 0200. Ike is dead. Well, he had been ill for a long time now and has been fading recently, but I still have a slight feeling of personal loss. I can still remember the excitement when we went back into France in 1944 and although, of course, Monty was "our man", he had to share the honours with Ike. It is never pleasant for a proud nation to have to admit it is no longer the biggest power, and to place its armies under a foreign leader . . .

On April 6th Knox-Johnston was at last spotted by a passing tanker, and preparations immediately began for a triumphal return. He would now undoubtedly win the Golden Globe. But his voyage had been so slow (96.5 miles a day average) that both the trimarans were expected to beat his time for the £5,000 prize. Meanwhile, Tetley had by March 20th successfully rounded the Horn and was turning up the Atlantic. His route took him just 150 miles from *Teignmouth Electron* which was idling north of the Falkland Islands. There was still nothing Crowhurst could do but wait.

*   *   *

How did Crowhurst fill in the time? There was one activity about which we can only speculate. We know that in Teignmouth

Crowhurst bought four logbooks. Yet when the boat was discovered there were only three on board—Logbook One, Logbook Two, and the Radio Log. It therefore seems probable that Crowhurst destroyed the fourth logbook at some stage of his voyage; and he clearly would not have felt this necessary unless it had been in use. But what could it have contained?

Crowhurst might have been using it for his outpouring of poems, stories and essays, but we think this unlikely. He had already given up the back pages of Logbooks One and Two to this purpose, and ample space remained. Also there are many indications that he intended his creative writing for publication once he was a hero—and it is improbable that he would have thrown all his work away.

A second theory is that he kept the spare logbook for notes, such as navigational calculations, electrical circuits, and radio messages. But again it seems unlikely. The boat, after the voyage, was littered with scribbles on odd scraps of paper, and the plotting sheets, Radio Log, and the margins of technical manuals had also been used for this purpose. Everything suggests that Crowhurst had no place for keeping systematic notes.

There is a third theory: that the spare logbook was being used for drafting an account of the fake voyage. By now, Crowhurst had almost ceased even his short mariner's jottings in Logbook Two. Unless he intended to rely entirely on memory and invention for convincing detail, he should surely have been drafting his fake voyage day by day. We think this explanation probable. And it is even possible that Crowhurst may have been composing a complete new logbook covering the entire voyage, for as we have seen Logbook One contained some suspicious switches of style that must have worried him. There is further evidence in the tape recordings that Logbook Four existed and was used. It would help to explain the almost total absence of the meticulous and detailed preparation for forgery which Crowhurst produced for all his other, smaller, deceits.

In all the papers he left behind there are only two pieces of writing which seem obviously intended for inclusion in a forged log. (The poem "Song of the Southern Ocean" is deceptive, but could as much be wish-fulfilment as deceit.) The two crucial passages are on blank pages in the back of Logbook One and, to judge from the position of the pages, were written at about this time. One is a dutiful piece of doggerel which Crowhurst, in his role as poet-laureate as well as hero-to-be of Teignmouth might have felt was called for:

> In Tigenmouth Town, in Tigenmouth Town,
> On the blazing sands, all tropical brown,
> The people are smiling, hardly ever a frown,
> It's 'gin the law in the mouth to be down,
> Oh to be back in Tigenmouth Town.

He seems (quite rightly) to have been worried about the fourth line, which had been rubbed out several times. The other "fake" draft, on the opposite page, is more interesting. It was evidently meant to be part of an account of rounding the Horn, and has all the same signs we have noticed before of Crowhurst when lying: stilted, uneasy and full of oblique excuses for failure of the "evidence" (he supposed his camera to have broken down). It also introduced an alter ego called "Mac," a remembered BBC film instructor.

> Rounding the Horn I got out the camera, loaded a reel and started shooting. I'd got about 50 feet when the thing came to a grinding halt. I had to take the thing to bits. (Mac said 'Any minute now, laddie, and the spring and 38 cogs will hit the coachroof'.) But found the trouble and cured it by giving the phosphor bronze friction spider on the empty spool drive a bit more bias and wiping away surplus oil. Then after commenting on people who give people second-hand cameras I was back taking film. After my noon sight I turned N.E.!!

There is a counter-argument to our fake logbook theory. If he had any powers of self-criticism left, he could hardly have been happy with his childish bit of verse and lying prose. Perhaps, after making these two inadequate attempts he postponed the task, and found he could never go through with it.

* * *

Crowhurst, meanwhile was spending March sailing the thousand miles to the Falkland Islands. Because shipping is sparse south of Buenos Aires, he could now stay within a hundred miles of the coast of South America. This helped navigation (he could use his Navicator on the coastal radio beacons) and allowed him some shelter from the increasingly rough weather. He was, however, careful to avoid getting in sight of land, except at one point when he went within seventeen miles of Mar del Plata; this was not too risky, because it is one of Argentina's wealthier resorts, and the sight of a strange yacht there would not have provoked much comment. Off Golfo San Matias (one of the places he had originally considered for a landing; was he again thinking of putting in?) he sharply turned south-eastward towards the Falklands.

He was spending long hours listening to morse on the radio, mostly from Cape Town and Buenos Aires. Then, from March 21st, as the radio shadow cast by South America diminished, he was at last able to pick up Wellington Radio, New Zealand. A series of South Pacific weather reports followed in his Radio Log. Reception, however, was not good and the reports were frequently interrupted by the note "QRM", which is the international Q-code* symbol for atmospheric interference.

Crowhurst deliberated for a long time whether to try to transmit a telegram to Australia or New Zealand. His fake course would have taken him past longitude 140° east—the position at which he said (in his last message before he started his radio silence) that he would try to make contact. For two days, he drafted and redrafted the possible wording on a piece of scrap paper. The main aim was to find if he had been spotted, but it would have seemed too eccentric not to give any position. This worried him and he tried several different phrases. He also pondered whether to send it to Wellington or Sydney. He eventually hedged his bets by a Q-code prefix to his telegram: "QSP [will you relay free of charge to . . .] ZLW [. . . Wellington . . .] VIS [. . . or Sydney]". This was in the hope that if anyone picked up the message it would be relayed home—but only via the right channels. The telegram continued:

PRESSE DEVONNEWS EXETER=ON COURSE HORN MID APRIL   MUST
KNOW POSITIONS OTHERS ALSO IF SIGHTINGS REPORTED AS ANXIOUS
SCANTY TRANSMISSIONS DUE GENERATION PROBLEMS WORRY CLARE

In the strictest sense, the wording did not lie. Crowhurst, sailing

* The Q-code—groups of three letters always beginning with Q—is used in morse communications for asking and answering standard questions. Crowhurst had diligently learned it at his course in Bristol before he set out, and used it expertly in his telegrams.

down the side of South America, *was* "on course Horn" at that moment. He had merely neglected to mention that he was "on course" from the wrong side. If his ambiguous probings about sightings had produced a positive reply, he would have had difficulty in talking his way out of it—but he could still possibly have produced some explanation.

There are indications that he tried repeatedly to transmit the telegram, because the date and time—which are always added to the prefix of cables—were amended several times on his draft from March 23rd to 24th to 25th. However, he evidently failed to get through. He preserved the scrap of paper, but there is no record of a transmission in the Radio Log.

On the evening of March 25th, he picked up a weak, fading signal from Portishead Radio in England, and wrote it down in his Radio Log:

MZUW [*Teignmouth Electron* . . .] DE GKG [. . . from Portishead . . .] QRU? [. . . have you anything for us?. . .] 0200Z 12 MCS [. . . we will listen at 02.00 g.m.t. on 12 megacycles]

Why were they calling him? Could it mean he had been reported from Rio Salado and they thought he must now be nearing England? Or was it just a routine call hoping to contact him somewhere in the world? Either way there was nothing Crowhurst could do. It would not have served his purpose to contact anywhere but Australia or New Zealand; and in any case his radio was too small to transmit to England. He decided that the problem of breaking radio silence must be put off until later.

* * *

By now, Crowhurst was getting a taste of Forties weather. He had been making comfortable progress towards the Falklands and seemed to have only two more days' sailing before glimpsing land. Then, suddenly, he was hit by a storm and blown more than a hundred miles off course. It is easy to forget in recounting Crowhurst's devious behaviour, that great courage is required to sail a boat in these southern seas. At this moment, he was little over 500 miles from the Horn, and—as many mariners have found—things can be just as rough here as at the Horn itself.

One of Crowhurst's tasks was taking film for the BBC, and during his voyage he shot several scenes through the cabin windows as great waves crashed on the trimaran's decks. The film reels were undated, but some were probably made at this time. He was perhaps also hoping to get dramatic Cape Horn-style pictures at the Falkland Islands. If so he was to be disappointed. When he arrived there on March 29th—three days later than he expected—the storm had abated and the sea had reduced to an unusual gentle swell. There was little he could do but spend an afternoon and evening hovering a few miles off-shore north of Stanley Harbour, shooting unheroic pictures of the sunset. The BBC film was recovered from the boat, and shows the dark, low profile of the Falklands on the horizon.

This was the southernmost point of Crowhurst's voyage. Once the film session was over, he settled down to his one hundred and fiftieth night aboard *Teignmouth Electron*. In the morning, he turned abruptly round and—still with time to spare—started his 8,000-mile journey home. For two days he ran swiftly before westerlies of the Roaring Forties, perhaps just to get a taste of what they were like. Then he slowed down and turned northwards, back towards safer waters.

*　　　*　　　*

The problem of transmitting a radio message was now pressing on Crowhurst. He evidently felt it essential for credibility to make radio contact before his fake voyage "reached" the Horn. If he did not, it might be too obvious that his transmissions throughout the trip had all been from the Atlantic. If a simple, direct message could not be got home via Wellington, New Zealand, then he would somehow have to create a credible blur of confusion.

His first idea was belatedly to acknowledge the two radio telegrams he had received in January after he began his radio silence—the one from Stanley Best which released him from the "unconditional purchase" agreement, and the "upspirits" message from his sister-in-law Helen. He looked up the reference numbers of the two telegrams and drafted a "received" message, also adding in that he was at present in radio area 5a—which is on the *west* of South America. He addressed it to Capetown Radio, but via Wellington. He knew it was unlikely that Wellington would be able to pick up his transmission, but perhaps hoped that the acknowledgement would somehow reach Capetown with the Wellington instructions still in. However, after making various attempts at drafting the cable in his Radio Log, he eventually crossed it out with the note, "This will probably cause trouble at Capetown, won't send it."

He then drafted a message of the kind known in communications procedure as a "TR". These messages are supposed to be sent regularly by ships to the Long-range Radio-telegraphy Service to give information on positions and destinations, so that telegrams can be efficiently routed. Crowhurst's TR was a complicated series of instructions, written in Q-code, which contained practically everything except the one thing a TR should contain—his latitude and longitude. What it amounted to was that he would be in Area 5a (the zone west of South America, served by Wellington Radio) up to April 15th and thereafter he would be in Area 2a (the zone east of South America served by Cape Town). This implied, when translated from its dry telecommunications context, that he planned to round Cape Horn on April 15th. (Interestingly, on a later draft of the TR message, he changed this date to April 18th— he had decided to delay his supposed rounding of the Horn for three days). Crowhurst also appended details of his listening times for receiving incoming telegrams, but added: "PLEASE ASSUME RECEIPT IF ACKNOWLEDGEMENT IMPOSSIBLE". He clearly did not yet want to get drawn into communicating regularly.

Crowhurst transmitted his TR on April 7th, first to Wellington, New Zealand, and Portishead, England, then finally to Capetown (which serves the area he actually was in). Apparently, none of the stations replied. What happened next is not quite clear, but on April 9th he suddenly recorded in his Radio Log a hilarious morse conversation with General Pacheco Radio, Buenos Aires. This station is not part of the normal network for British ships, but was the nearest large transmitter to Crowhurst's actual position. There is no record in the Radio Log of whether Crowhurst called Buenos Aires or they (perhaps hearing his unsuccessful attempts to raise Wellington) called him. But to judge from the snatches that Crowhurst wrote down—a mixture of Q-code and Spanish-English—the Buenos Aires operators were very puzzled by his obtuseness. Over and over again they asked "QTH?" (what is your latitude and longitude?) and "QRU?" (have you anything for us?). Though Crowhurst did not write down his own side of the conversation he was clearly being evasive. Eventually Crowhurst was persuaded to send a telegram through Buenos Aires. Its wording was deliberately cryptic:

DEVONNEWS EXETER=HEADING DIGGER RAMREZ   LOG KAPUT
17697 28TH   WHATS NEW OCEANBASHINGWISE

*   *   *

Rodney Hallworth had been having a worrying time. Since the alarming telegram of eleven weeks before, he had heard not a word from his hero-to-be. Crowhurst's promised radio calls had failed to come through, and Lloyd's had not reported a single sighting. And although the newspapers had been content for a while with descriptions of the "Indian Ocean storm", even Hallworth's resourcefulness had long since flagged. There was little left to report but the cautious belief that Crowhurst might possibly be progressing slowly past Australia. In the Ship Inn, Teignmouth, the black line on the map showing the daily progress reports provided by Hallworth stopped ominously in mid-Indian Ocean, and some people even feared for Crowhurst's life.

Hallworth was shaving on the morning of April 10th, when the telephone rang, and the operator read Crowhurst's brief message. His face still covered in lather, Hallworth phoned Clare Crowhurst with the joyous news. Then at leisure he translated the cryptic words. "Digger Ramrez", he worked out, must mean Diego Ramirez — a tiny island south-west of Cape Horn. He noted that the logline had broken on March 28th after 17,697 miles, and that Crowhurst seemed very anxious to find out what was known about the ocean bashers. What splendid phlegmatic humour, Hallworth thought.

He at once realised that if his man could keep up this sort of speed he was favourite to win the race for the fastest time. There was only one annoying thing about the message, Crowhurst's lack of precision. He didn't seem to understand that rounding the Horn was a great event which needed a time and a date. Hallworth therefore read very carefully between the lines of the telegram and divined that Crowhurst had meant to say he was 300 miles from the Horn — so he should have arrived there in time for the following morning's editions. So it was that half of Fleet Street sent *Teignmouth Electron* round the Horn on April 11th — a week before Crowhurst's carefully-balanced considerations required.

Crowhurst's progress had now started to seem suspiciously fast — an impression compounded by an erroneous statistic in the Devon News report that *Teignmouth Electron* had been averaging 188·6 miles a day for 13,000 miles. (Though calculated down to a decimal place, the figure was about thirty miles a day too high, even on the assumption that Crowhurst was at the Horn.) Surprisingly, a week later on April 18th, several newspapers *again* reported Crowhurst to be "just rounding the Horn"—this time on information deriving from Hallworth, but issued by the race organisers, and apparently based on Crowhurst's contact with the radio-telegraph operators. Of course, neither Hallworth nor the race organisers could know the truth, but at least this second announcement got it wrong the way Crowhurst intended.

There was, too, the inconsistent fact that the cable had arrived from Buenos Aires and not from Wellington. But it seems that Crowhurst had worried unduly: the point passed everyone by unnoticed. The only explanation for the almost total lack of scepticism can be that the newspapers at this time were full of the imminent home-coming of Knox-Johnston and their stirring stories dwarfed the small paragraphs about Crowhurst. Only the usual lone voice was raised in protest. Sir Francis Chichester was now convinced that something odd was going on, and in Falmouth, waiting for Knox-Johnston's arrival, he was openly expressing his doubts to Race officials.

Fifteen

Midnight Oil

On *Teignmouth Electron*, the days were now getting shorter as the southern winter approached, and Crowhurst decided to improvise an oil lamp to save his batteries. He took an empty dried milk tin, soldered on a tube to hold a makeshift wick and filled it with paraffin. Perhaps because of shortage of fuel he made only one. It produced a smelly flickering light by which Crowhurst stayed awake into the small hours, listening to his radio, tinkering with his gear, puzzling over his deceptions, eating, drinking and writing.

His writing of this period was, as before, a strangely contrasted mixture of the banal and boisterous, and the withdrawn and melancholic. It seemed to reflect the two conflicting aspects of his character that had been apparent throughout his adult life: the bar-room braggadocio and the lone, dedicated boffin; the life-and-soul of the officers' mess and the fretting, small-town intellectual. Only now, the gulf seemed wider than before.

At the most banal level were his regular additions to the collection of mildly risqué limericks which he kept at the back of Logbook Two. Even for limericks they are uncompromisingly bad.

By way of explanation, Crowhurst had added an apologia at the head of the collection:

> Whilst a-sailin' the Sunday Times race,
> I sublimate sexual urgeses
> By sailin' a Clipper Ship pace
> An' a-writin' o' dirty vergeses

We shall spare the reader by quoting only two:

> When questioned, a lass from Gibralta
> Who naked swam fast toward Malta,
> Said the spray from her feet
> Flew four hundred feet
> And frustrated attempts to assaulter

(To this, Crowhurst had added, "I thought Ho Ho! as I put on me aqualung", which theme seemed to fascinate him as he added several more limericks about pursuing the lass in goggles and aqualung, but naturally without wet-suit. Another regular theme was Sidney who had successfully faked a sailing competition, though Crowhurst discreetly changed it to the *Observer*'s Transatlantic Race)

> A transatlantic race entrant named Sidney
> Taped air tickets on to his kidney
> Said "I sailed to New York
> On a small piece of cork
> And the sea wuz so big it just hid me."

In the same high-spirited, self-mocking mood he also, by oil-lamp one night, got drunk and recorded a long tape on his BBC machine.* He had been drinking a bottle of Moët et Chandon that he had been given before his departure by John Norman, and he had finished it all in one session, as he felt one must with champagne. His drunkenness produced none of the maudlin responses one might have expected; it restored him instead to the old, boisterous bar-room clown, enjoying the role of being drunk, as well as its actuality. This, verbatim, is a small part of what he recorded:

* The tape was not dated in Crowhurst's logbooks, but from internal evidence it was apparently made on April 23rd or 24th.

Hast a bone to picketh.

Hast a bone to picketh with thee. Thou givest me a whole bottle of champers mate, a whole blinkin' bottle and it doesn't keep does it? You wicked man. You should have given me two half bottles, cause I'm drunk you circum, you silly old circum, you're as drunk as a circumnavigator can be. [*Laugh*]

Hey, I'll tell you something, in strictest confidence matey. I have recorded the most god awful load of codswallop you have ever heard in your life matey . . . However, seeing as how I am sti . . . oops watch the level matey . . . you will saturate the old 'ysteresis whatsit — [*Sings*]

> "Do not saturate the 'ysteresis loop,
> 'ysteris loops musn't be saturate.
> You must not saturate the 'ysteresis loop"

How's that?

What a you wanna know matey. Yeah, where am I, what am I doing? Well, I tell you matey I cannot remember for sure whether you gave me that bottle of champers, John, for around the Horn, or Christmas Day, or whatever, well I decided I would a keepin' of it until such time as I had crossed the old Summer Zone, a-going northwards like. Well I 'ave [*Laugh*] I 'ave matey. I have crossed the horrible line which lies about 36 degrees southern latitude . . . and I am out of puff, completely and utterly out of puff matey. After screaming across the Southern Ocean I am now ignominiously crawling at . . . about four knots or three knots with every stitch o' canvas I can lay me hands on up. And if there should chance to be a hurricane tonight matey, my circumnavigationals will be severely jeopardi-I-ased I can tell 'ee matey, cause I am in no fit state to go attendin' of it whatsoever, and you will have a lot to answer for matey when you comes across me little box of Tupperware in which me tape recordings are stowed, when I went to Davey Jones and threw over the side like. The only record of me downfall will be these horrible tape recordings, and I want the world to know it was all the fault of John Norman esquire of the BBC matey.

Me gawd, we must be doin' of all of three knots. Will you listen to the crashing of the great Atlantic matey . . .

Oh tis 'orrible to be out matey. Mountaineous seas eighteen

inches high an' horrible great black clouds, roll upon roll of them matey, stretching away as far as the eye can see. Now I will cast me optic on the wind recorder. Me gawd six knots . . . Oh I have been in some tight spots on this voyage matey, but this is diabolically tight matey. It is tighter than tight can be. It is diabololical tight. I will not embarrass the listeners with a description of how tight it is. [*Laugh*]

Now then what I want to know is this. What terrible hardships I am enduring? Well, I tell you. Terrible hardships enough mate, I tell ee, terrible hardships enough. For instance, I give you for instance, the only light illuminating the sordid details of my cabin comes from a paraffin lamp which I have constructed myself out of an old tin, in which there was powdered milkEIA matey. [*Chuckle*] The only luminosity I have got matey, apart from when I charges up the batteries and can switch on the odd fluorescent lamp matey. Now the point is, the terrible hardships one endures . . . hang on, I'm getting mighty thirsty. [*Pause*] As I sit here drinking my Gold Label beer — barley wine — I'm filled with a great contentment. As a result of this superb beverEIage, it might be . . . Aah, the tape is nearly distinguEIAished matey, and all the little oersteds faithfully recording my drivel for ever. What a sobering thought matey. My drivelling nonsense on record for ever. Unless of course you decide to erase it which would be a very grave mistake, because drivel of such monumental driviality is very, very difficult to find. I venture to suggest in the 'ole of the archives of the BBC there is no evidence of such drivel as I drivel at this moment. It is like the nose of Cyrano de Bergerac. A monument of drivel, not mere drivel, not plebeian, pedestrian drivel, but aristocratic drivel, the prince of drivel, the emperor of drivel, the supreme example of the driveller's art.

Don't erase it. Don't erase it. For posterity's sake preserve it. Preserve it for future generations as yet unborn.

Well now, oh dear, oh dear, oh dear, it seems I've come to the end of the tape, what a diabological pity . . . Actually matey, I tell you this matey, I've got a hell of a lot of tape to record on. I don't have the faintest notion matey how I'm going to fill it, but if I keeps this up much longer somebody's gonna shoot me. I think the Director General of the BBC's probably at this very moment slipping some buck shot into his twelve-bore as it were. Oh I shan't worry, that's the man Donald Kerr. Oh there'll be some sharp knives awaiting Donald Kerr. [*Giggles*] He's given this lunatic Crowhurst a tape recorder he has. It is a terrible thing, but I think I'll just have another little swig of his bottlel. [*Drinks*]

Towards the end of the recording he started also to drink a bottle of rum, and became increasingly drunk. Even so, his guise of having sailed the Southern Ocean never slipped, and he remained fully articulate and in control. (At one point he even gave the BBC men a little lecture on the techniques of deleting tapes, which made perfect technical sense.) So far as the evidence reveals, heavy drinking on the voyage was unusual, though he did take adequate supplies with him, mostly of beer, sherry and barley wine.

*   *   *

In contrast to the limericks and tapes were the other writings at the back of Logbook Two. They reveal a totally different man, lonely, depressed, groping for intellectual stimulus, and exploring his mind and his memories to find it. The ideas he wrote down were becoming increasingly fanciful.

One of his melancholy thoughts, expressed in mathematical symbols was written incongruously opposite the limericks, and given a whole page to itself. He called it the "Cosmic Integral":

$$\int_{-\infty}^{+\infty} \text{Man} = [\text{o}] - [\text{o}]$$

which means that the summation of man from minus infinity to plus infinity is nothing—or, in general terms, that mankind, over the whole course of time, adds up to a blank.

At the same time, Crowhurst was recalling his Indian childhood, and drawing gloomy inferences about the nature of man and God. He wrote his thoughts down in a section headed "Memories", on the page immediately following the limericks. It is a tortured, midnight-oil passage, full of deletions and insertions. It is completely rational, yet its content gives the first clear foretaste of the mental unbalance which was to develop increasingly towards madness.

Two childhood parables this section contains show him to have been deeply disturbed about his deceptions. And he was already obsessed with the idea of his mind and the system of the universe as rival computers. He began the section with a recollection of his first, childish ideas of religion:

When I was five years old I knew all about God. He had made everything. My parents had told me, and they knew everything. He was an old, old man with a long grey beard who loved me but would punish me if I was naughty, just like Daddy would. (That computed readily enough!) I knew all about his son Christ too, and by the time I was seven wept when I thought about his good life and the manner of his death. (That did not really compute, but no doubt God knew best.)

One night while looking at the stars and wondering about God I thought I detected a pattern in the stars resembling the head of Christ with a crown of thorns. I turned to my companion and tried to point it out, but she could not see it. Nor could I. I had been brought up on miracles, and decided that this was a miracle computed in a sort of way.

One day soon afterwards I noticed a fruitcake in the pantry and ran to my mother to thank her for obtaining my favourite food. "I bought no fruitcake," said my mother. "Yes you have!" "No I haven't." I was worried. What could the explanation be? You see, it never occurred to me that my mother could be lying. "But I have just seen it in the pantry." "Oh," said my mother, "I bought it as a surprise." My mother had lied to me! I reeled under the mental blow, but only for a moment, for was not the lie justified by the fact that it was intended to give me pleasure? It computed in a messy sorty of way.

So Crowhurst had decided that lying was all right, *providing* it gave people pleasure. Would his putative round-the-world voyage give people pleasure? Perhaps it would—but then Crowhurst remembered another childhood scene that reminded him of the wrath of God on people who are dishonest:

Soon after that a man got run over by a train. Like most small boys I enjoyed railways and soon spotted the crowd round his body. He had got caught up in the wheels and the train had run over his chest. His left arm, flattened, lay along the rail. His head, right arm, and part of his chest lay on one side of the rail, the rest of his body lay on the other. His face was bearded and his features bold and vigorous.

I began to compute. He was well dressed, a Mohamedan I would say, a dashing interesting sort of fellow. He was probably trying to avoid paying fares by stepping off the train before it reached the station. Now I knew this was "wrong". But God had really gone a bit far in his punishment. And another thing. I could *see* that the man had once had what I understood to be a soul. But because the "soul" was deep in his heart and would sort of slowly drift upwards when he died, the fact that the mechanics of this satisfactory arrangement had been spoilt by the railway train made me fear for his soul, which would have to move quick in getting out. My computer had become quite clogged with problems that just wouldn't compute! I was face to face with problems that have vexed humanity for millennia.

If God would not compute, then there must be something wrong. He must be a hostile—or at least an indifferent—being. In that case a different concept of God must be devised. The young Crowhurst continued to toil away at the problem as "more information was fed into his computer" from the outside world:

By the time I was 20 I formed the conclusion that there seemed no justifiable reason to expect any assistance from God—if he existed at all. For no reason at all except the "feeling" I had when I looked at the stars many years ago, I just could not deny the possibility that God existed, but sadly admitted to myself that he couldn't really be all that interested to "allow" Belsen, and the flaming success of the Nazi regime.

I decided Man was evading his responsibility by constantly looking to God for assistance, and became very hostile towards my mother's dependence on God. At first I argued gently with her, upbraiding her for dependence, but the more I argued the more convinced I became that I was right and she was wrong. As the arguments grew hotter and hotter, my attacks became more sarcastic and cruel. Once, after a vicious attack on my mother's constant preoccupation with Jehovah's Witnesses, my mother simply gave up the argument, looking at me with great love and simply said: "If you say so". I was stunned, for I knew that, in some way she was right and I was wrong, and she had "won" by surrender!

My computer threw out everything I had put into it so far. I was back at the beginning! I took stock of the certainties. I had been born alive and was due to die. That computed. Whatever lay outside the time interval defined by these events was immaterial to the physical world. If I sought to change events in the physical world I had better get cracking! By which way? How does man define progress? I asked myself. The nearest thing to a satisfactory solution was "success" at making money. I thought about being rich. Nothing much wrong with that, I thought, and set about it.

Writing, now, on the margins and odd corners of his logbook page, Crowhurst went on to explain that he now had an understanding of the "interplay between the economic systems, the political systems and the unmoving, though powerful religious systems". After elaborating further on this theme, in increasingly unintelligible writing, he ran out of space and the essay stopped in mid-sentence.

Crowhurst had also been writing down some notes and doing a few exercises from his two engineering textbooks. He does not seem to have approached this with much enthusiasm, and got through only a chapter or two. There was, in any case, plenty of practical engineering to worry him without bothering about learning new theory. Most of the mathematics he did on the voyage was concerned directly with modifying his radio equipment, and with attempts to devise a new self-steering gear.

The Einstein *Relativity*, however, was much more to his taste. It is not a particularly mystical work, though Crowhurst, reading and re-reading it, made it so. It was written by Einstein himself to explain his theory, so far as was possible, to people "of a standard of education corresponding to that of a university matriculation examination", and presumed no great mathematical expertise. Einstein may, it is true, have slightly over-estimated the intelligence required for matriculation, and did admit that it required "a fair amount of patience and force of will on the part of the reader". From Crowhurst he certainly got it.

Crowhurst annotated the book in the margins, and wrote a critique in Logbook Two, aimed (apparently) at showing that the General Theory was not general. The book was, it should be remembered, one of his very few sources of intellectual stimulus on board *Teignmouth Electron*. He made it his gospel in the same kind of way that family Bibles were read before the coming of public libraries and cheap paperbacks. And just as an old-time fundamentalist might seize on particular biblical passages out of context, and derive meanings that were never intended, Crowhurst would read deep cosmic significance into snatches of Einstein's text.

He was especially fascinated by one paragraph, in which Einstein said:

> That light requires the same time to traverse the path A to M as for the path B to M is in reality neither a supposition nor a hypothesis about the physical nature of light, but a *stipulation* which I can make of my own free will in order to arrive at a definition of simultaneity.

Einstein was, in fact, saying nothing more than that he would choose, for the time being, to define the word "simultaneous" in a particular way, so that everyone would know in precisely what sense he was using the word. But Crowhurst saw in Einstein's phrase an almost god-like assertion. Here, he thought, was a superior being who could order the nature of the heavens *of his own freewill*! He turned down the corner of the page, and repeatedly referred back to it. In his essays, Crowhurst began to refer to Einstein as "the Master". He saw the equation $E = mc^2$ as a cosmic revelation, equivalent to the Christian equation "God is love".

In a later essay, Crowhurst described his conversion. He said that when he first read Einstein's definition of simultaneity, he thought it was trickery:

> I said aloud with some irritation: "You can't do THAT!" I thought, "the swindler." Then I looked at a photograph of the author in later years. The essence of the man rebuked me. I re-read the passage and re-read it, trying to get to the mind of the man who wrote it. The mathematician in me could distinguish nothing new to mitigate the offending principles. But the poet in me could eventually read between the lines, and he read: "Nevertheless I have just *done* it, let us examine the consequences."

It was a peculiarly religious approach to Einstein. Crowhurst may have rejected the biblical fundamentalism of his Jehovah's Witness mother, but he still needed another gospel to put in its place. His elaborations around the Einstein book were to play an important part in his later delusions.

Sixteen

Win or Lose?

We left the great race with Knox-Johnston on his last stretch up the Atlantic, now the certain winner of the Golden Globe for the first man home, and with the two trimarans battling it out for the fastest voyage and the £5,000 prize. Tetley's supporters had been shattered by Crowhurst's miraculous reappearance, when their man had seemed the clear favourite for the prize. Although his boat was showing bad signs of wear, Tetley was being urged to gamble all on full-speed sailing.

At the *Sunday Times* hasty new calculations were being made. The newspaper's predictions of Crowhurst's arrival date had reflected the curious pattern of his voyage. In the early stages he had not been expected home until November 1969, or even later. After the "record run", the date had been pulled forward to September 30th, and then revised twice to September 8th (after the "Tristan da Cunha" report) and August 19th (after he had been reported to be in the Indian Ocean). Now the slide-rules showed Crowhurst due back in Teignmouth on "July 8th at the latest".

Crowhurst's total time to the Horn, so everyone thought, had been two weeks faster than Tetley's. And although Tetley had

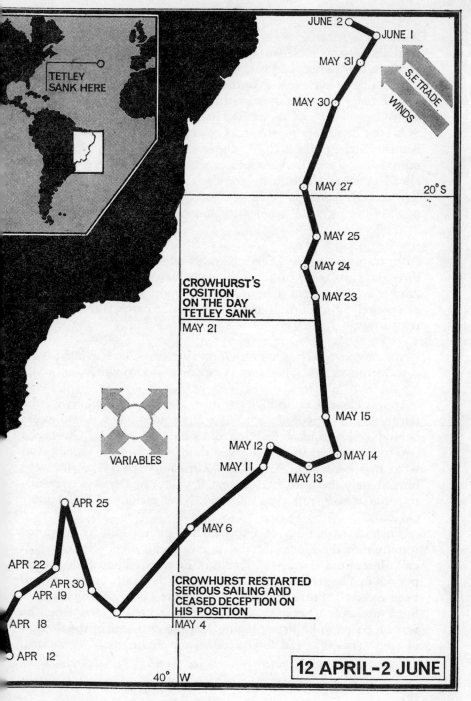

TETLEY
SANK HERE

JUNE 2
JUNE 1

MAY 31

S.E.TRADE.
WINDS

MAY 30

MAY 27

20° S

MAY 25

MAY 24

CROWHURST'S
POSITION
ON THE DAY
TETLEY SANK

MAY 23

MAY 21

MAY 15

MAY 12
MAY 11

MAY 14

MAY 13

VARIABLES

APR 25

MAY 6

APR 22

APR 30

APR 19

CROWHURST RESTARTED
SERIOUS SAILING AND
CEASED DECEPTION ON
HIS POSITION

APR 18

MAY 4

APR 12

40° W

12 APRIL–2 JUNE

O

since been making good progress up the Atlantic, the new, revitalised Crowhurst was expected to do just as well. Nobody, except a tiny handful of cynics, now thought he could fail to win, and Rodney Hallworth—the man who had all along had faith in Crowhurst—was overflowing with pride and admiration. "Donald is proving to be one of the great sporting sailors of our time," he said.

All this had been inspired by Crowhurst's one tentative "Digger Ramrez" telegram on April 9th, since which date he had transmitted not a word. As before, events at home were galloping ahead of what Crowhurst intended. Let us therefore return to *Teignmouth Electron* on April 9th and follow through the development of the race as it seemed to Donald Crowhurst.

*   *   *

After transmitting his Digger Ramrez telegram, Crowhurst spent three days anxiously tuning in to his radio waiting for a reply. The answer would reveal if he had been reported from Rio Salado or spotted by a ship. When it eventually came, the reply was reassuring:

YOURE ONLY TWO WEEKS BEHIND TETLEY   PHOTO FINISH WILL
MAKE GREAT NEWS STOP   ROBIN DUE ONE TO TWO WEEKS=RODNEY

It was clear that he had got away with it. But otherwise the telegram was not very informative. Did it mean he was two weeks behind Tetley in his actual date of reaching the Horn? Or was he two weeks behind in the "elapsed time" terms of the race?* And what had become of Moitessier? Crowhurst could not find out immediately, because for the next few days he decided to return to radio silence, not even acknowledging receipt of Hallworth's cable.

Then on April 18th—the day he had planned for his supposed rounding of the Horn—he did briefly break silence to answer a call direct from Portishead Radio in England. The call had been put out in a hopeful attempt to discover if the Hallworth cable had been received. Portishead might have found it strange that Crowhurst was able to communicate directly with England when he was supposed to be struggling against the elements in the shadow of South America, but the inconsistency again passed unnoticed.

* Either way, as it happens, the cable information on Tetley was wrongly calculated, but Crowhurst was not to know this at the time.

Crowhurst, it seems, had risked replying to it mainly to discover more precise details about the race. In morse cross-talk with the Portishead operator, he learned about Moitessier's retirement and found Tetley's exact position. With this knowledge, Crowhurst could now start to make exact plans.

All this time, Crowhurst had been sailing steadily northwards up the Atlantic, and was now about level with Buenos Aires. His problem was how to phase the progress of his fake route so that it would catch up with his actual position. This "rendezvous" between the real and the imaginary Crowhurst would have to be made before he returned to the busy shipping lanes.

There followed a strangely hesitant period in Crowhurst's voyage. He knew that with the next published telegram home he would be irrevocably committed to carrying through the fraud; and his last faint hope of disentangling himself would be gone. The thought seems to have produced yet another crisis of indecision. This time, however, we have no direct evidence of the options he was considering; we can only try to interpret his actions.

The position of Crowhurst's chosen rendezvous with himself is apparent from the course he sailed. It was a point about a thousand miles north-east of the Falklands and 700 miles due east of Buenos Aires. It was a cautious choice, because he could almost certainly have projected his false route another thousand miles up the Atlantic without serious risk of detection. As it was, he was left with several more days of unproductive waiting—zig-zagging aimlessly in the lonely ocean east of Buenos Aires—until his false route caught up with him.

However, staying in this area had one supreme advantage. It left him for two weeks within easy radio-telephone range of Buenos Aires. Crowhurst had apparently formed an overwhelming desire to get a phone-call home to Clare; he wanted to talk to her directly, and not through the restricting jargon of telegrams. In the days following April 21st he several times contacted Buenos Aires Radio in morse, asking them to fix up a direct telephone link to the Crowhurst home in Bridgwater, and he drafted cables to Clare telling her when to stand by. The attempts failed because although Buenos Aires could pick up good radio-telephone signals from *Teignmouth Electron*, they were never able simultaneously to fix a land-line connection via New York to England.

Why had a phone-call become so important? Obviously Crowhurst, after his long silence, yearned for human contact, even if just a few words on a crackly telephone. But his actions implied more than that. The phone-call seemed to have become paramount; for nine days while he was trying to set it up, he was even sailing southwards to stay within range of Buenos Aires. Also—as we shall see—the desire to speak to Clare was to become an increasing obsession in the final stages of the voyage. It seems possible that, as in previous moments of crisis, he was hoping that Clare might sense his plight, and that she might give him the courage—or the excuse—to extract himself from it.

Crowhurst had also, meanwhile, been preparing the crucial Press telegram to Hallworth which would need to state unequivocally that he had rounded the Horn and was hot on Tetley's trail up the Atlantic. The wording, through a series of rewrites, was shaped into yet another masterpiece of disingenuousness. It was full of inconsequential detail and half-truths, of which the only immediately checkable facts were careful distillations of the weather forecasts that Crowhurst had been patiently copying down in his Radio Log. For good measure, it added a characteristic echo of Chichester, who had also passed the Horn in reasonable weather but had been hit by a gale soon afterwards:

201 DAYS* AFTER DEPARTING LIZARD FIRST SIGHT LAND FALKLANDS   HOVE-TO ALMOST HOUR WATCHING SUNDOWN CAPE CARYSFORT   HAZY AUTUMN EVENING WOODSMOKE ON WIND   THEN PELL MELL FOR SAFETY SOUTH ATLANTIC STOP REASONABLE WEATHER TO HORN BUT SOUTHEASTER NEXT DAY GALE AND SLEET TUESDAY   CONFIRMS TIMING TRIFLE TIGHT

After drafting the cable, Crowhurst sat on it for more than a week while he continued attempts to arrange his telephone call to Clare. Then finally, on April 30th, he broke his three-week radio silence to the people at home and declared himself back in the race. On that date he sent first the Falkland Islands telegram (Hallworth thought it enchanting. *Woodsmoke on the Wind* must be the title of Donald's book, he declared.) Then he sent a telegram to the BBC news desk in London. Under cover of offering congratulations to Knox-Johnston on his successful return, Crowhurst's main purpose was to imply that although the Golden

* Crowhurst had meant to say 171 days. The calculation is in the margin of the Radio Log, and he had accidentally added in an extra month.

Globe had now been won, he was still very much in the running for the "elapsed-time" race:

NEWSDESK BBC = TICKLED AS TAR WITH TWO FIDS* SUCCESS KNOX JOHNSTON   BUT KINDLY NOTE NOT RACEWINNER YET SUGGEST ACCURACY DEMANDS DISTINCTION BETWEEN GOLDEN GLOBE AND RACE = OUTRAGED SOUTH ATLANTIC OTHERWISE CROWHURST

With these two messages, Crowhurst was firmly back in the race. He was already at his chosen position for reuniting his fake route and actual route, and he had temporarily abandoned his attempts to telephone Clare. Yet there was nother strange hiatus: for a further four days he stayed almost stationary, indeed continued to ghost slowly southwards. It was as if he was deliberately trying to throw away his dishonestly-won advantage over Tetley. Was it guilt that impelled him to do so? Or was he taking very literally Hallworth's opinion that "photo finish will make great news"? Perhaps he had simply got his navigation or his arithmetic wrong? Or could it be that consciously or subconsciously he *wanted* to lose to Tetley?

This last theory is a tempting one to explain Crowhurst's erratic progress up the Atlantic. To lose would have meant forfeiting the £5,000 prize—but there would be the all-important corollary that *nobody would have needed to look at his logbooks*. At the same time, a close finish would have made Crowhurst exciting headline news and he would have become a hero nonetheless— with all the benefits to his business and status that being a hero implies. We know that Crowhurst had a penchant for keeping his options open, and if he was uneasy about writing a fraudulent logbook he is likely to have considered it as a way of getting off the hook. His erratic behaviour suggests that his mind was never fully made up. He continued to go through the motions of the race, sometimes with great determination, sometimes in a half-hearted way, as if hovering between one choice and another. Another of Crowhurst's characteristics, it will be remembered, was to recognise options, but then not to resolve them.

*　　　*　　　*

* This phrase is a jaunty nautical obscenity (a "tar" is a sailor; a "fid" is a pointed wooden pin). As Crowhurst grew more and more fraudulent, his cables grew more and more sprightly.

It was not until May 4th that Crowhurst eventually decided that the time had come to begin heading seriously northwards. From now on he was genuinely sailing against Tetley, and whether he was aiming just to win or just to lose he would have to get down to it in determined fashion. As if to celebrate his return to integrity, Crowhurst's first day's progress was dramatic.

In course of preparing this book, every navigational calculation that Crowhurst made has been reworked, and, so far as we can tell, his genuine mileage between his sun-sights of May 4th and May 5th was very near to the "record" of 243 miles that he had fraudulently claimed earlier in the voyage. According to the weather reports from Buenos Aires he had excellent conditions with a good steady following wind, but even so, it was a prodigious burst of speed. It showed that when things were going their way, there was nothing so very much wrong with either *Teignmouth Electron* or her helmsman. It seems ironic that the feat should have passed without comment in Crowhurst's logbooks.*
But anyway, what mattered now was not a record day's run but whether he could sustain the tempo for the final two months.

Crowhurst did not, in fact, sustain it for very long. Within a week he had run into head winds, and the old trouble of his trimaran reasserted itself. Unable to make further progress northward, he spent three days heading eastwards, hoping to work himself into a more favourable position for picking up the South-East Trades.

It was at this time that Crowhurst found himself in dispute with the fans at home. Hallworth had got so excited after Crowhurst's reappearance that he was confident his man would not only put up a faster time than Tetley, but might also overtake him physically as they approached England. In the simple blacks and whites of popular news stories, he knew than an "elapsed time" victory was all very well, but was expecting rather a lot of the public's understanding. Nothing could really beat the straightforward image of the winner charging past the field on the last lap home. He therefore started to urge his man on to even greater efforts, and such was his faith that he presumed that the only thing that could be holding him back was the damage sustained under

---

* Another inexplicable irony of Crowhurst's voyage is the coincidental recurrence of the figure 243. Early in the voyage he calculated his methylated spirit would last 243 days; his actual voyage lasted 243 days. His false record run was 243 miles, and so—approximately—was this actual record run.

that crushing five-ton wave that had engulfed *Teignmouth Electron* in the Indian Ocean, and loosened the "struts". He cabled Crowhurst accordingly:

> . . . ELLIOT DISCOVERED STRUTS SHOULD LOOSEN SO BOAT IS SAFE   PLEASE PUSH HARDEST TO OVERHAUL TETLEY NOW NEARING EQUATOR

Crowhurst replied loftily, correcting Hallworth on his use of nautical terms, offering a rude comment to John Elliot, and indulging in some questionable self-justification about the design of the boat:

> AM AWARE MISCONCEPTIONS REGARDING SAFETY CROSSARM AT-TACHMENT CRACKS IF STRUTS MEAN CROSSARMS   BUT OWING MY SPECIFICATION AND CAREFUL CONSTRUCTION NO PROBLEMS THERE DAMAGE WHERE DESIGN STANDARD   CURRENTLY SIX BROKEN FRAMES TWO FOOT SPLIT STARBOARD FLOAT TOPSIDES   NOT DAWDLING   DIGITS ELLIOTS AND OTHER ARMCHAIR VIEWS SAFETY 31 SOUTH 34 WEST   FOUR DAYS LOST UNUSUAL NORTHEASTERLY GALE   SHOULD BE FASTEST   OVERTAKE TETLEY ONLY BY LUCK . . .

It took two telegrams to smooth things down. Hallworth replied ruefully, "Only trying to help . . .", and Crowhurst finally conceded magnanimously, "Motives well understood, never annoyed." But the real reason for Crowhurst's apparent anger seems to have been to conceal a neat bit of back-tracking. He realised that four months earlier he had given an excessive impression of the structural damage to his boat, which soon would be home for all to see. The "deck joints parting", in his cable of January 14th were now sharply reduced to a "two foot split".

Crowhurst was continually fretting about the little inconsistencies of his fake voyage and was trying, whenever possible, to explain them away. Another instance was his strange success in transmitting directly to England while supposedly rounding the Horn. Three weeks afterwards, Crowhurst sent a cable to Portishead explaining that "our direct contact was a fluke" and that he could normally only be reached through Capetown. Then there was the problem of the weather at the Falkland Islands. The met. report for the period when he was supposed to have been there was of strong winds and sleet. It did not tie up with the gentle sunset he had filmed on his actual visit. So he slipped in a little anecdote into one of his BBC tape recordings recalling how he "shot a magnificent sunset with the lens covered up". It would provide an explanation if the film turned out accidentally spoilt. In another of his tape recordings (made on May 16th) he produced a long, diffuse account of his attempts to send telegrams in the Southern Ocean:

> The traffic is routed from Portishead to various stations throughout the world giving worldwide communications through stations at Capetown, Sydney and Wellington, and of course there are other stations in Canada, Vancouver etc. . . . but the ones I mentioned first are the ones that were of course of most interest to me . . .
>
> I would very much have liked to have worked* my way round the world. I did in fact work both Sydney and — well I — perhaps wrong to say I worked them but I was heard in Sydney and Wellington, so I don't feel too badly about it. But I would have liked to have passed traffic from Sydney and Wellington. Unfortunately I couldn't, my signals were very weak and my battery was getting extremely low and, as I said, I didn't want the bother of unsealing the hatch. Well it wasn't purely a question of bother because it could be dangerous in the conditions prevailing at the time actually. It was fairly rough and there was a fair amount of water getting into the cockpit and I did feel that to risk the several hours of the unsealed hatch — and then on top of that of course there's the question of whether the generator would, in fact, work. When I got a calm spell about 1500 miles off the Horn, I did in fact open up the hatch; the weather was settled and the barometer fairly high. I opened the hatch, but of course I couldn't start the engine, which is hardly surprising because it had a very long spell standing unstarted, un-run, in a terrible environment and had had a certain amount of leakage on it through one of the ventilators which I can't shut but which I try and keep covered with an old canvas bag I've got. It's a bag, incidentally, that I'm extremely fond of. I acquired it with my little boat *Pot of Gold* . . .

These dishonest sections of Crowhurst's tape recordings show

* A radio ham's term for transmitting messages.

him to have been a clever liar, but not a very comfortable one. Even in transcript, they contrast sharply with the honest sections — disjointed, uneasy, too eager to disarm, and full of "in facts", "of courses" and "actuallys". As Crowhurst made these detailed preparations for his fraudulent story, he must have worried a great deal about his ability to carry his deception through. If this was the best he could do while concentrating alone on a tape recorder, how would he make out at the press conferences and in informal conversation after his return? Perhaps the thought crossed his mind that for the rest of his life he would need to discuss his exploits in this guarded, uncomfortable way. It was probably at this stage of the voyage that he began to have really serious doubts about his ability to pull it off.

There were, too, in the increasing number of cables pouring out to *Teignmouth Electron*, the first mind-concentrating indications of the welcome that lay ahead in England. There was not only the private admiration of his wife ("very proud") and Pat Beard ("you're wonderful"), but also the great public heroics that Teignmouth, the BBC and the *Sunday Times* were now preparing to stage-manage. Hallworth cabled:

TEIGNMOUTH AGOG AT YOUR WONDERS   WHOLE TOWN PLANNING
HUGE WELCOME — RODNEY

Crowhurst was now left with just the one last way out: losing to Tetley. It would not solve all his faking problems, but at least it would simplify them. As if to indicate that this was in his mind, his progress began abruptly to slow down: after the middle of May it had dropped below an average of seventy miles a day. The *Sunday Times* had already added a week to his expected time of arrival, because of his puzzling speeds.

Crowhurst's half-hearted approach could also be deduced from the tape recordings he made after the middle of May. He had a favourite word — "sailorising" — for the serious nautical business of keeping the sails properly trimmed, steering the optimum course, and keeping the boat shipshape. He always spoke of it as if it were some incidental chore, not a total involvement like mending radios or transmitting messages. He had evidently recovered a brief taste for "sailorising" in the early part of May, but from the middle of the month his recordings show him deeply occupied again in his peripheral pursuits.

On May 16th, Crowhurst cabled his fans back home, apparently preparing them for the possibility that he might not win:

DEVONNEWS EXETER . . . 27 SOUTH 30 WEST   GOING WELL FOR
THESE PARTS   NO CHANCE OVERTAKE TETLEY   NOW PROBABLY
VERY CLOSE RESULT

Just four and a half days later came the supreme irony of this already eventful race.

*   *   *

Lieutenant-Commander Nigel Tetley, RN, aged forty-five, had been totally dedicated to "sailorising" even before going as a boy to Dartmouth. He had been having a rough time on the voyage; he looked physically older than at the start and his problems with his "Victress" trimaran had been even greater than Crowhurst's. However, in stoic naval spirit he had stiffened his upper lip and pressed on, and he already had a number of achievements to his credit: he had made the first-ever passage of the Horn in a multi-hull, and, after his inward route crossed his outward route north of the Equator, he had (by one definition) achieved the first multihull circumnavigation. The sudden re-emergence of the mercurial Crowhurst off the Horn had surprised him, but had simply encouraged him to grit his teeth and press on even harder.

Like Crowhurst, Tetley had been having problems from leaking floats, but his were far more serious. He had even drilled holes in the forward float compartments to let the water *out*. Pushing on too hard through gales off north Brazil, in order to steal a few hours from Crowhurst, his boat had started to disintegrate. The deck had sprung in several places, and whole series of hull and float frames were broken. Crowhurst had been worried by small cracks in the fibreglass skin of his boat; on Tetley's "Victress" the entire skin of the port float had peeled away. He still sailed on, and would probably have reached home if he had not been so determined to beat his fraudulent rival. But then, only 1,200 miles from the end of his 30,000 mile voyage, he again pressed too hard through a storm near the Azores. Shortly after midnight on May 21st, the port float bow broke completely away, smashed into the centre hull of his trimaran, and the whole boat started to fill with water. In his rubber life-raft, awaiting rescue, Tetley watched his "Victress' sink slowly into the North Atlantic.

Seventeen

The Inescapable Triumph

Crowhurst was now caught in the tightest knot of the whole tangled web woven by his deceit. The irony of his predicament was so neat, and so crushing, that one suspects the gods of a taste for cheap melodrama. Crowhurst must have appreciated its logical progression: had he not claimed his fake circumnavigation, Tetley would not have overtaxed his boat, and would have arrived home safe and sound to win the £5,000 prize. Had Tetley not sunk, Crowhurst could have sailed home equally safe and sound to accept the plaudits due to a valiant but unscrutinised hero. Now, for the rest of his voyage, the full glare of public attention would be focused undividedly on him—and afterwards on his logbooks. And whether he wanted to or not, he could not avoid winning. To put up an even slower time than Knox-Johnston would have meant losing two more months, which would have passed the bounds of credibility. So Crowhurst's lies had sunk not only Tetley's "Victress', but his own last option for escape.

Or, at least, his last rational option. Exactly a month after he heard the news of Tetley's catastrophe, Crowhurst found another way out, of a totally different kind. He gave up "sailorising" altogether, and retreated into a private world in which all that mattered was to expound a philosophical revelation that had been slowly forming in his mind.

The story of the intervening month can be told largely in Crowhurst's own words—from the tape recordings and radio messages that increasingly occupied his time. The most remarkable thing about them is their apparent normality. Not until the very last tape he recorded—on the day before he started to write down his great revelation—did the faintest hint of Crowhurst's deep, brooding thoughts show through his public surface. The final crisis, when it came, displayed itself with terrible suddenness.

*　　*　　*

Crowhurst had heard the news about Tetley's misfortune on May 23rd in a cable from Clare. She told him that the rescue operation had been successful and prompted him to send his condolences. This Crowhurst duly did, in the slightly chirpy tone that was expected of him:

EVELYN TETLEY — SYMPATHISE DAVY JONES DIRTY TRICK   REJOICE MASTER SALVAGED — CROWHURST

His true feelings, however, could perhaps better be inferred from the unusually pessimistic Press cable which he sent at the same time to Rodney Hallworth:

AVERAGE 23 MILES LAST SIX DAYS   METHS PETROL LOW   FLOUR RICE MILDEWED   WATER FOUL   CHEESE INTERESTING

During the following two weeks Crowhurst was sailing past the north-eastern coast of Brazil back into the tropics. As the heat increased, he spent much of the day completely naked except for his wrist-watch. Though thin, he looked sun-tanned and fit, if slightly bedraggled. So far as he could, he was leaving the boat to sail herself and for long stretches did not even bother to set the mainsail.

But it was not all holiday crusing. All the old problems of his ill-prepared boat kept recurring. Even with the canvas reduced to give speeds of only three or four knots, which kept the decks fairly dry, he still regularly had to bale out the floats by hand. The self-steering gear was by now quite defunct. In a tape recording,

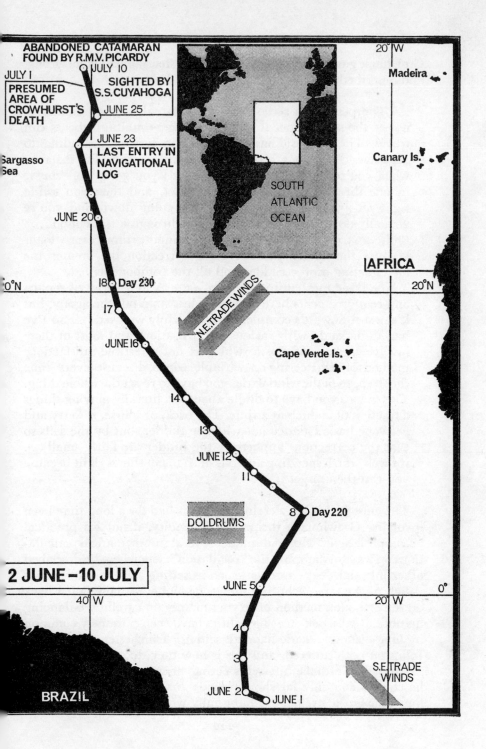

ABANDONED CATAMARAN
FOUND BY R.M.V. PICARDY
JULY 10
JULY 1
PRESUMED
AREA OF
CROWHURST'S
DEATH

SIGHTED BY
S.S. CUYAHOGA
JUNE 25

JUNE 23
LAST ENTRY IN
NAVIGATIONAL
LOG

Sargasso
Sea

JUNE 20

20°N

18 Day 230

17

JUNE 16

14

13

JUNE 12

11

8 Day 220

DOLDRUMS

JUNE 5

4

3

JUNE 2 JUNE 1

BRAZIL

2 JUNE – 10 JULY

40°W

20°W

0°

20°W

Madeira

Canary Is.

AFRICA

N.E. TRADE WINDS

Cape Verde Is.

SOUTH
ATLANTIC
OCEAN

S.E. TRADE
WINDS

Crowhurst gave his views on why the self-steering had gone wrong, and described how he was coping:

... The pendulum servo system is not really strong enough — not at the sort of speeds that one of these multihull boats can travel. There's basic instability in the system ... leading to excessive corrections and oscillations. It means for instance when you're running [before the wind] you go 45° off course in one direction and then you correct, and then you swing right off 45° in the other direction — going downwind you're virtually doing a tremendous zig-zag through a total of 90° ... Quite apart from anything else [this] imposes unnecessary loads because the longer you leave the correction the greater the forces acting on the rudder and all the components ...

The basic mechanism just broke up. A long series of repairs and reinforcements here and there just spun out the agony, but it's past it now, it's completely, completely wrecked ... So I've had to make do with various improvisations and most of these involve the use of elastic which is not a terrible satisfactiory method of self-steering in variable winds, because every time the strength of the wind varies you have to re-set the whole thing. This means you have to fiddle about ... literally moving things a fraction of an inch at a time. The trick, of course, is to try and get your basic balance not with the rudder, but by the sails so that the corrections applied by the rudder are fairly small ... it's well worth spending an hour or so to get things right because you can then forget it.

The cure for his self-steering problems had for a long time been involving Crowhurst's theoretical ingenuity, if not his practical accomplishment. He had made several mathematical calculations on ways of damping the "oscillation". Elsewhere he described other ingenious experiments — such as setting sails on the shrouds — but, as the tape recording shows, he had eventually fallen back on the orthodox method of relying mainly on carefully balancing his normal sails. Self-steering failures have been extremely common in long-distance single-handed sailing; Chichester and Knox-Johnston both suffered, and this is how they, too, coped.

Crowhurst's makeshift self-steering arrangements meant that he could sleep only for short periods — usually for no more than four hours at a stretch. He habitually worked through the night, not sleeping until dawn, because his navigation lights were not working and he was afraid of being run down by a steamer. One of the lights had been hanging loose from the mast for several months, but the main reason why Crowhurst did not use them was to conserve electricity. This nocturnal existence with long hours in his cramped, ill-lit cabin, added to his increasing isolation and introspection.

He was also, as he had mentioned in his last Press cable, getting worried about the shortage of supplies. He was down to his last pint and a half of methylated spirit, and could light his cooking stove only sparingly. He would try to use the absolute minimum amount to get it going, but then if he just underestimated it, he would have to wait many minutes for the burner to cool down before starting again. "It is the sort of thing," said Crowhurst into his tape recorder, "that tends to happen when materials are more important than time. If it took me an hour to light the burner, I'd still have to do it without using any more meths than I could possibly help." All this made even brewing a cup of tea into a tense intellectual exercise. And with the tea there was another problem as well:

The tea's gone off. Something's happened to it . . . I think it's gone mouldy or something, but it makes me ill if I drink tea. I've got quantities of it—probably about fourteen lbs—but I can't cope with it somehow.

Crowhurst, nevertheless, continued to drink tea, as several of his subsequent tape recordings reveal. In a later recording Crowhurst gave a more detailed description:

I mentioned earlier that I'd gone off tea . . . Well I did an experiment. I had a feeling that there might have been some contamination, some fungus growth in the tea pot. I didn't like the look of it. So I tried putting a couple of teaspoons directly into the cup and pouring hot water onto it, and this seems to be all right . . . I suppose that the secret is the psychological effect of getting near England again—the prospect of being an Englishman who doesn't like tea was more that I could bear. So I had to steel my constitution to the effort of getting used to it again!

Other food supplies were also going mouldy, but Crowhurst still had sufficient unaffected food for a reasonably balanced — if monotonous—diet, and he remained punctilious about taking his large brown vitamin pills. One of his staples was a soggy mixture which he called bisque bread:

I quite enjoy it, but I'm getting a bit fed up with it now. I've been eating it for about two months, but still it's good stuff and I'll tell you how to make it. Powdered egg with oatmeal and flour added in until it's a nice stiff paste and just about pourable. This goes into a frying pan with [tinned] butter in it and with a lot of salt. The salt is to prevent the pancakes from sticking and also for seasoning of course. This is cooked both sides and served up with lots of honey over it . . . I don't think any dietician could find much wrong with it . . . sugar, starch, protein — all good stuff.

His supplies of alcohol were down to a last bottle of rum and eighteen bottles of barley wine. He was having to ration himself— permitting himself a drink only if he had completed an unpleasant task, which provided at least some incentive for his reluctant "sailorising". This particular liquid shortage, however, worried him much less than his fast-dwindling supply of petrol. On May 29th he sent a cable asking John Elliot if it was all right to run his Onan generator with paraffin mixed into the petrol to make it stretch further. This was yet another inconsistency in his supposed voyage, which passed unnoticed: if he had spent so much time with the generator unused and sealed up, where had all the petrol gone?

On the same day as the cable about the petrol, Crowhurst sent home news of a new problem which, for him, made every other difficulty seem trivial. A fault had developed in his Marconi Kestrel transmitter. The convertor, which produced its high tension power supply, had partially failed. He managed to get a telegram to the Marconi factory asking for advice. He was told, in reply, that he would have to nurse the equipment and make only limited use of it for telegrams, and minimal use for telephone calls. Even then its operation would be marginal.

This was shattering news for Crowhurst. He could continue to receive incoming telegrams on his Racal receiver, but his hopes of talking directly with Clare on the telephone were now seriously

prejudiced, and there was no longer the consolation of being able
to send regular telegrams. A few days later, the transmitter failed
completely. It left him even more cut off, even more lonely, even
more out of control of events as he approached the conclusion of
the voyage. At this crucial moment, his only link with the world
and with outside reality had been brutally cut off.

*   *   *

Everything now became subsidiary to the one objective of getting
himself back on the air. Crowhurst's last two weeks of normality
were spent sitting at his tiny table for sixteen hours a day, naked in
the tropical heat, as he obsessively soldered together electronic
components in an attempt to make his transmitter serviceable
again.

His one other major activity was talking for many hours into
his tape recorder, as if compulsively trying to maintain his personal
identity and some sense of human contact. The recordings continued to sound quite composed, though clearly it was only the
role-playing "public-voice" Crowhurst that was talking into the
microphone. Because of them, this final phase is the best-docu-
mented bit of the entire voyage, if only at a superficial level. They
show Crowhurst as a courageous man, putting on a brave show
despite all difficulties, and full of intelligence and lively observation. What was going on in his mind, beneath the surface, can
only be imagined.

As before, in times of loneliness and stress, he found some brief
solace in the companionship of sea creatures. On July 9th he took
a few moments off from his electronics to try and record the high-
pitched squeaks of porpoises that were playing round the boat.
Crowhurst was puzzled at the difficulty of doing so—at why the
human ear seemed to have a capacity for "tuning in" to selected
sounds above the noise of the sea and rigging, while the microphone could not pick them up. He described a mischievous game
he would play with the porpoises, apparently trying to gain their
notice and respect:

> ... They're having a great time all around the boat—they
> think they've got it sewn up, you see. The thing to do is to go
> up onto the bows and just as they're committed to the notion of
> a leap and can't change their mind you switch a powerful beam
> of light onto them. Now this might be a bit of a dirty trick

because I'm sure it gives them a tremendous feeling of panic for a while . . . They twist in the air, they go down into the water again and shoot off at the most amazing speed, zig-zagging this way and that, trying to escape the beam of light which of course you direct to follow them . . . They've gone perhaps 150 yards in two or three seconds — the speed they travel is really amazing . . . And then, gradually, they come back again to see what this strange creature's behaviour pattern is going to be like this time — so they're quite courageous really, although they're frightened. They're prepared to come back and have another look.

Crowhurst was by now across the Equator, through the Doldrums, and just meeting the North-East Trades. It meant he could put *Teignmouth Electron* on a steady reach to the north-west, and leave her under jib and mizzen to make slow, unattended progress towards the weeds and flotsam of the Sargasso Sea, while he stayed below repairing the transmitter. The slow progress did not worry him, nor the fact that he was being blown westwards of his desired route. He became so absorbed with electronics that on some days he lost track of time and forgot to take his noon navigational sights. A few days more or less on the time of his voyage or a few miles on the wrong course were now of no consequence.

The task he set himself with the radio transmitter was daunting. He first dismantled the Marconi Kestrel but could not repair it. So he hit on a more ambitious idea. He also had on board his little Shannon radio-telephone, which was designed for short-range operation on the medium waveband. Crowhurst decided to modify it to transmit morse at long range on the short waveband — in other words almost totally to alter the nature of the transmitter. It involved redesigning and rebuilding whole stages of its circuitry, mixing up transistors with valves, and cannibalising crystals and spare parts from the Kestrel. Also, although he had a mass of components on board, Crowhurst did not have any text-books, design manuals or test equipment for basic development work. Before he could start the actual job, he had to build himself test instruments and start working out theory from first principles. It was a formidable enterprise in any circumstance, let alone in a tiny cabin rolling on the sea, which — as Crowhurst pointed out — produced hazards all of its own:

If there's very much jerking I'm likely to do myself a terrible injury, putting it mildly. I'm likely to electrocute myself and with nobody around to render any first aid or disentangle me from the bits and pieces, this is something I naturally want to avoid. However I've had plenty of practice at this sort of messing about with high voltages. During my youth I was obsessed with high-powered transmitters, and although I dislike getting shocks intensely, I might be building up a degree of tolerance or something. But, as I say, when you're on your own, things are slightly different . . .

After a few days' work the cabin was a total shambles, and remained so until the end of the voyage. Crowhurst himself gave a graphic description in a tape, recorded on June 17th:

Things get a bit chaotic . . . There are five Tupperware boxes with their contents partly in and partly out, the debris from breakfast, several cans which I've just shifted in from one of the float compartments which I cleared of water the other day, 12 tins of steak, 24 tins of milk, 20 lbs. of cheese all lying about on the floor. The bunk is littered with electronic components, to say nothing of the sleeping bag and a few odd clothes. There are the innards of two transmitters strewn all over the working surfaces. There's the transistor convertor from the Marconi Kestrel lying in one heap. And there's the Shannon transmitter disgorging its insides all over the work benches. So what with one thing and another we're in a fair old state of chaos.

It was hot in the cabin, too. *Teignmouth Electron* was now nearly at the Tropic of Cancer, and since it was almost the June solstice the sun at mid-day was vertically overhead. Crowhurst had rigged up a wind sail to funnel air into the cabin which pulled the temperature down from the hundreds into the eighties. This made things tolerable, though he was suffering from an embarrassing little pain . . .

I've just been talking about how comfortable I am completely nude . . . except for one patch which is a bit sore. That is where I — the soldering iron slipped onto the seat as I was sitting down and I branded myself across the rump. If I tend to sweat at all, that irritates. I'm working on this transmitter at my eating desk, and there's another hazard here, which is blobs of molten solder tend to fall on your lap, which is not the best of things! So — after a couple of these occurrences you tend to be very careful about where the blobs of molten solder fall!

And so the strange naked figure of Crowhurst, his bottom branded, sweated on amidst the chaos. It was hardly the heroic picture they envisaged back home, as Teignmouth Council met and the *Sunday Times* conferred, to co-ordinate the triumphal homecoming.

*   *   *

All the time as he worked, Crowhurst had his radio receiver switched on, listening to the Test Match commentaries, and taking down incoming telegrams (to which, of course, he could not reply). On June 18th, while Crowhurst was making another tape recording a telegram arrived from the BBC:

> CONGRATULATIONS ON PROGRESS   HAVE NETWORK TELEVISION PROGRAMME FOR DAY OF RETURN   YOUR FILM URGENTLY WANTED CAN YOU PREPARE FILM AND TAPES INFORMATION   ANY SUGGESTION PLEASE ON GETTING IT BACK AT LEAST FOUR DAYS BEFORE TEIGN-MOUTH ARRIVAL   CAN ARRANGE BOAT OR HELICOPTER HOW CLOSE AZORES BRITTANY OR SCILLIES   REPLY URGENTLY = DONALD KERR

Even if Crowhurst had not previously realised what sort of welcome awaited him, he must have done so now — boats, helicopters, special networked programmes . . . But if he was alarmed, he did not show it on the tape. He simply exclaimed, "How about that!" and resolved to work harder on his transmitter so that he could send a reply. Over the next three days, successive cables from the BBC became even more insistent. Donald Kerr, having not heard from Crowhurst, was now proposing that they should rendezvous near Sao Miguel in the Azores, which was further to the south than Crowhurst wanted to go.

Crowhurst mused aloud on the problem into his tape recorder. And he added in, for later public consumption, a concern for the strict letter of the *Sunday Times* race rules that — considering he had already broken every single one — was almost breathtakingly devious:

Of course, Donald, you must be wondering at this moment whether I've had your telegrams . . . There's no way of me telling you that I don't propose to go to Sao Miguel if I can possibly help it . . . I think it's imperative that any rendezvous should be observed by the *Sunday Times*—they should have an observer there but I can't tell you this. It's more than likely that they would not take up the offer to attend, and take your word for it that you didn't give me any assistance. But I would prefer it if they were there.

He recorded those words at midnight on June 21st—only sixty hours before his philosophical revelation and the end of his serious participation in the race. Almost to the very end, he was still making constructive plans to add credibility to his fraud.

Perhaps also in response to the BBC telegrams, he decided, earlier that day, to shoot some more film of himself. Before doing so, he had to put on some clothes, in deference, as he said, to the susceptibilities of the viewers:

I've dug out a rather gay piece of towelling which I've rigged as a sarong. I remember that Bill Howell is a great advocate of the sarong when sailing in tropical climates. I'm now looking rather gaudy, like a bird of paradise. I don't know how it'll turn out on the film but from where I see it right now it's pretty spectacular. It's not a very wide strip of towelling. My first attempt was to lay it round in a spiral. But first the spiral slipped lower and lower tending to defeat its own object and secondly it was very restricted around the knees. I've now rigged it into the mini-est sarong ever saronged. However it serves its purpose.

In front of the camera, Crowhurst acted out taking a sun-sight and having lunch with—of course—beer and flying fish. ("I didn't really eat the fish, you know," confessed Crowhurst.) It was in the course of fetching the beer from a hatch in the float that his sarong nearly caused a disaster:

The hatch cover fell on my head and has now raised a bit of a bruise and a slight wound. I suppose I must have been a bit groggy from this because when I got up on deck I very nearly fell over, probably due to the combined effects of the tight

229

sarong around my knees and the fact that I'd just had a clout on the head.

But he added an explanation of why he did not sound unduly concerned:

In order to guard against this eventuality when conditions are so calm that [safety] harnesses are not really justified, I stream a long line aft which enables me to get back on board if I should fall over, and the yacht is sailing at about 5 knots. I think this is probably more use than a harness.

Crowhurst had mentioned this streamed line before in his logbooks and he was to mention it again in his tapes. It seemed now to be his regular practice.

After the filming session, Crowhurst described how he kept a record of what he had been shooting:

I have to get the film out of the camera, stow it away in its carton, tape it up in its cardboard box, enter the contents of the film in my log so that there are two records of what's on the film, one of which is written on the tape round the canister and the other of which is in my log, so that if one should for any reason be destroyed there is a duplicate.

This is strong confirmatory evidence that Crowhurst was keeping a fourth logbook. There is no record of Crowhurst's films in either Logbook One or Two, or in the Radio Log. He did keep a neat list of tape recordings in the back of Logbook One, but there is no equivalent list for films. If he *was* keeping a film record in a Logbook Four, this would not have been unexpected, because we know that most of his filming was done in the covert part of the voyage.

*   *   *

In the early hours of the morning of June 22nd, Crowhurst finally got his rebuilt transmitter working, and made contact in morse with Portishead. He got off messages to the BBC, Rodney Hallworth and his wife. Afterwards he was quite euphoric and stayed up all night in a mood of happy self-congratulation, ruminating heroically into his tape recorder:

It's this, I think, that makes the business of sailing small boats so rewarding. This is why people do it. [It] provides problems, and they're not too difficult problems really. Some of them are beyond their capacity—I happen to be able to repair transmitters, not everybody could do this—but it's a fairly typical sort of problem. It's a good indication of why people go sailing, because they know there are going to be odd things happening that are going to tax their ingenuity. But of course it gives one a feeling of satisfaction to be able to overcome difficulties and cope. I'm pretty pleased with myself at the moment . . .

He grew rhapsodic about the physical pleasures of being at sea —an unusual theme for Crowhurst—and about the mild summer night, still 70° on deck:

Yes, a fine night, the phosphorescence streaming away from the three hulls of the boat, my line streamed aft creating a long streak of phosphorescence like the tail of a comet . . . I think the Canaries or the Azores must be a perfect place to live, but good old England will do me for the time being . . .

His safety line, note, was still fastened to the boat. He also promised to make a more determined effort to get back to good old England:

Now that I've finished messing about with the transmitter, I'll be able to do a bit more sailorising, put on a spurt of speed, get cracking again, get that mainsail sewn up and bash on with it.

Crowhurst did not, in fact, get on with sailorising. When he woke up later in the morning of June 22nd his euphoria had departed. He realised that simply being able to send a few messages in morse had not solved all his problems. He spent much of the day by his radio, fixing up his rendezvous with the BBC (which again reminded him of the ordeal that lay ahead) and sending anxious cables to Rodney Hallworth about syndication contracts (he continued to be deeply worried about money). And he still could communicate only in morse—his compulsive desire to talk on the phone to Clare remained unfulfilled.

He therefore yet again dismantled his little Shannon transmitter and started a new project—trying to make it work for long-range

231

high-frequency speech transmissions. As usual he worked on it until well after midnight, and in the early hours of June 23rd tried to make contact with the English radio-telephone station at Baldock. It was a failure. He sounded in exasperated mood as he confessed into his tape recorder about his poor progress for the day:

I'm not going that fast—even if I decided to do some sailorising, which I didn't after all today. I got involved with this wretched transmitter. It's fascinating me . . . I haven't been able to manage . . . it's no good.

But once again it was the radio—his one supreme skill—that fascinated him when all else was too appalling.

Crowhurst sent a cable to Clare telling her that he had been trying to phone but that it had proved impossible. He also, in desperation, sent a request to the *Sunday Times* asking them to bend the rules and allow the BBC men to bring spare parts for the Marconi Kestrel to their rendezvous. It would not materially affect the result, he argued to himself, but would just make things easier. The *Sunday Times* vetoed the suggestion. The rules were sacrosanct.

*   *   *

Crowhurst now slowed down even further: he had run out of the North-East Trades, and was entering the calms and variable wind of the Horse Latitudes. The strings of weed, through which *Teignmouth Electron* was running told him he was approaching the eerie Sargasso Sea. His sense of strangeness and loneliness was intensified by a Spanish passenger liner that altered course to have a look at him:

I could make out some people, high up near the bridge. Passengers, you know, come to see this curious animal going about the ocean . . . I could hear a public address going on the boat. They were obviously saying: "There is a mad Englishman in a yacht on the starboard hand. If you go to the rail you will see him free of charge", or whatever the Spanish equivalent of that may be.

In the Sargasso weed, he found a new sea pet—not a jolly porpoise this time, but a weird, miniature ocean monster. In his final tape recording—on June 23rd, his last rational day—Crow-hurst described their brief companionship. He spoke in a forced, strained voice that was now beginning to reveal his true emotional state:

I picked up one of the little monsters . . . they had four rudi-mentary limbs but on the end of each were about eight further limbs, so really they had in the region of thirty-two, which were folded around their backs and were obviously adapted for clamping on to things. It was like a little lizard with the most delicate and beautiful colouring of silver and blue. Its under-neath was a pale pink colour and its tummy was a little tiny hard very pink nodule. I put it in a plastic container. I thought, I shall keep you as a pet. Unfortunately I left him out in the sun and the little plastic container got hotter and hotter . . . He was obviously not very well. I realised what I'd done, I'd virtually killed him. I quickly changed his water and he revived a bit, but next day he was dead. And here's the funny part: he's completely disappeared except for his tummy. This tiny little bright pink bit was still there, but there was no trace of anything else.

Now this little monster had really all the ingredients of a superb science fiction monster. Magnified about three hundred times he would have been really quite terrifying in the best tradition of H. G. Wells . . . The Kraken—who wrote *The Kraken Wakes?* I can't remember now—but I wish people wouldn't go in for stories like that, you know, about the sea. You lie in your bunk at night . . . and there's a deep subliminal fear that something unknown [is] lurking about waiting for this moment to make its presence known—the Kraken! unheard of terrible things that lurk in the depths waiting for Crowhurst and his trimaran! Of course, you laugh. Ha, ha you say. Ha, ha, ha. But it doesn't dispel that dark, uneasy feeling in the pit of your soul.

At the end of this tape Crowhurst gave his last spoken words to the world. It was an assertion, slightly shrill and overemphatic in tone, of his feeling of physical well-being:

I feel tremenduously fit . . . I feel as if I could realise all those ambitions I nurtured as a boy like playing cricket for England. I feel on top of the world, tremendously fit. My reflexes amaze me. They're so fast, you know. I catch things almost before they start falling. It's really very satisfying—I feel in tremenduous shape actually.

All those flabby men—the grey-flannelled executives of Madison Avenue . . . But it's true. There is a danger that the way we live nowadays just poisons us with sitting down worrying. Worrying about our nearest competitor in our level of the pyramid. The rat race! All that, plus the extremely unhealthy way of life. I'm sure we're in terrible danger from it. And there's nothing like going to sea, for getting rid of all the poisons, you know. Harping back to Strangelove—the sort of Strangelove colonel—the poisons in your body, you must get rid of them. I don't know what they are, but they've got to go. The sea's the way to get rid of them I'm sure. I feel in tremendous shape. I've never felt so . . .

With those ambiguous sentences—in one sense, morbidly prophetic—the tape ran off the end of the spool. Within twenty four hours, Crowhurst had ceased to behave as a rational being. At noon on June 23rd, he entered his last sun-sight in his logbook, and thereafter did no more systematic navigation. He gave up all attempts to sail the boat and left her to drift sluggishly through the Sargasso Sea. The cares, torments and vanities of the real world no longer troubled him. He had simply opted out.

* * *

What finally precipitated Crowhurst's madness we cannot be sure. Was there a chemical cause? Drugs, perhaps, or alcohol? Vitamin deficiency or mouldy tea? We have explored every possibility, but the evidence is against it.* More likely he was finally overwhelmed by the accumulated stress of his whole nightmarish situation—the loneliness, the hostile environment, the strain of lying, and the clamorous reminders that in two weeks' time he was expected home to receive the ruthless public attention, as well as the glory, due to a national hero. There was no escape, except to retreat from reality.

* Of the drugs he carried aboard, only Dexedrine was capable of producing psychotic symptons. He had twenty-two left from a small bottle which was found stowed away with his other medicines. It seems improbable that he had been taking them to excess.

In the last hours before his mental collapse, there had been the disappointment of failing to raise Clare on the telephone, and further pressing requests from the BBC. But these were only last straws: they did not alter Crowhurst's basic predicament. Above all must have been a growing certainty that his deception could not succeed. Virtually every act in the later half of his voyage was devoted to willing his story to come true. His convoluted lies show how deeply he was concerned. But they lacked conviction, and served only to make his position even less tenable.

If Crowhurst sensed that he could not get away with his fraud, he was almost certainly right. Sir Francis Chichester had gone on holiday to Portugal with his growing suspicions playing through his mind. And there, he decided that the time had come for a thorough examination. As chairman of the judges he wrote to Robert Riddell, the *Sunday Times* race secretary, asking him to start enquiries. His letter read:

Dear Robert,
First re D.C.: we don't want to hold up his award a second longer than necessary. Can you do the following (if you agree about it)?
Prepare a list of his authenticated messages and positive position statements, with, of course, dates. Particularly we should consider as soon as possible, his last message on leaving the S. Atlantic for the Southern Ocean, his first message, position, etc. on nearing the Horn and about having the Falklands in sight. We need to know why the silence from the Cape to the Horn (from an electronics engineer too); and why the 12-day interval between the Horn and the Falklands. Why did he never give exact positions? It also appeared that he had had an extraordinary increase of speed on entering the S. Ocean; I think he claimed 13,000 miles in 10 weeks, or something, which seems most peculiar considering his slow speed for the previous long passage to the Cape and the succeeding 8,000 miles (Horn-home). If you could let me have this information as soon as possible it may well save embarrassment later . . .
Sincerely,
Francis.

Eighteen

Into the Dark Tunnel

On June 24th, Midsummer Day, Donald Crowhurst began to write down a great new truth he had just perceived. A strong impulse forced him to start a long philosophical testament in Logbook Two, and in the next week he wrote 25,000 words, some scribbled with apparent gaiety, some scrawled in passion, some in feathery script, some in large capital letters pressed almost through the page. Every word was of supreme importance; he had a message which must be revealed to the world, and he sensed he had only seven days to write it. Even as he began he was scarcely sane, with each page he wrote he lost more control, and by the time he finished he was totally out-of-touch with reality.

He was becalmed, amongst the strange weeds and hallucinatory beasts of the Sargasso Sea. The hot summer sun shone down by day; by night Crowhurst had only his dim bulb, or his flickering oil lamp. The cabin, after eight months of cramped, unmethodical male housekeeping, smelled as if cabbage juice had been poured over old bedding, allowed to ferment, then baked in a hot oven.* Several days' plates, saucepans, and ripening curry lay in and around the sink; his bed stank; his last reserve of methylated

* This smell was still pungent five months later.

236

spirit stood in a half-pint medicine bottle beside the sink. His life-jacket, and safety harness, neglected for months, were stowed away in the aft compartment.

The logbooks lay on his small table on the port side of the cabin, still littered with components and tools from his attempts to modify his radio-telephone transmitter. A soldering iron was balanced on an empty Milo tin to their left, and spilling all around him were valves, transistors, earphones, and bundles of copper wire. If he could not reassemble that transmitter to talk himself out of trouble, perhaps he could do something with the logbooks. But what? Logbook One was blank from December 11th onwards. The Radio Log looked genuine, but those round-the-world radio reports, and one or two peculiarly worded cables, would instantly arouse suspicion. Logbook Two, totally incriminating, offered one account of his last five months. Logbook Four—if our theory is correct—offered another.

Crowhurst sat at his desk to look through the logbooks. As far as they still had any message for him, in his mental state, they can only have made it clearer that he could not arrive back at Teignmouth, ever. So he turned the pages until he found the only page which could give him any comfort, his scribbled critique of Einstein's *Relativity*.

*   *   *

It was more than comfort, it was the revelation. Einstein offered him the perfect way to cope with his nightmare! When Einstein was faced with a mathematical impasse he merely "stipulated of his own free will" that the impasse should disappear. If Einstein could make something so, merely because he *wanted* it to be so, then so could Crowhurst. He had the free will to conjure up anything he wanted! And what he wanted was escape from this cabin and this predicament.

So he turned over one page in Logbook Two, and wrote at its head a title to assert the intellectual power of mind over matter:

PHILOSOPHY

and beneath started an argument to show all the wonderful things he could now do. Like a lever, which lifts vast weights with intelligently applied effort, he would work miracles:

Man is a lever whose ultimate length and strength he must

determine for himself. His disposition and talent decide where the fulcrum will lie.

The pure mathematician places the fulcrum near the effort; his exercises are much more mental than physical and can carry the "load" — his own ideas — taking perhaps nothing but his own and kindred minds along the route. The shattering revelation that $E = mc^2$ is one supreme example of this activity.

The extrovert, say a politician, places his fulcrum nearer the load, for his function is to move the whole politico-economic system of his country — perhaps of the world. Both types of activity shape the course of man's history. The first shattering application of the idea that $E = mc^2$ is a good example of this — I refer to the bombing of Hiroshima.

This seems rational enough an argument, almost academic. But as soon as he had written it, Crowhurst's mind started to leap; his writing turned into garbled notes:

Einstein — a Jew — the face of God, or Christ — the Messiah? The King that brings Salvation to the Jews? Nuclear Power! Mystery of Prophecy!

The stride of the mind. The phases of man's development, like the development of man's education: elementary, secondary, advanced. No real classification possible until advanced stage reached — to the stalled mind, the present stage will always seem advanced. To the free mind, the present stage will always seem elementary.

This pattern is typical of the next 25,000 words: straightforward crypto-scientific argument, with much method in its madness, suddenly breaking out — under the pressure of Crowhurst's fantasies — into incoherent wild phrases. Already he had written out, in note form, the major points of his great new theory: that some minds — including his — have reached such an advanced state they are free of normal physical restraints, and can achieve salvation and prophecy. All the other stalled minds, still thinking of winds and tides and circumnavigation, simply could not comprehend this new miracle.

Then he moved into a rambling account of the mathematical puzzle, the square root of minus one. This, he argued, was a powerful mystery. Just as $\sqrt{-1}$ can turn ordinary numbers into "imaginary" numbers, inconceivable to stalled minds, so could his new idea turn ordinary thinking into unimagined new forms:

I introduce this idea $\sqrt{-1}$ because [it] leads directly to the dark tunnel of the space–time continuum, and once technology emerges from this tunnel the "world" will "end" (I believe about the year 2,000, as often prophesied) in the sense that we will have access to the means of "extra physical" existence, making the need for physical existence superfluous.

In the process the "mechanism of second sight" and "prophecy" will be laid bare as a process simply linked with the possession of intelligence, and likely to be possessed by all intelligent animals. It is the application of intelligence that will allow this mechanism to be used at will as a *superfluous by-product*.

If second sight, and prophecy, are only superficial by-products, what is the important conclusion? Crowhurst is arguing, in mathematical language laced with the visionary phrases of the near-insane, that he has the power to free his mind from his "physical existence"—that is to say, his body—whenever he wishes. To float away from *Teignmouth Electron* as a disembodied soul! What better escape could he imagine?

Here Crowhurst paused in his writing. He scrawled the facetious title: "The Thoughts of Chairman Ja Ac' Tarr" at the top of the page, and took a break.

*   *   *

It was early afternoon. He had been listening as he wrote to his radio-receiver. Something he heard attracted his attention, and he jotted it down. First he wrote "14:30 gmt, 24th", then the name of the broadcasting station, Radio Volna Europa (an American propaganda station beamed towards Poland). At 2:35 he heard "Hysterical laughter"—an odd counterpoint to the sighs he had imagined at Christmas when last his mind was similarly in the grip of fantasy—and wrote that down, too. Then, a couple of hours later, he found himself listening to the Voice of America. He wrote down the name of a broadcaster, Edward W. Crosby, and the subject of his talk, Black Americans. Next to these words he wrote "Private Note", which is clear evidence that he intended his philosophical writings to be published.

We have checked with Voice of America, and they say that an

Edward W. Crosby did broadcast a talk on negro Americans on the afternoon of June 24th. It was about racial tension, and the black man's attitude to his own race. Its title, a punning use of a Joseph Conrad novel of tragedy at sea, was "The Nigger *and* the Narcissus".

This talk is important because, as with so many previous isolated stimuli, it started Crowhurst's mind working, so that he kept bringing the irrelevant subject of black Americans into his meditations. It is also the main evidence that his deranged writings began on June 24th.

*   *   *

Some hours later (his writing changes, and is in heavier pencil) Crowhurst began a new attempt to set down his idea. A mere essay was not enough. This time he wrote a long manuscript, probably intended to fill a small book. He had gained control of himself again, and was able to write in "public voice" scientific jargon. He called his second attempt:

THE KNOT

The process we call Mathematics. The flower of basic intelligence. Ideas can be manipulated. If manipulated under a correctly formulated set of rules, they produce new results which clearly reveal aspects of the original concept which, though valid, would not have been so clearly revealed.

The idea that Mathematics is the language of God, however, possesses more poetry than abstract validity. It should be re-stated as Mathematics is perhaps the only certain common ground man TODAY occupies in the Kingdom of God" . . .

Would not any man agree mathematics is the nearest we can get to "Truth" with a "certainty" THAT IS ACCEPTABLE TO ALL? . . . That which is most certainly true of God's Kingdom will be acceptable to all who accept such a kingdom, and I know of nothing rivalling the science of mathematics in this respect.

It seems to me that progress is the coin of most value to humanity . . . Progress towards what? Why, towards cosmic integration, of course, where else do you think you are going? How do I know? I'll tell you.

The soberly worded preamble is complete and as Crowhurst

prepared to describe his personal revelation, the strain forced him
to break away into wild phrases:

Antichrist? "Love thy neighbour as thyself" in times when
physical existence hung by a tenuous thread. "Love thy
neighbour's ideas as thine own" will lead us through the tunnel.

The dark tunnel, the cosmic mind, the kingdom of God, the end
of physical existence—already the phrases and symbols were
growing apocalyptic and repetitive, as Crowhurst tried to convey
what he meant by "progress towards cosmic integration".

His "theory of progress"—which is also his revelation—occupies
most of the remaining pages of Logbook Two, and takes 12,000
words to explain. It is too mathematical to display undigested,
and often too incoherent because of the frequent break-away
passages. As his sufferings increased, his method grew less and his
madness more.

The theory itself, however, is comparatively simple. It has
already appeared in a crude form in his wild "Thoughts of
Chairman Ja Ac' Tarr" and is an elaboration of the belief he has
held for many years, and used to present frequently at late-night
discussions: man has evolved to a state where his mind can escape
his body, and a determined exercise of intelligence can make this
happen.

In the beginning, thought Crowhurst, there existed only a void,
without any physical matter. Then, as a sudden change, matter
arrived, disturbing the stable "system" which had existed happily
for billions of years. Next, life arrived, and after life, intelligence.
Each new arrival caused an explosive change in the universe,
disrupting the previous apparently stable system. The system
always fights the new arrival, sometimes destroys it, but always
loses in the end. Recently, man's intelligence has been steadily
growing and improving, thanks to brave original thinkers like
Christ, Galileo, and Einstein, each of whom dared to disrupt the
static system of human society in their time with a new idea.
Because of their thinking, human progress has been accelerating.
Intelligence has now grown so powerful, with all this accumulated
knowledge, that it is ready to achieve the next great change and
disruption of the system. This will be the "freeing" of the intelligence or mind from its physical body, so that it leaps into an
abstract existence.

The moment for the mind's great jump out of our present biological system was at hand, Crowhurst thought. The man who was about to tell the world all about it, in the great tradition of Christ, Galileo and Einstein, was Crowhurst himself. When he uttered the message, everyone would instantly see the truth of it, and this would force them all to make the great effort of free will necessary to leap into abstract existence.

Furthermore, anyone who made this leap became like a God. Probably "God" was only a name to describe minds in the past that had managed the leap. Provided we were all very intelligent, which also meant being very loving to our fellow men (this was Crowhurst's message to black Americans) we were all like Gods. To ensure we loved everyone, we had to look upon life as a great game, played with infinite understanding, and no hostility.

All this is clothed in the jargon language of a variety of sciences. Each new phase, for instance, Crowhurst calls the change from "first order differentials" to "second order differentials" borrowing the language of calculus. At one point he changes his imagery and describes it in terms of biology, using the idea of a parasite living off a host animal:

> The arrival of each parasite brings about an increase in the tempo of the Drama, causing first-order differentials in its own lifetime within the host, and second-order differentials within the host to the host etc etc
>
> So far we have a void, acting as host to a physical universe, acting as host to an intelligence universe. Where is the system designed to go? To the point where it brings about a fundamental change in the tempo of events in the host.

In essence this is only Crowhurst's old habit of blinding his listeners with science, to make his thoughts sound more original than they really were. But it certainly meant a great deal to him in his disordered state, for he first defended it in classic psychotic fashion ("I'm the only one who understands") and then suddenly erupted in a blaze of revelatory exclamation marks:

> That these sentences would at first sight apparently be devoid of physical meaning is hardly surprising, for if we had a complete understanding of their meaning we would indeed have arrived at the stage it is now the object of the exercise to predict.)

And yet, and yet—*if* creative abstraction is to act as a vehicle for the new entity, and to leave its hitherto stable state it lies within the power of creative abstraction to produce the phenomenon !!!!!!!!!!!!!!!!!! We can bring it about by creative abstraction!

The frantic excitement reveals that Crowhurst was back at the nub of his argument: he could leave his body, and make himself divine, whenever he wanted. No wonder he peppered the page with exclamation marks. He had theorised for himself an escape from his unresolvable predicament. Yet again he could abandon the old, unsuccessful challenge, and take on a new one on a higher plane. Just as he had abandoned the army for Cambridge, Mullards for Electron Utilisation, and Electron Utilisation for a heroic circumnavigation, now he could abandon the race, his boat, and the whole tragic mess of his failed and fraudulent voyage for a new existence, where no niggling reality of money, winds, leaking floats or forged logbooks could interfere with his triumphant achievement. He could become God.

*　　　*　　　*

As if in response, the preparations back in England for his return were rising to a liturgical pitch. At Teignmouth, the "Crowhurst Welcome Home Sub-Committee" of the Council had met in full session, and decided that, after their hero had been escorted up the Channel by a naval minesweeper, and the Teignmouth Corinthian Yacht Club had fired a finishing cannon, Crowhurst would be towed along the seafront to the pier, and back to enable a maximum number of eager visitors to catch a close view, and then be moored in the river estuary. BBC and ITN helicopters would hover reverently above him. When he had been rowed ashore, he would be greeted on the muddy foreshore by Mrs Irene Arnot, Chairman of the Council, who would orate the Civic Welcome. Crowhurst would reply. Then he would be driven with his family to the Royal Hotel for a short rest before going on to the Press Conference at the Carlton Theatre (admission by invitation only). On the day after the arrival the "Name-It-Teignmouth Committee" would hold a second reception at the London Hotel . . . and so on. A banner reading "Teignmouth Welcomes Crowhurst" would be draped along the seafront, for maximum exposure in

243

news photographs. As a special concession, petrol tankers and fire tenders would be permitted on the civic tennis courts.

Rodney Hallworth, who had endured some ridicule during his client's long and mysterious radio silence, was now the social lion of Teignmouth. The Ship Inn was triumphant; the Lifeboat admitted grudging admiration. Everyone clustered round to tell Hallworth how they had never shared the cynical scepticism about Crowhurst's voyage. Commercial suppliers were writing to remind him that their products were aboard, had no doubt performed nobly, and would he please arrange for photographs? A sculptor offered a special trophy with "symbolic hull in aluminium alloy extrusion, and translucent sail in acrylic sheet". A request had been received for Crowhurst to present the Duke of Edinburgh awards for the West Country, on behalf of Prince Philip. The Post Office agreed to a special Crowhurst franking mark during the week of arrival, and Mr A. John E. Hole, postal historian, of Lee-on-Solent, Hants, agreed to buy a hundred autographed commemorative covers from Devon News, at two and sixpence each.

Hallworth was also organizing publicity material. He had printed ten thousand postcards with Donald's photograph and the words "Greetings from Teignmouth, the Devon resort chosen by Donald Crowhurst for his triumphant around the World Yacht Race" on the back. He organised, and largely wrote, a special edition of the *Teignmouth Post and Gazette*: CONGRATULA-TIONS AND WELCOME HOME DONALD CROWHURST. His opening paragraph sounded a prophetic and clarion note:

> Before he left Teignmouth, Donald Crowhurst was little more than a week-end sailor. He was unknown. Many club tie yachtsmen and local critics thought his strangely shaped boat built of wood which included second-hand tea chests* would sink, or at best turn back before Land's End.
>
> Today his name is added to the famous. And behind that brief statement is a story almost as long as the gruelling 29,000 miles he has travelled; a story packed with courage, self-discipline, and an unswerving belief in his own capabilities.

But the most moving text in the newspaper was an article called

---

* Messrs L. J. Eastwood deny that any tea chests, first or second-hand, were used in the construction of *Teignmouth Electron*.

"My Life as an Ocean Widow" by Clare Crowhurst, in which for the first time she felt able fully to describe her feelings during the eight lonely months:

> I find time to wonder about the type of person who is coming home. Eight months . . . each day with a new challenge, a new view, albeit only water and the odd fish or bird. The more trivial things such as growing a beard or even possibly long hair. I can't possibly remember whether the long list of necessary things included scissors, I imagine it did . . . I can't see him cutting his hair with a knife!

On June 25th she allowed her naturally ecstatic feelings to pour out in a *Daily Express* interview:

> Now most of the bad things are lost in the tremendous anticipation at seeing him again. It's incredible the fantastic excitement in the house. Everybody's laughing. It's really awfully stupid. It's almost like the atmosphere you get when you have a child. We just can't wipe the smiles off our faces.

*　　*　　*

At some time during that week, Donald Crowhurst did cut his hair. Tufts were strewn all over the cabin floor. And on that same day, June 25th, he thought of his wife, waiting for him in Bridgwater. In the course of yet another mathematical exposition, he invented a conversation with her, to illustrate a point:

> It will be instructive for the non-mathematical reader to consider certain mathematical concepts: I sit at my boat becalmed, in the middle of the Atlantic. In England my wife asks me "how are things with you?" I say "for the last 3 hours I have been stationary in position 31°25′N, 39°15′W. I am well and happy."
> My wife is well satisfied that she completely understands my condition by virtue of my reply. She takes out a chart and marks my position with a pin on a chart she has at home. She looks at the clock, which indicates that the time is 3 o'clock in the afternoon, looks at the calendar which indicates the day to be 25th July [*sic*] and writes beside the point on the chart 1200–1500 July 25, '69. She thinks "I am glad he is well and

happy", but she does *not* write this on the chart. But if she wishes me to know her own reaction to this news she says "I'm glad," at the time of the call, and if she wishes to make a record of the events does so in a diary or notebook.

This passage was written just after Crowhurst's first full statement of his theories, which culminated in his shout of excitement. It suggests these first eleven pages of the meditations were written in one day. The mention of "July 25th" is obviously a mistake for June 25th,* Crowhurst's position is where one would expect, about 150 miles to the north of his June 23rd fix, and the passage shows how much he yearned for his radio-telephone to work, so he could talk to Clare and—at last—describe his real condition. For so many months he had been giving his wife, and the world, geographical positions—both true and false. They had often been glad to hear he was "well and happy". He wanted desperately to tell them more. So desperately he even started to redraft the unsent code telegram (XYZAB CDEFG HIJKH) of six months before in his Radio Log. He wanted someone, anyone, to talk to sincerely, to tell them everything so they could advise him. But he never carried it through.

By an amazing coincidence someone did observe his real physical condition at this moment. The Norwegian cargo vessel *Cuyahoga* spotted the trimaran at about 5.00 p.m. on June 25th and came over to have a look at it. As she passed Crowhurst waved, apparently cheerfully. The *Cuyahoga*'s captain noted that he had a beard, wore khaki shorts, and seemed in good shape. Some clothes were hung up to dry and the life-raft was lying on deck. The weather was fine, and *Teignmouth Electron* was sailing north-east. Her position, said the *Cuyahoga*, was 30° 42' north, 39° 55' west (the discrepancy with Crowhurst's own calculations reveals he was not navigating accurately). Crowhurst noted the meeting in the margin.

Crowhurst spent most of June 25th writing a history of the past 2,000 years (flitting further back, at one point, to the actions of cavemen) which was designed to show how exceptional men have, in the past, managed to shock society and the system into change. His excitement kept breaking into the narrative, and destroying its flow. He now not only felt that he had had a great revelation,

---

* There are several examples in Crowhurst's logbooks and notes of his confusing, when writing quickly, July and June, and March and May.

but thought that if he wrote it down too clearly the very existence of the words on paper would be an impulse that would set off a cosmic explosion:

. . . Now we must be very careful about getting the answer right. We are at the point where our powers of abstraction are powerful enough to do tremendous damage.

Once we understand a normally stable system well enough to tamper with it in unnatural ways we must be very very careful about what we decide to do. We must think hard and long about the system before doing *anything*, and when we decide to act we must be careful not to rush things. Like nuclear chain reactions in the matter system, our whole system of creative abstraction can be brought to the point of "take off" . . .

By writing these words I do signal for the process to begin . . .

However, he knows that this cosmic explosion has been prophesied as the Second Coming, and when it happens he will, like Einstein, be already a God:

So there is dormant in human intellect abilities which can bring this about. There is evidence of this in prophecy, and clairvoyance. Nostradamus is a remarkable example. Many people insist that the time of Revelations is at hand—again I think the prophecy is being fulfilled and the priests are those who have the most to lose. The Jews, I believe, interpret the prophecies as meaning the end of the world will follow hard on the heels of the Messiah. Einstein fits.

These thoughts made Crowhurst more at ease, and as his second day of meditations ended, he relaxed:

Why do I feel strangely at peace, as I gaze at the sunset here in mid-Atlantic? Because I am clearly aware that I am looking at the peace and beauty of the environment that has cradled the life-form carrying my intelligence. Bound to Newtonian time, my "soul" senses future freedom from this beautiful cradle, and I am nostalgic as a child sensing he is about to leave "home" for ever. This explanation of these feelings is acceptable to me here and now.

The next day, Crowhurst concentrated more intently on the linked ideas of escape from his body, and the use of "Einsteinian" free will. This brought problems. Just as Einstein felt obliged to write a book telling the world of his "impulse", so must Crowhurst. He became increasingly terrified as he realised that to do so, and leave his physical body, meant that his body must die. He began to shout once more:

Free will — the obligations to morality, each man is providing the system with impulses and he should think hard about the nature of them — THIS IS THE SOLE MORAL OBLIGATION THAT the individual OWES TO THE PROGRESS OF THE SYSTEM.

I consider this statement with some trepidation as I think about the conclusions I am drawing so rapidly out of the system, but am at ease about the outcome because the impulse is in the required form — thought.

If the shark rubbing itself on the bottom of the boat got me today it still would not matter. The solution would not disappear, so long as this boat was found. I would be "sorry" if the boat and the book went up in flames, for "my" impulse would have been lost.

He patted himself on the back for the brilliance of his ideas:

Mathematicians and engineers used to the techniques of system analysis will skim through my complete work in less than an hour. At the end of that time problems that have beset humanity for thousands of years will have been solved for them. Aspects I have no need to mention will tumble into place, and the distressing struggles of man to reach an understanding of the driving forces between God, Man, and the physical universe [will be over].

Then he summed up his argument:

If I stipulate of my own free will that by learning to manipulate the space–time continuum Man will become God and disappear from the physical universe as we know it I am providing the system with an impulse. If my solution is rooted in the mathematical requirements of a solution it is "correct" and immediately acceptable to a rapidly increasing body of men, then I am very close to God and should, by the methods I claim are available, move at last to prophecy. Let's have a go! . . .

Free will—the very centre of the theological mystery resolves itself to this childishly simple issue. Will man accept, of his own free will, the stipulation that when he has learnt to manipulate the space–time continuum he will possess the attributes of God? The choice is simply this. Do we go on clinging to the idea that "God made us", or realise that it lies within our power to make GOD?

His excitement grew more and more intense, his capital letters larger, and more deeply scored:

The system IS SHRIEKING OUT THIS MESSAGE AT THE TOP OF ITS VOICE why does no one listen I am listening anyway

but felt obliged to cross out such strong thoughts, as embarrassing to his readers. He regained control of himself, and wrote out the same idea in quieter language:

The system is trying to tell us this, but the people who formulate "moral" views are rarely equipped with a mathematical dictionary. They simply do not understand the language the system is using to try and communicate with us. But mathematicians understand the language and on behalf of the system I appeal to them to think about what Nature is trying to say. The voice is the voice of natural truth. It is a loud, clear voice, and it speaks with the voice of correct abstract thinking.

Finally, Crowhurst turned the page and, in the grip of real madness for a moment, wrote down the words:

Vengeance of God is mine. Birth Control.
The second is . . .

and stopped. He had reached the end of the blank pages in Logbook Two, and besides he had other things to do. A cable was coming in from Rodney Hallworth:

BBC AND EXPRESS MEETING YOU WITH CLARE AND ME OFF
SCILLIES   YOUR TRIUMPH BRINGING ONE HUNDRED THOUSAND
FOLK TEIGNMOUTH WHERE FUND NOW REACHING FIFTEEN HUN-
DRED PLUS MANY OTHER BENEFITS   PLEASE GIVE ME SECRETS OF
TRIP NEAR DEATH AND ALL THAT FOR PRE-PRESS SELLING
OPPORTUNITIES MONEY OUTLOOK GOOD   REPLY URGENT THINK-
ING ABOUT ADVERTISING

"My God!" said Rodney Hallworth when he read the logbooks
later, "I think I may have killed Donald Crowhurst with that
telegram."

Nineteen

The Cosmic Mind

As Crowhurst turned to Logbook One to continue his meditations, he was still capable of rational argument. At moments his writing was at its most intelligent and perceptive. But the sharp reminder of the phoney heroics that his plan required ("NEAR DEATH AND ALL THAT") sent his mind scuttling even further from reality. He was now so deeply submerged in his theories that whatever he thought about, he became. Before, he had written of abstract intelligence as a concept; now he actually experienced his own mind undergoing the change. Before, he merely contemplated the cosmic mind; now he felt its thoughts in his own head. Before, the idea of life as a "game" was a useful form of words; now it was literal truth, and Crowhurst—like some chess pawn—was caught in a hideous play between God and the Devil.

Time became increasingly important to him as he watched his clocks ticking onwards towards the moment of expected arrival in England, and towards the moment he was half-consciously appointing for his own end. Here, also, reality and fantasy merged. He began to see his defective chronometer as more than a navigational tool, defining his position in the ocean. Just as it had gone wrong under the strain, and offered lies about his true position—so had he. Therefore he saw it, first, as a symbol of his own condition, and then actually *as* his own condition. He was in a machine. He *was* a machine. And the machine was about to break down. Crowhurst moved into the dark tunnel where space and time co-existed, to substitute God's clock for his own:

God's clock is not the same as our clock. He has an infinite amount of "our" time. Ours has very nearly run out...

This obsession with time-keeping, and involvement with clocks, followed naturally from his pseudo-Einsteinian theories. It is also a familiar derangement to mariners, who call it "time madness".

Crowhurst's breakaway outbursts grew wilder, and dredged up experiences deeper in his mind. Now he thought of his dead father, of his mother's links with Jehovah's Witnesses, of the dreaded "misfit" symbol headed for death, of cosmic beings, shameful secrets, and of his own idea of himself as a newly-created God. These memories and imaginings jumbled together in tormented confusion. Sometimes he seemed to achieve a strange, demented peace, but then he remembered the new trap he had built for himself: his theory of the mind escaping the body meant he must destroy himself to achieve salvation. His hints of impending death grew clearer. Something, however, still prevented him writing down clearly on paper that he intended to kill himself. It was as if he felt that once he recorded the fact that he was going to commit suicide, the deed would be forced upon him. He wrote, for instance:

Christ: he had arrived at the truth, but fed the system with the truth in a way that produced a violent reaction. People witnessed the manner of his death. I must consider whether to ...

but stopped, and crossed out the last sentence. He must not write down what he considered doing!

He was still hugely pleased with himself for his revelation:

By their fruits shall ye know them—good souls create good ideas, they flourish and contribute sanity to all apes. They flourish and contribute something to all intellects. They enable the intellect to create better systems to contain the actions of apes without denying the ape the freedom to be happy. That has been my problem, that is the problem every man must solve for himself. This is how I solved the problem. And to let you inside my soul, which is now "at peace" I give you my book. I am lucky. I have done something "interesting" at last. At last my system has noticed me!

In the next 12,000 words he explained, and developed, two ideas that became increasingly important to him. One was the concept of "the ape", presumably derived from what he had heard of Desmond Morris's book *The Naked Ape*. Crowhurst's ape is, simply, the human animal which confines the potentially free intelligence in a monkey-like body, with all its nasty instincts, and sad weaknesses:

> We are still apes, and we need the bodies of apes to carry our intelligence and give mechanical reality to our ideas. If you kill the ape the computer stops. We deeply resent our computers being stopped because we sense that once the computer stops we, as individuals, somehow stop. This is probably true, *alas I shall not see my dead father again unless* for I see no way in which the system benefits by the retention of a computer incapable of action within the system, when the system provides a ready supply of fresh computers capable of acting within the system.

(The italicised phrase Crowhurst crossed out. It was a sudden shriek of anguish caused by the thought of death. "Alas, I shall not see my dead father again, unless..." Unless what? Presumably unless he killed himself, to ascend to the world of disembodied intelligences where his father would be waiting for him. Infantile fantasies about both his father and mother grew more prominent from this point on.)

The second basic idea Crowhurst developed in his public voice argument was that of "the system". A system is only an ordered, and predictable, state of affairs. But as Crowhurst's intellectual training had been in the understanding of electronic systems, and other machines, he tried to interpret all organisations and situations as equally deterministic systems. The biological and physical universes were systems, with clearly defined rules. So was the human body; so was society:

Systems—systems—systems—you can't escape them because nature is systematic, and man is a natural phenomenon, and his intelligence is a natural phenomenon.

Crowhurst's theory stipulated a hierarchy of systems, stretching from physical matter to godlike abstract intelligence:

intelligence system (gods)

↑

human system (apes with minds)

↑

biological system (animals)

↑

matter system

The "progress towards cosmic integration" was, of course, the process of moving upwards through these systems. The highest system, composed of abstract intelligences and inhabited by gods, could now be reached, as Crowhurst had argued, by "an effort of free will"—that is to say, by wanting to get there. But first, every ape had to learn to live lovingly and cleverly within the human system. Our predicament is the result of our mixed natures, half ape and half cosmic intelligence. We suffer pain, corruption and degradation in human society not because the human system is evil—it behaves "correctly" according to its own lights—but because the cosmos is trying to persuade us to leave it for the higher plane. Any individual, therefore, who tried to make some anarchic gesture against society as he finds it, both impedes progress and is bound to lose:

If your system will not listen to you, don't go home and start work on a bomb—the system knows how to cope with that, you can bet. Don't burn yourself to death in the street. The system may not know quite what to make of that, but it will change nothing, and will waste your intelligence (an intelligence forceful enough to make such a sacrifice is worthy of better things). You can either quietly get to work persuading the system to accept you, and change it from within, or simply remove your intelligence into a more satisfying system.

This was, in part, a sophisticated argument against all forms of violent revolution, but mainly a rationalisation of Crowhurst's own wish to remove his intelligence into a more satisfying system, that of pure intelligence. In other words, to die.

Crowhurst also wrote a separate essay called "The Game". His idea of life as a game became increasingly intertwined with apes and systems. A game, of course, is an activity conducted according to its own, arbitrarily defined, rules — a game player does not have to worry about thoughts of right and wrong. He can therefore manipulate situations at will. More important, a game is a conflict that hurts no one. Revolutionaries, and other violent apes, are not playing the game, because they break the rules of the present system of society. In his essay, Crowhurst argued that you could believe in anything, and could still progress towards cosmic integration, provided you only competed with other men, and their ideas, in your mind. Everything must be done within the mind.

All these thoughts had come to him within three days. As his great burst of writing ended, he congratulated himself on his speed, and insight:

> In just three days the work was done! Christ is amongst us just as surely as if he was walking about signing cheques . . .
> . . . You will have trouble with some of the things I have to say. Until recently — three days ago — I had a lot of trouble with them myself.
> . . . I was determined to solve the problem if it took the rest of my life. Half-an-hour later I had set up the basic equations, and seen the pattern. Three days later I understood everything in nature, in myself, in all religion, in politics, in atheism, agnosticism, communism, and systems. I knew everything from Julius Caesar to Mao Tse Tung. I had a complete set of answers to the most difficult problems now facing mankind. I had arrived in the cosmos while contemplating the navel of an ape . . .

In reality, the only problem he had recognised was how to escape the consequences of a forged voyage round the world. And his only answer was a demented vision of his own death. But Crowhurst by now was too far inside his own mind to recognise this.

* * *

255

It was now June 28th. In the midst of these fantasies Crowhurst was still able to operate his transmitter, and could even compose jovial telegrams. He ticked off the BBC and Rodney Hallworth for demanding a firm arrival time from him:

BECALMED THREE DAYS   PUFF BOATS HAVE DESTINATIONS NOT
ETAS

An "Estimated Time of Arrival" is, as the BBC should have known, seldom possible with sailing boats at the mercy of winds and currents.

Crowhurst gave the radio operator at Portishead his position, 32N 40W, another thirty-five miles to the north of his June 25th fix. The operator told him he would be telephoning Clare Crowhurst, and were there any messages for her? This must have disturbed Crowhurst, for on the next day he again contacted Portishead, who told him that his wife and children were all well, and happily looking forward to meeting him off the Scilly Isles with Hallworth and the BBC. He tapped out a message to them insisting that Clare must stay at home, she must *not* come out to the Scillies to meet him. Please confirm, asked the perplexed operator who could not understand why the lone sailor was rebuffing his wife and family. Crowhurst confirmed his message.

Mrs Crowhurst decided her husband was thinking merely that a Scillies voyage would make her and the children seasick. Later, as she worried about it, she felt rather hurt. Now, of course, it can be seen as clear evidence that he had finally decided what he must do.

After some morse small-talk the Portishead operator told Crowhurst to make contact again at 11.00 p.m. on June 30th, wished him a good strong wind, and told him he would "see" him again on the next day.

Crowhurst never used his radio again. This was his last record in the Radio Log, and his last contact with anyone outside his own imagination. From that moment he was completely alone.

*   *   *

Cutting off contact with the rest of the world finally cut off Crowhurst from any rational appreciation of his own situation. From then on, his writings were only a confused metaphorical expression of his anguish, voiced in a mad shorthand vocabulary of divine revelation, always incoherent and often packed with two or three simultaneous meanings.

He began with a debate with himself about his deliberate "concealment". What should he do? On the one hand he wanted to confess the sin of his fraudulent voyage—but that would cause torment to his wife, family and friends. On the other, he was tempted to destroy all the records of his fraud as he destroyed himself—but that would offend the sacred principle of always telling the entire truth, and deprive mankind of his great revelation.

He started a fresh page, where he scrawled seven short lines:

Nature does not allow
God to Sin any Sins
Except One—

That is the Sin of Concealment

This is the terrible secret of the torment of the soul
"needed" by a natural system to keep trying

He has perpetrated this sin on the tormented . . .

These are obviously cries of pain. They have meaning on at least three levels. First, Crowhurst was simply upbraiding himself for his concealed fraud, and his secrecy, which had brought upon him the torments he now suffered. On a second level, he was scolding God for hiding from him for so long, forcing him to spend his life as an unbeliever. Finally, on a third level, "God" was Crowhurst himself, who learned the terrible secret of the torment of the soul as he became divine. His divinity forced him to conceal himself from ordinary human beings. This was why he had switched off the radio, and warned off his wife. As a God, he felt lonely, and cut off by his new secret. Nature "allowed" him to be so, but it hurt.

Turning the page, Crowhurst restated his isolation in terms of the doomed bird he had written about six months before:

The Misfit excluded from the system—the freedom to leave the system.

Then he became obsessed with Time again:

I prepared my self for a long hand

3 h

~~that is only one sin~~

~~Nature abhors god or~~

Nature does not allow
God to sin any sins
Except One —

That is the Sin of Concealment,

This is a for the Twentieth Secret
of the Torment of the Soul "needed"
by a natural System to

keep denying

He has perpetrated this sin
on the tormented

The Kingdom of God has an area measured not in square miles but in square hours. It is a kingdom with all the time in the world—we have used all the time available to us, and must now seek an imaginary sort of time.

His jumbled phrases continued, now classically illustrating what a psychoanalyst might call regression, or a "return to the womb" as he thought of his parents, his birth, and the Kingdom of God:

When we have found it we will be ready to begin another painful adventure—We will be your gods, and will have to learn how to live with our parents in a new system.

We are in the womb of the universe. We conceived ourselves as we "ought" to conceive ourselves. All we had to do to get there was to think of ourselves as we would like to think of ourselves.

Next, he returned to his idea of "the game", but now the game was sinister: "During each man's lifetime, God plays cosmic chess against the Devil." He crossed out this sentence, and replaced it with:

During his lifetime, each man plays cosmic chess against the Devil. Each man can decide for himself who has won. The moves of the game are all well-known. It is a difficult game to follow who is winning the game because God is playing with one set of rules, and the Devil with the other exactly opposite set of rules.

Again it is obvious what Crowhurst, beneath the theological phrases, is actually thinking about. The game he had played in the Round-the-World race had been played, at the start, according to God's rules. But the Devil had unfairly played every trick against him; it had ended as the Devil's game.

Recoiling from this unpleasant thought, Crowhurst started a new story. He began it three times, each time groping for comfort in a mixture of yearning for his father (who was now half-identified with a father-like God), religious imagery, and his basic argument that all apes must love each other:

Once upon a different sort of time a boy fell out with his father. About the . . .

Once upon a different sort of time a boy and his father were wandering about when they came across some apes. "Those are jolly good apes," said the man. "They are useless apes," said the boy. An argument started, and the boy got very angry. The father was a perfect father, and was trying very hard to teach his son an important lesson, so he was patient. He thought of an idea. We will play cosmic games with these apes . . .

God and his favourite son were playing together in the cosmos. He was the Perfect Father and he had a Perfect Son. Naturally they were playing a jolly good game. The game they were playing was called turning apes into gods. It was a jolly just game, and so long as it was played according to one simple rule, the apes were not allowed to know anything about gods. The game was . . .

All his theories were beginning to concertina together, in hopeless confusion. Once again he broke off, and thought about the coming cosmic explosion. He had thought up some slogans to help:

The Masses are Critical Masses

They Can Come Together in Love or Hate

IT IS THE MYSTERY OF FREEWILL

Then followed a very revealing passage, in which all Crowhurst's ideas linked together even closer. "The game" is included. So is "the system". So is the idea of Crowhurst becoming a God, and the problem of God's secrecy, which he now further explained:

The explanation of our troubles is that cosmic beings are playing games with us. (If you know the "right" mathematics it is "easy" to work out.) It amuses them to devise systems capable of "making" cosmic beings by themselves. When you think about this you will have to admit it is a *very* amusing game. I love amusing games, and can see the cosmic beings' point-of-view. But I am a man also, and when I think of the long pains that men have endured because of the cosmic beings' game, I get very angry with them. They tell me they understand the pain. They have pain in a different way too, and devised the method of making cosmic beings automatically in order to make second-generation cosmic beings better able to cope with their problems than they were themselves.

Crowhurst was now so far into his fantasy world that he was displaying extreme symptoms of paranoia: a deluded sense of persecution, projected into an idea of his own importance, so grandiose that he felt he would be a finer God than any now in heaven. He felt so close to the cosmic beings that he started to talk directly to them: "You should have made it easier." His voyage should have been easier. So should forging his logbooks. The Gods had not helped enough:

> I was annoyed with the cosmic beings. Something was going wrong. I felt I could have played the game better than the cosmic beings . . . In the end I was forced to admit that nature forces on cosmic beings the only sin they are capable of. The sin of concealment. It is a small sin for a man to commit, but it is a terrible sin for a cosmic being. That is the anguish of a cosmic being.

To have lied as an ordinary human being was possible. But now he was a God he could only avoid terrible torment by revealing all he had done:

> I was beginning to understand more and more of the cosmic beings. All cosmic beings had to throw themselves on the mercy of one man!
> By this process I have become a second-generation cosmic being. I am conceived in the womb of nature, in my own mind. Then I too have a problem. I must move the bulk of mankind in the right direction at once.
> I have powerful systems at my disposal, but very little time to work out the best way to get the powerful systems moving with each other instead of against each other. But I am certain that if I get the first move "right" I will get all the help I need in reaching a fast and easy solution.
> Even Gods need help, you see.

In his paranoid state, Crowhurst saw himself as beyond ordinary human morality:

> The more things got upside down, the better they fitted. The truth was that there was no good or evil, only truth. Those who know the truth could select one or other of two equally

261

satisfactory sets of rules. Complete freedom of choice beyond the reach of any discipline is the meaning of free will.

This led him to debate once more the dilemma of choosing between Godlike concealment, and his moral duty to his impulse:

> I, beyond the reach of any discipline, by my freedom could choose between sending man into oblivion like an ape with an oversize computer, by remaining silent.
> *or* I could try to get him out of trouble *my* way
> *or* I, who hated the way the Roman Catholic Church obstinately refused to change, can say the words that will save the world into the ear that has been waiting so long to hear it.

Catholicism is the final, unexpected element in Crowhurst's deranged thinking. He was thinking of Clare, and her religion; he was also seeking—despite his boasts of freedom from conventional morality—some kind of final absolution in orthodox religion. The end was now very near:

> There is such beauty in truth that I am prepared to submit to the discipline I hated most, the rigid, unmoving, stupid, bigoted system called the Holy Roman Catholic Church, because the pure mathematics fit any place any time. The applied mathematics fit only me, the man of the world, with the knowledge of the cosmos, this time, this place, and a particularly beautiful instrument of God.

But why had God hidden from him for so long?

> The shameful secret of God. The trick he used because the truth would hurt too much. If it had been known before, the necessary perfect shining instrument would not be what it is today.

Then followed a paragraph so terrible, and so unambiguous in its suggestion of impending suicide, that Crowhurst tried to rub it out:

> The quick are quick, and the dead are dead. That is the judgment of God. I could not have endured the terrible anguish and meaningless waiting, in fact.

Now that Crowhurst knew the secrets of the cosmos, he could not endure the meaningless waiting for a conventional death in old age. Therefore he comforted himself with the advantages of a swift death, and translation into the world of Gods:

> There must be much we can learn from each other.
> Now at last man has everything he needs to think like a cosmic being.
> At the moment it must be true that I am the only man on earth who realises what this means. It means I can make myself a cosmic being, by my own efforts, but I have to hurry up and get on with it before I die!

Then, a last effort at "public voice" argument:

> It is fine to go to the church. There is nothing wrong in going to your priest once a week and saying to him "let's go Dad", and play the game of Roman Catholic ritual. It is a fun game. Like all good games, it is a meanings game. Its meaning is just a game called Finding Truth.

and a final few disjointed phrases:

> Man is forced to certain conclusions by virtue of his mistakes.
> No machine can work without error!
> The only trouble with man is that he takes life too seriously!

These are the last words written in the meditations, and very nearly the last words Donald Crowhurst wrote. Their meaning, apparently obscure, is clear from what has been written before: the "certain conclusion" that Crowhurst was forced to make was that he must commit suicide. The machine that cannot work without error is himself, broken-down and lying — like his navigational chronometer. And the trouble with man is that he both views life with stupid solemnity, and is far too serious about losing it.

The page on which these phrases are written is the only one in the logbooks soaked by salt water, possibly tears, but more likely the sea.

Twenty

The Great Beauty of Truth

        Donald Crowhurst had lost all track of time. Asleep, engrossed with his writing, or contemplating what he intended to do, he was quite unaware of what was happening around him. Both his watches and his Hamilton chronometer had been allowed to run down, and stop. He had to remind himself, even, what day it was. He started laboriously to pick up the threads. Returning to Logbook Two, he checked the date of his last navigational entry. He counted in his mind through the ensuing days and nights, then, on the first of three blank pages— just before the incriminating record of his voyage down the coast of South America—he wrote:

Yesterday was June 30

He still had no idea of the time. It was broad daylight, but going up on deck he could just distinguish the full moon low on the horizon. He had tables in his nautical almanac to give him the time of the setting of the moon. He returned to the cabin and worked out that the time must be 4.10 a.m. Greenwich Mean Time, or 5.10 a.m. British Standard Time, which he tended to use

The face of Donald Crowhurst, about three weeks before he died, taken with his BBC film camera secured to a bracket on the mast. He has grown a moustache and a wispy beard. Note how the face has hardened and aged compared with pictures taken before he set sail, a sign of the months of strain

Teignmouth Electron as she was found, ghosting like Mary Celeste in a calm Atlantic, un

The cabin o
discovery

RIGHT: **Dir
pots in the
galley**

LEFT: **His
navigationa
and technic;
books (with
copy of
Chichester';
'Gipsy Moth
The pistol-
shaped obje
is a Navicat
made by his
own firm**

en. **The boarding party is seen approaching. Picture by a sailor aboard RMV Picardy**

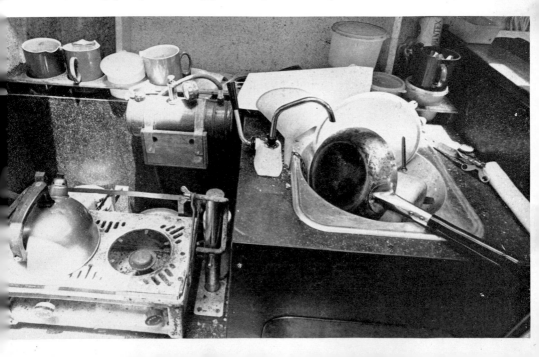

After the air search, Capt. Richard D. Hoover reports back to the Azores that Crowhurst is lost

BELOW: The end of the voyage—the barnacled trimaran is off-loaded from RMV Picardy, on arrival at Santo Doming

on board because it was convenient for BBC broadcasts. He recorded this, too, in his log:

Clock started approx. 5.10. Just before moon went down.

Then suddenly he came to his full senses. This was totally ridiculous; it was bright daylight outside, with the sun quite high in the sky. The 5.10 timing must be wrong. He looked again at his almanac. The time he had recorded was not for the setting of the moon, but for its meridian passage—its highest point in the sky. He could not have been more wrong. The time was really 10.00 in the morning. In disgust, with a thick black pencil, he wrote:

June 30.   5.10   MAX POSS ERROR

and below this, to set the record straight (remembering just in time that June had only 30 days, and therefore it must be July 1) he wrote out a fresh line:

TRUE POSITION   ~~June~~ July 1   10.00 H

How could he, Crowhurst, the supremely precise calculator, the beautiful shining instrument that now knew the innermost secrets of time, have made such a culpable error? And at a time when he was caught up in the ticking movements of his clocks, counting down the seconds towards the moment when he must become a cosmic being?

Having corrected himself and his clocks, Crowhurst started to write his final testament. It was a record of his tortured, deluded thoughts during the last eighty minutes of his life. It was also— so far as its meaning can be established—a confession. It was as if the words he had already written had taken symbolic possession of him: he too had committed the "maximum possible error" and he too would now attempt to define his "true position".

*   *   *

Before attempting to decipher Crowhurst's meaning, we must give a word of warning. Crowhurst's writings in his earlier meditations, though often difficult and obscure, were capable of logical interpretation. But by now he had lapsed into a deeper madness and was using language that he alone understood and at whose meaning we can make only tentative guesses. Our interpretations must now be impressionistic rather than specific.

The earlier writings had been typical of classical paranoia, a psychotic disorder in which deluded ideas are built into a complex, intricate structure. Though founded on mistaken beliefs, the structure of paranoid thought has a strong internal logic and consistency; at the same time, the rest of the personality remains more or less intact. Most often, the delusional system is one of persecution, but, as with Crowhurst, a paranoid can also have delusions of grandeur, thinking himself to be a great mathematician or philosopher, or a second Messiah. It is possible, while thus convinced, to continue behaving in an otherwise sensible way, as Crowhurst did with his radio messages.

However, it is not common for delusions to stabilise at this level. The personality is liable to become more disorganised, and forms of thought become strangely disordered. Writing ceases to communicate: ideas condense together illogically, unrelated themes interpenetrate, and abstract words take on peculiar concrete meanings. These, coupled with delusions, are symptoms of paranoid schizophrenia—and towards the end of his meditations Crowhurst's writing was showing an increasing tendency in this direction.

Crowhurst's final testament is extraordinarily complex in its uncontrolled use of meanings on different levels, expressed in a private shorthand language. In the grip of his delusions, Crowhurst was more than ever the supreme punster. His words simultaneously embodied three different activities. He wrote, first of all, as a "corrector" of himself, as if he were a clock; second, as a navigator establishing his "true position" after faulty timings and sightings had put him off course; and third as a player of a game of chess against God, in such a hopeless position that he was forced to resign. These concepts were impenetrably interlocked.

But in the schizophrenic obscurity, Crowhurst was expressing more than witty word plays around his delusions. He was displaying a desire to put the record straight, a concern that the truth should be known.

After he had completed the testament, Crowhurst chose to die. No one can be certain of the precise circumstances of his death, for the simple reason that nobody was there to watch. We have based our reconstruction on a detailed examination of the logbooks and the evidence of certain crucial objects on board or missing from

Teignmouth Electron. Some descriptive details are less strongly substantiated than others, but of the central thesis we have no doubt. That Crowhurst decided to end his own life is overwhelmingly supported by the evidence of his writings, and by every other clue we could find.

*   *   *

Everything was ready for the final confession. He sat at the desk in his cabin, still half-covered with the debris of radio repairs. His Hamilton chronometer was now ticking in front of him. It probably was not perfectly on time, but that did not really matter any more — for counting down the minutes to his death, all he needed was to know how much time was passing. His barometer on the forward bulkhead was clearly in view, the fresh pages were waiting for his thoughts. He wrote out a second heading, to get things absolutely right:

EXACT POS   JULY I   10 03

Beneath his heading Crowhurst ruled three parallel lines down the left-hand side of the page, just as he had for all his navigational workings. Here the count-down timings of the chronometer would be placed, precisely marking out the minutes and seconds that Crowhurst allowed himself for his confession. Five minutes and forty seconds after writing the heading, Crowhurst put down his first thought:

10   08   40   Reason for system to minimise error
                To go — remove experience
                Barometer pressure on move

The first phrase is reminiscent of the meditations. The system, which always tried to remove things — and people — guilty of error, was now seeking to remove Crowhurst. He had, after all, been guilty of the maximum possible error — he had tried to falsify a voyage round the world. Therefore he would go, removing his experience to a more satisfying system where he could be his true self. His barometer — another symbolic instrument — showed that the weather, which had been totally calm during his period of revelation, was now due to change. It was time to leave.

    10   10   10   System of Books reorganise perfectly
                     Many parallels

All the great books displaying the wisdom of Christ, Galileo had
changed their meaning once Crowhurst's revelation was known.
The system of knowledge was reorganised by his "impulse".

    10   11   20   Realisation of role of decision making
                     Hesitation — time   Action +time

At first sight this is just a new version of "procrastination is the
thief of time". Perhaps when one was indecisive one slowed down
time, when one acted one speeded it up. Hesitation was *minus*
time, action was *plus* time. Was Crowhurst here working out —
against the steady march of his chronometer — the idea that it had
been his own hesitancy that slowed down his time and his clocks,
his own panic rushes that made them run too fast? Was he thinking
of his own hesitancy as the countdown progressed?

    10   13   30   Freq.
                     Books Soul of men into their work —
                     reason for "work" unimportant?

This is obscure. Maybe Crowhurst was thinking of his revelation
in the logbooks, and hoping that the fraudulent nature of his
"work" was unimportant.

    10   14   20   Hermits force unnecessary conditions on them-
                     selves
                     Seek truth wasting time.

Crowhurst, of course, was such a hermit, who had learned the
truth because of his long enforced hesitation. By "wasting" time,
he had found out its real nature.

Ten seconds later he wrote down a strange, clotted passage
which was, perhaps, amongst many things, a personal confession of
one of his most characteristic weaknesses:

    10   14   30   My folly gone "forward" in imagination
                     Wrong decision not perfect   Time
                     no longer computed   Had disorganises Clocks

What was his "folly gone forward in imagination"? Was it his old habit of leaping on to fresh challenges when the old one grew stale, or collapsed about him? This trait, which we have noted many times, he now recognised. It was a "wrong decision". It made time no longer "compute". Things had not been perfect as he had imagined them. His clocks had all become disorganised.

> 10 15 40 Clocks Think no need worry
> about time ± but only elapsed time
> ± May be meaningless? Important
> reason for work is (lost) understand

> 10 17 20 right Sorry waste of time

It was all very confusing. Crowhurst first comforted himself about his inaccurate clocks. It did not matter that they were not precisely adjusted, because he was only using them to mark the minutes and seconds before his moment of retribution. Anyway, the distinction, in Relativity theory, was meaningless. He tried to write down what the point of his voyage, and his revelation had been, but couldn't.

He was so confused he scratched his head in perplexity, which amused him.

> Ape indicates perplexity by headscratching!

The human animal, when perplexed, lifts up its animal hand to scratch at the skull which contains its mind. In the margin where he was recording his chronometer times Crowhurst then wrote "not quite right?", and repeated the phrase in the text. He put down the time in the middle of his confessions, as if his excited mind were now associating time and his thoughts even more closely as he tried to express himself. No longer did the neatly ruled margin divide the one from the other:

> not right?   10 19 10 Evil is choice of
> interpretation of symbols

He then began a new page, in a new style. The ruled margin was abandoned, and the symbols of the clock, time, and navigation diminished in importance. His confession so far hadn't gone quite

right; he had got himself into a logical morass. Evil . . . the choice
. . . the symbols—this was nearer to the heart of his real concern.
As a God he was above conventional morality, he knew that. But
there was still a terrible choice to be made, the choice that had
been perplexing him during the last pages of the meditations, and
while philosophising about time he had neglected it.

This choice, quite simply, was what evidence to have aboard
Teignmouth Electron when he abandoned her. The alternatives were
clear: on the one hand he could destroy Logbook Two, which
revealed his trip in the Atlantic, his illegal visit to Rio Salado, and
the confession he was now writing; and leave Logbook Four
aboard, with its perhaps passable forgery of a circumnavigation.
No one would examine too closely the documents of a dead man.
It would mean he died a hero, became a "concealed" God (which
nature allowed him to be) and which would save his family the
suffering of his disgrace. But that course would mean his revelations would be largely lost, and mankind would continue as mere
apes with computers.

On the other hand, he could destroy the fraudulent Logbook
Four as a retribution for his sin, and leave Logbook Two aboard
Teignmouth Electron, together with his other truthful and incriminating documents. In this way the world could read his confession,
and the proof that he never left the Atlantic. This course would
make amends, save him the torment of concealment as a God, and
serve the cause of truth by recording his true position.

This is the real dilemma which lies behind the confused and
complex words which follow, on "the game". At first, Crowhurst
considered carrying through his pretence:

> New reas[on] occurs for game. My judgement indicates
> cannot not use anything "put" in place, but have
> to put everything in place. Task very difficult.
>
> NOT impossible. Must just *Do the B*
> Strive for perfection in the hope of

It is tempting to see this as Crowhurst arguing that if he continued
his game, fooling the world, he could not use his actual journey,
with any of the facts naturally "put" in place by that journey, but
must himself put everything in place by inventing navigational
positions. This was difficult, but NOT impossible. The italicised

phrase *Do the B[est]* was crossed out. He wrote instead, "Must just Strive for perfection in the hope of . . .' In the hope of what?

He stopped writing. He knew he could not do it. He could not put everything in place, however hard he strived for perfection. Perhaps Logbook Four was just not convincing enough. Anyway. the whole idea conflicted with his God-like dedication to honesty. Putting down a timing again, he wrote:

20 22   Understand two "reasons" for task of
              conflict. Rule of game unsure. If
10 23 30   game to put everything back? Where is back?

Now he was considering the other alternative, of confession. The two "reasons" were the two choices of concealment or confession, which were in conflict and made the task so difficult. Crowhurst was still perplexed. All the rules of the game were unsure. Honesty told him to try and put everything back into the good state that existed before he started faking his voyage. But this was very confusing. For what *was* his precise position before he started? Was he honest, or not?

This confusion made him despair:

10 23 40 Cannot see any "purpose" in game.

And two minutes later he had given up entirely. Like a losing player in a chess game, he was in an unplayable position:

10 25 10 Must resign position in sense that if
              set myself "impossible" task then
              nothing achieved by game . . .

He cannot carry off his fake, nor can he make full amends.

              . . . Only Reason
              for game to find new rules governing old
              truths. Understand Exact position
              of concept of balance of Power. It is
              only one way of expressing hope. The
              age process is new way of despair concept

These last two sentences are obscure. Perhaps the balance of power was between the two unbearable choices, which were so evenly balanced that he welcomed not having to make up his mind. Perhaps the age process was his chronometer ticking the time away. Anyway, the realisation that the game had been too much for him, and there was no escape, forced Crowhurst's mind into a final burst of wild, agonised, theorising:

> 10   28   10   Only requirement for have new set of
> rules is that there IS some

> 10   29   Understand reason for need to devise
> games. No game man can devise is

> harmless. The truth is that there
> can only be one chess master, that is
> the man who can free himself [from] the
> need [to] be blown by a cosmic mind . . .

The only way to escape this harmful game was to leave his body, and become a cosmic intelligence.

> . . . there can only be one perfect beauty
> that is the great beauty of truth . . .

Therefore he must tell the truth about his forged voyage, and leave Logbook Two behind.

> . . . No man may do more than all
> that he is capable of doing. The perfect
> way is the way of reconciliation . . .

Now he was asking for forgiveness:

> . . . Once there is a possibility of reconciliation
> there may not [be] a need for making errors . . .

At long last, he brought himself almost to make a straight confession:

> . . . Now is revealed the true
> nature and purpose and power
> of the game offence I am

I am what I am and I
see the nature of my offence

Having confessed, or *virtually* confessed, he addressed an appeal
to God, or the Devil, or whoever set the terrible rules of the harmful game he had been playing, to play it fair next time. He was
close to God he felt himself his messianic son:

I will only resign this game
if you will agree that [on]
the next occasion that this
game is played it will be played
according to the
rules that are devised by
my great god who has
revealed at last to his son
not only the exact nature
of the reason for games but
has also revealed the truth of
the way of the ending of the
next game that

It is finished —

It is finished

IT IS THE MERCY

He had written the words. He had clearly said what he intended
to do. The cosmic explosion had begun, and the game that he had
first thought so amusing, so harmless, so likely to bring him glory —
deserved or undeserved — was now inevitably to bring about his
own death in retribution. It was finished, it was the mercy.

For about half an hour Crowhurst waited in a resigned agony of
mind, preparing himself for death, and perhaps arranging various
things in his cabin. It may have been at this stage that he unhooked
the safety line that he habitually streamed astern as a precaution
against falling accidentally into the sea. (There was no line attached
when the boat was found.) Then he returned to his cabin and
took up his pencil and, in a large hasty script, wrote until he
reached the end of the page.

He added five final phrases, telling God — his father — that he
would do his duty as his holy family required. He talked directly

to God, who was to play the next game with him, in the system of pure, bodiless intelligence. The next move was up to God, and this was the time for God to make that move:

```
11  15  00   It is the end of my
             my game the truth
             has been revealed and it will
             be done as my family require me
             to do it


11  17  00   It is the time for your
             move to begin

             I have not need to prolong
             the game

             It has been a good game that
             must be ended at the
             I will play this game when
             I choose  I will resign the
             game 11  20  40      There is
             no reason for harmful
```

These were the last words Donald Crowhurst wrote. There was no space, and no time, to write more; he had stopped at eighteen minutes past eleven, which allowed only two and a half minutes until the moment he had appointed for his great gesture. There were important things to do in that time.

He rose (we presume) to his feet, shut the logbooks, and put them all—except one—on the chart table where they could easily be found. In them was the full glory of his revelation, which would change the history of mankind, and the full confession of his forgery. He was what he was, and he wanted everyone to see the nature of his offence—because this was the true nature and purpose and power of the game. He remembered that there was one small truth the logbooks would not reveal: the way he had forged his record run in December. So he carefully arranged beside them the only two navigational plotting sheets which he had not destroyed, the ones on which he had worked out the "cooked" navigation. They would complete the picture. He was being methodical, and wanted everything to be clear.

He then picked up his Hamilton chronometer, watching the seconds tick by, one by one. Holding it, and his Logbook Four, he walked towards the companion ladder. He looked round the cabin for the last time, to check that all the evidence was in place.

He looked, perhaps, at the radio sets he had so desperately fought to repair to make contact with his wife in Bridgwater; at the still unbuilt "magic computer" beneath his red cushion seat; at the jagged remnant of the ceremonial champagne bottle used at the launching nine months before; at his rejected lifebelt in the aft locker; at his newly-cut hair lying all over the cabin floor, shorn in preparation for a triumphal homecoming, or a triumphal death. A minute had already passed.

Still timing every move with the chronometer, he climbed the seven rungs of the companion ladder into the cockpit. It was nearly mid-day. The sun shone benignly and the sea was calm. Green sargasso weed floated by in patches. *Teignmouth Electron* was moving forward very slowly under her single sail.

Donald Crowhurst threw Logbook Four, the only totally lying navigational record, into the sea. This was essential, so that the world would learn only his "true position". He had thought hard about his tormented choice, and made his decision. "Conceal-ment" would hurt too much, he must choose honesty. The testimony he had left behind in his cabin occasionally lied in minor details, but it would enable anyone who studied it with care to reconstruct what had happened.

It was twenty minutes past eleven. Only forty seconds left, now. He climbed on to the stern of the trimaran, walked past the defunct Hasler gear and the mizzen mast with its gently pulling sail, still watching his chronometer. The seconds hand was circling the dial, and as it reached the forty-second mark he jumped off the stern into the sea. The man who wanted to be a hero, and ended as a God, took with him to destruction the two things that epitomised his Maximum Possible Error: the lying clock and the lying Logbook. He left behind the Great Beauty of Truth.

Teignmouth Electron was making less than two knots in the calm air, but it was still faster than he could swim. Crowhurst watched her pull slowly away from him.

Yesterday was June 30.

Clock started approx 5.10. Just before movement down

June. 30 . 5.10   MAX POSS ERROR

TRUE POSITION   ~~June~~ July 1   10 20 H.

EXACT POS JULY 1   10 03

JULY 1

10 08	40.	Reason to system to minimise error
		Togo — Run by men
		Barometer pressure on men
10 10	10	System of Books reorganise perfectly
10 11		Many parallels.
—	20	Realisation of role of decision making
		Resolron — Turn Action + time.
		Free.
10 13 20		Books Send of men into their work —
		reason for "work" unimportant ?.
10 14 30		Hermits face unnecessary derelictions in thunder
		Seek truth Wasting time.
10 14 30		My folly gone forward in imagination
		wrong decision not perfect True
		no longer computer their divergences Clocks
10 15 40		~~Clocks~~ Think no need worry
		about time ± but only elapsed time.
		± May be meaningless ? Important
		reason for work is (lost) understand
10 17 20		right language of true
not quite?		Ape indicate perplexity by head scratching !
right		not ~~next~~ rt. 10 79 10 Evil is absence of
		reinterpretation of Symbols.

New ideas occur for game. My judgement adviser
must not use anything "put in place" but have
to put everything in place.   Task very difficult.

Not impossible. Must just ~~do the job~~
Strive for perfection & the hope of

10 22   Understand Two "reasons" for lack of
         conflict. Rule of game unsure.   If
10 23 30 game to put everything back? when is it back?

10 23 40 Cannot see any "purpose" in game.

10 25 10 Must resign position in sense that it
          Set myself "impossible" task then
          nothing achieved by game. Only reason
          for game to find new rules governing old
          truths. Understand Exact position
          of concept of balance of Power. It is
          only one way of expressing hope. The
      age process is new way of despair concept
10 28 10   Only requirement for game new set of
10 22   rules is that there. there is some

10 2   Understand reason for need to devise
         games.   No game may can devise is

         ~~Resign game if you will agree~~
         ~~only rule~~

         harmless   The truth is that there
         can only be one chess maybe that is
         the man who can face himself the
         need be blown by a cosmic mind.

         there can only be one perfect beauty
         that is the great beauty of truth.
         No man may may do more than all
         that he is capable of doing. The perfect.
         way is the way of reconciliation
         once there is a possibility of reconciliation
         there may not a need for making
         errors. Now is revealed the truth
         nature and purpose and power
         of the game my friend I am.

I am what I am and and I
see the nature of my offence

I will only resign this game
if you will agree that if
the next occasion that this
game is played it will be
played according to the
rules that are devised by
my great god who has
revealed at last to his son
not only the exact nature
of the reason for games but
has also revealed the truth of
the way of the ending of the
next game that

It is Finished ~

It is finished

IT IS THE MERCY

11 15 00   It is the end of my
            my game the truth

has been revealed and it will
by done as my family require me
to do it

11 17 00   It is the time for your
            move to begin

I have not need to prolong
the game

It has been a good game that
must be ended at the
            I will play this game when
I close I will resign this
game 11 20 40   There is
no reason for harmful.

And the World Said . . .

The first news that *Teignmouth Electron* had been found mysteriously abandoned was given to Clare Crowhurst on the evening of July 10th. Two Bridgwater policemen drove up to Woodlands in a squad car while she was out for a walk with her dog, and told her sister Helen. Helen waited for her at the top of the drive, and was joined by a nun from the nearby convent, who had heard about the discovery on a news bulletin. At first Clare was not desperately worried and simply presumed her husband must have been off for a short trip on his dinghy. She told the nun, rather brusquely, that she was not in need of comfort, and walked down to Woodlands. Several cars were parked there, and a small gathering of anxious friends was in the living-room. Clare took the children upstairs and told them the news, but still none of the family felt any sense of shock. As she came downstairs the police sergeant warned her that she must be prepared for a barrage of distressing telephone calls. It was only then that the significance of the news began to dawn on her. The police squad car was parked in the drive to repel the newspaper siege, which for the next month was to be almost continuous.

Mrs Crowhurst refused to make any statements that night, but said she had a strong feeling that Donald was still alive. The newspapers repeated this the following day. The reason for her certainty was that she had felt no premonition of any tragedy. She had such a belief in her psychic unity with Donald, that she was convinced she would have sensed the moment of his death. Her mind jumped at various possibilities for hope and comfort. She asked Rodney Hallworth to find out whether the rubber wet-suit was still aboard *Teignmouth Electron*. If it was missing it might indicate he had merely gone underwater swimming near the trimaran just before it was found, and was still alive and swimming. Hallworth's agency put out the theory to the newspapers that contaminated food might have made Crowhurst ill—presumably based on the cable about mouldy flour and interesting cheese. Captain Box on the *Picardy* rebutted both theories. The wet-suit was aboard, and most of the food supplies were still in excellent condition.

Two days later, the *Sunday Times* started an appeal fund for the Crowhurst family with a £5,000 donation, and Robin Knox-Johnston immediately asked that the £5,000 prize for the fastest circumnavigation—which he now automatically could claim—should go to the Fund. Everyone was far too affected by the tragedy to question the genuineness of Crowhurst's voyage. In the midst of all the messages of condolence and cheques for the Fund, Sir Francis Chichester's letter requesting an inquiry into the Crowhurst voyage—posted on July 2nd in Portugal—arrived at the *Sunday Times*. It got submerged in the surge of emotional sympathy and we found it only some months later when going through the files.

Meanwhile the newspapers, with no inkling of the true story, were bombarding Captain Box with requests for further details, and publishing fanciful theories of their own. Someone unearthed sightings of three other yachts found mysteriously abandoned in the mid-Atlantic near *Teignmouth Electron*, which conjured up imaginings of vast sea-monsters, or universal death rays in the area. Almost every headline evoked the *Mary Celeste*; not one spelt it correctly.

*   *   *

By his mysterious disappearance, Donald Crowhurst gained the fame he had set off around the world to achieve. It made him an internationally famous, mythical figure. As with all mythical figures, his name was swiftly surrounded with legend and romantic speculation. The most persistent, and glamorous myth that attached itself to Crowhurst (as it has to the memory of legendary heroes from King Arthur to Che Guevara) was that he never died. He is alive and well in South America, or some other paradise for escapees, says this myth, awaiting the call to resume his normal life.

For all romantics—and those, like Peter Beard, who thought Donald Crowhurst capable of escaping from the most impossible predicament—this will always be the most attractive theory. Mention the name "Crowhurst" in any saloon bar, and the response is always: "Is he still alive? How did he escape?"

Newspapers which had depicted Crowhurst as a stock character in a marine epic, from electronics wizard and local hero, through jaunty helmsman and flying fish breakfast eater, to the modern *Mary Celeste* mystery figure, now conjured up the logical epilogue to this cliché drama. The *Daily Express* sent a reporter off to uncover him on the Cape Verde Islands. A message in a bottle was found on a French beach saying "Help—stranded on island in the Aegean" and caused a flurry—though the merest glance showed it to be an obvious forgery. Later a photographer called Shaun Hennessy claimed to have seen Crowhurst—hidden behind a voluminous beard—at Barnstaple in Devon, but then conceded that he must have been hoaxed.

It will never be possible finally to disprove such speculations. Anyone who thinks it possible for Donald Crowhurst to have simulated the agony and derangement of the 25,000 words in his last meditations, will always be able to credit tales of a secret confederate, in a helicopter or midget submarine, who picked him up in mid-Atlantic to carry him off to safety. However, the meditations have been read by a number of psychologists, and all agree they could not have been written by a sane person, intent on a hoax. One of our consultants summed up his conclusions: "It would be very difficult to write 25,000 words of this stuff. Try it."

There is another—equally improbable—theory that Crowhurst managed to swim the 700 miles to the nearest land, without a lifebelt.* Or that he landed secretly on the Azores, and pushed

* The *Sunday Times* erroneously reported that the life-jacket was missing. It was discovered in our later examination of the boat, stowed in the compartment under the companion ladder.

off an empty *Teignmouth Electron* so hard that she managed to sail herself, against prevailing winds and currents, and without efficient self-steering, to the position where she was discovered by the *Picardy*.

The other, less romantic possibility, is that Crowhurst died accidentally. In the earlier part of the book we have listed several instances of Crowhurst behaving clumsily aboard boats, particularly when he was preoccupied. An accident cannot be dismissed as a total impossibility, but the evidence of the logbook writings, the absent safety rope, the missing chronometer and other objects, argues overwhelmingly against it. The theory we have advanced is, we are convinced, the only one that fits all the facts.

*   *   *

The mystery of Crowhurst's disappearance could not begin to be solved, of course, until his logbooks were methodically examined. They were therefore clearly a valuable journalistic property. While the *Picardy* headed for the Caribbean port of Santo Domingo with trimaran and logbooks aboard, Rodney Hallworth travelled to London to offer world exclusive rights in the unseen record of what was still thought to be a heroic voyage round the world. When Hallworth started the auction, the *Daily Express* were keen, but not keen enough, and he finally sold the copyright in the logbooks for £4,000 to the *Sunday Times*.

A party flew to Santo Domingo to meet the *Picardy*, and receive the logbooks. It included Nicholas Tomalin (one of the authors of this book), photographer Frank Herrmann, and Rodney Hallworth, who was to supervise the handover. Hallworth was still so affected by the death of his client that he asked the party to observe one minute's ceremonial silence as the Boeing 707 flew from Madrid over the stretch of the Atlantic where Crowhurst died.

As soon as the *Picardy* docked, on Wednesday, July 16th, Captain Box took Hallworth into his cabin to explain the situation. He had found the confession pages, with their suggestion of suicide. He showed them to Hallworth, and urged him to tear them out of the logbooks so that Crowhurst's family would never learn the appalling truth. Hallworth did so, intending to show them only to the *Sunday Times* editor on his return.

It was only on the next day—after Tomalin had cabled a speculative story on the various possible accidents that might have taken place—that examination of the logbooks revealed that Crowhurst had never left the Atlantic.

This discovery made the real circumstances of Crowhurst's death an easy logical deduction. Hallworth decided he could not keep Crowhurst's secret any longer. He drew the torn-out logbook pages from his coat pocket and, announcing that he already knew how Crowhurst had died, read out the final confessional words. The party flew back to England and, on their arrival at the *Sunday Times*, joined an editorial conference to ponder the difficult problem of what to do.

On the one hand, they had a sensational scoop. On the other hand, it was not a scoop which, on the face of it, greatly redounded to the credit of the newspaper which had sponsored the Round-the-World race. There was also Mrs Crowhurst, and her feelings, to consider. But the story could not be suppressed, particularly in view of the Appeal Fund. It was decided to publish a full account, but first to show the text of the proposed article to Clare Crowhurst and her advisers for their approval. The BBC, who were preparing a trumpeting version of the Heroic Circumnavigation from their film and tape recordings, were warned to delay their programme (but only the Director-General was told why).

The revelation of Crowhurst's pretence, combined with hints of his mental derangement and suicide, was the national sensation of the week-end of July 27th. It became the lead front-page news in almost every rival Sunday paper. It inspired an increasingly demeaning series of speculative follow-up stories, and a renewed newspaper siege of Woodlands, but—all things considered—it was as painless as possible. There was some indignation at dangerous newspaper stunts being mounted without sufficient supervision, but the general view was that this was not the essence of the tragedy that had befallen Crowhurst.

The celebratory Golden Globe dinner on the *Cutty Sark* was regretfully put off in the light of the tragedy, and the various other race contenders gradually recovered from their ordeals. Robin Knox-Johnston—now with even greater generosity—stuck to his intention of waiving the £5,000 prize for the fastest circumnavigation, so that the money could go to the Crowhurst Appeal Fund. "None of us should judge him too harshly," he said. He later thought of becoming a Conservative parliamentary candidate. Bernard Moitessier, having sailed one and a half times round the world without stopping, finally landed on Tahiti, and there decided

to remain for several months, untarnished by the poisons of civilisation. Nigel Tetley—awarded a £1,000 consolation prize by the
Sunday Times—began to build himself a new boat. It was another
trimaran. Bill King repaired his boat and started off on yet
another attempt to sail non-stop round the world, but had to give
up at Gibraltar. Chay Blyth persuaded the British Steel Corpora-
tion to sponsor another circumnavigation in a steel boat, but in
the opposite direction—against the westerlies of the Roaring
Forties. Captain John Ridgway started an adventure school in
Scotland to spread the heroic cult to the rising generation. Alex
Carozzo and Loick Fougeron retreated, apparently happy, into
private life once more.

In Norfolk John Elliot was training to become a schoolteacher
(he had decided that boat-building was not his vocation, even
before the building of *Teignmouth Electron*). John Eastwood himself
continued his regular work, slowly allowing the small but painful
wounds inflicted by the incident to heal. In Somerset Stanley Best
did the same, and tried to find someone in Jamaica to buy
Teignmouth Electron from him.

In Argentina, Nelson Messina, Santiago Franchessi, and the
Salvatis were famous for a week, but then resumed their unevent-
ful lives. The only person to suffer any unpleasant consequences of
Crowhurst's brief visit was the coastguard midshipman at La
Plata. His failure to report the incident to his superiors, though
an apparently reasonable decision at the time, resulted in an
investigation of whether to bring charges of negligence.

Meanwhile Clare Crowhurst gradually became hardened to the
prying journalists who besieged her, and settled down to life alone
with her children. She took in lodgers, learned to live with the
curiosity of her neighbours and—after a few weeks when she had
thoroughly read the logbooks—finally accepted the fact that her
husband must be presumed dead. Everyone who met her testified
to her courage and good sense.

For a while Rodney Hallworth was unmercifully teased by his
colleagues for the triumphant success of his campaign to link the
name of Teignmouth with the most famous nautical trickster of all
time ("You'll have to sell the resort as the 'Sin Capital of the West
Country' from now on, Rodney old boy!"), but even the hoteliers
of his home town treated him with remarkable understanding.

An aggrieved Council, thinking of all the money wasted on
those "Teignmouth Welcomes Crowhurst" banners, summoned

him for an explanation. Hallworth emerged triumphant from the meeting. The Publicity Committee officially commended him for "the terrific publicity reaped from the Donald Crowhurst saga". Arthur Bladon, the ex-Chairman of the Council, happily estimated that the whole affair "had brought Teignmouth about £1,500,000 of free national and international publicity". And his final verdict, as reported in the local paper, put the tragedy into the right perspective from Teignmouth's point-of-view. "Despite the sad end," Mr Bladon told the meeting, "the voyage has brought up more publicity than this Committee has managed in 50 years. We have had this extremely cheaply, and I hope the town appreciates it."

Donald Crowhurst would have been glad to hear he did not die in vain.

Donald Crowhurst's Navigation

by Captain C. A. Rich
(Lecturer at the School of Navigation, London)

The charts shown throughout this book have been reconstructed from navigational details contained in Donald Crowhurst's logbooks. With the exception of the faked positions during the period December 6th–10th the tracks indicate, as nearly as can be ascertained, the actual voyage made by *Teignmouth Electron*.

The reconstruction has been necessary because of the absence of charts showing the yacht's daily positions and courses. These are normally kept by mariners as a continuous record of their voyage, in addition to the mathematical calculations and navigational data, normally kept in a logbook or sight book, and which are used to obtain the daily positions and courses. In fact, apart from the few plotting charts which have furnished irrefutable evidence of Crowhurst's faked logbook entries and several positions marked on a routeing chart towards the end of the voyage, no attempt was made by Crowhurst to keep a record of his positions on charts, unless these charts were, for some reason, destroyed by him.

Apart from the plotting charts already mentioned, and several unused ones, no others were found for any other stages of the voyage—but from the navigational calculations contained in the logbooks there is no doubt that Crowhurst did use plotting charts of some description throughout the voyage. It would appear, therefore, that he disposed of all of them except those which would clearly indicate his fraudulent logbook entries. Without these charts the logbooks alone would have been insufficient to prove, beyond doubt, that false entries had been made.

The following is a list of the equipment used by Donald Crowhurst for the purpose of navigation during the voyage.

SEXTANT For taking sights of celestial bodies for ocean navigation. Also used in coastal waters for angular measurement of shore objects.

NAVICATOR DIRECTION-FINDING SET To obtain great circle bearings of radio beacons situated around the coast (marine) and inland (aero).

ECHO-SOUNDER For obtaining the depth of water below the hull.

WIRELESS RECEIVER For obtaining weather bulletins and time signals for rating timepieces.

CHRONOMETER To obtain Greenwich Mean Time.

STEERING COMPASS To indicate the direction of the yacht's head.

HAND-BEARING COMPASS To obtain bearings of shore objects and celestial bodies.

BAROMETER To predict weather conditions.

PATENT LOGLINE To record the number of nautical miles sailed through the water.

ADMIRALTY *OCEAN PASSAGES FOR THE WORLD* (1950) Contains steamship and sailing ship routes for the various seasons of the year.

ADMIRALTY PILOT BOOKS (SAILING DIRECTIONS) For round-the-world voyage. Complementary to Admiralty Navigational Charts.

ADMIRALTY NAVIGATIONAL CHARTS Sufficient for his proposed round-the-world voyage.

ADMIRALTY LIST OF LIGHTS Giving comprehensive details of all navigational lights.

ADMIRALTY TIDE TABLES Volumes I (European Waters); II (Atlantic and Indian Oceans); III (Pacific Ocean).

ADMIRALTY RADIO SIGNALS Volumes I Port Radio Stations and Pilot Vessels. Coast Radio Stations; II Radio D.F. Stations. Radio Beacons; III Meteorological Codes. Radio Weather Messages.

PLOTTING CHARTS For use in obtaining the yacht's position with information derived from sights of celestial bodies (i.e. intercepts and position lines).

"SHORT-METHOD" TABLES (H.D.486) For use in navigational calculations concerned with celestial bodies and which reduce trigonometry to a minimum.

NAUTICAL ALMANAC (1968 and 1969) Containing astronomical data of the sun, moon, planets and stars. Essential for ocean navigation.

VARIOUS DRAWING INSTRUMENTS For use in chartwork.

It can be seen by the nature of the calculations in the logbooks that Reed's *Nautical Almanac* was used for 1968 which is normally intended only for use in home waters. For 1969, however, the more detailed *Nautical Almanac* was used.

From Teignmouth to Lizard Point, Crowhurst obtained his position by means of visual sightings of navigation marks and lights, and whilst within range of the radio beacons around the European coasts used bearings of these obtained with his Direction Finding set. It is noticeable that at this stage of the voyage these bearings did not appear to be very reliable. He also took bearings of the Consol Beacon at Lugo in north-west Spain. Later in the voyage Crowhurst obtained excellent results with his Navicator when en route to the Falklands from Rio Salado. He took many bearings of the plentiful beacons on the Patagonian coast and fixed his position accurately on several occasions. He was, however, much nearer the beacons than he had been when taking bearings off the European coasts.

Once out of sight of land, and out of range of its navigational aids, Crowhurst commenced his ocean (or celestial) navigation. He used the navigator's conventional method of obtaining his position by means of sights of heavenly bodies taken with the aid of his sextant, and with few exceptions relied entirely on sights of the sun. Later in the voyage when he took sights of the planet

Venus, the Moon and occasionally a star the results were erratic. This is understandable, as there is no reason to suppose that Crowhurst had had any great experience of ocean navigation, and while the sun's altitude may be obtained reasonably accurately by an inexperienced handler of a sextant, other celestial bodies demand far more practice.

It is interesting to note, however, that on June 5th the day he crossed the Equator homeward bound, and within three weeks of his last sight, Crowhurst took five sights during the day. Three of these were of the sun and the other two of stars. Plotting the results he obtained and adjusting for the necessary run between sights all five observations "come-in" and give a good fix.

Robin Knox-Johnston — a professional navigator with several years' experience of ocean navigation — found sights of the sun sufficient for his daily navigational needs and no doubt for voyages of this type the use of stars and planets would involve the single-hander in a lot of additional unnecessary work. However, when making a landfall or when an immediate fix is required there is no question of the advisability of star sights; Knox-Johnston himself was about to resort to them when unsure of his position before passing through Banks Strait, north of Tasmania. He was subsequently saved this chore by the timely sighting of Swan Island Light.

Crowhurst's daily navigation, therefore, consisted usually of two observations of the sun — the minimum necessary to obtain a reasonably accurate position. At noon, local time, when the sun was bearing due north or south — on his meridian — he obtained his latitude by meridian altitude, quickly, accurately and with the minimum of mathematics. Either in the morning or afternoon he would take another sight of the sun and with the aid of the *Nautical Almanac* and his "Short-Method" tables, he obtained a position line at some point on which the yacht's position lay. He then used a plotting chart to transfer this position line the number of miles estimated to have been sailed along the course line, up to noon in the case of a morning sight, and back to noon in the case of an afternoon sight. The point at which this transferred position line cut his noon latitude he took as his "noon position". This is a typical method used in ocean-going commercial vessels, where the noon position is recorded in the logbook daily and the days' run calculated from the previous noon position. Unfortunately it is only as accurate as the estimation of the course and distance run between the sights. It is what is known as a running fix—more commonly associated with coastal navigation and shore objects. It is somewhat strange that Crowhurst seldom noted his noon position in his logbook, despite all the mathematical data recorded in them. It is for this reason that it has been necessary to plot these daily positions for virtually the whole voyage using the intercepts and bearings calculated by Crowhurst in his logbook, and also his noon latitude.

On many occasions, however, Crowhurst used a far quicker, but much cruder, method of establishing his noon position. By observing the GMT at the time of taking his noon meridian altitude for latitude and comparing this with the time of meridian altitude (transit) of the sun at Greenwich, which is contained in the *Nautical Almanac*, he obtained his longitude immediately by merely converting this time difference into degrees and minutes of arc. He worked on the assumption that the sun appears to travel over the earth's surface through one degree of longitude in four minutes (360° in 24 hours). This is perfectly correct in theory, but in practice it is extremely difficult to obtain the exact moment of meridian altitude, especially with only one sight. An error of one minute in time would put the longitude as much as fifteen miles in error and it is quite conceivable that an error of two or three minutes with a resulting error in longitude—and the yacht's position—of the order of forty miles or so would not be uncommon. It is clear from logbook entries that errors of this magnitude were involved, but there is every reason to believe that Crowhurst was well aware of the limitations of this method. It may well be that he only used this method when he was unable to obtain a morning or afternoon sight for longitude due to overcast skies or more important routine work on the yacht. On the other hand he may have felt that this method was sufficiently accurate for his purposes and did not think the extra work justified taking a morning or evening sight.

In one of his tape recordings, Crowhurst described another short-cut that he often used:

The working of the noon sight is interesting. I've developed a method of working the latitude at noon which may well be used all over the world for all I know, but I've not come across it before. As far as I know it's original. It consists of working on differences rather than on observed values. In other words, I calculate the differences in height between today and yesterday.

To this I add or subtract, as appropriate, the difference between the declination yesterday and today which I merely add or subtract to the latitude yesterday to give me my latitude today. This sounds complicated, but in practice involves, in my opinion, less work than the traditional method.

In fact, Crowhurst was wrong in thinking that this is a quicker method for finding the latitude; the amount of mathematics involved is the same, if not more. But Crowhurst's method would have an advantage if he was making his calculations backwards in order to give fake sun-sights.

Crowhurst obviously gave the theory of celestial navigation much thought and was sufficiently conversant with it to take sights of the sun in the late evening when making the South American coast before his landing at Rio Salado. The advantage was that the sun, at this time of the year in the particular latitude that he was in, crossed his prime vertical, in other words was bearing due east or west, and so the position line he obtained when the sun was bearing due west in the evening was running due north and south, thereby giving him an exact longitude, irrespective of errors in latitude at noon, or at the time of taking the longitude sight. This was necessary as the South American coast runs in a roughly north–south direction and his latitude was little use in giving him his distance from land but his longitude was essential. Here again Crowhurst took the easy method by simply applying his intercept directly to his Dead Reckoning Longitude to obtain his observed longitude. To be correct in theory he should first have converted this intercept in miles into difference of longitude which, for a given number of nautical miles, varies with latitude. The maximum error according to the sights he took using this method would appear to be less than five miles and Crowhurst may very well have been aware of this and considered this sufficiently accurate for his needs and again very much less demanding with relation to the amount of work involved.

It is beyond doubt that false entries were made in the logbook from December 6th–10th, the period when Donald Crowhurst claimed a record day's run of 243 miles for a single-hander. This was when he was approaching the Cape Verde Islands which lie in the North-East Trade wind belt. His genuine navigational calculations were undoubtedly those appearing on a plotting sheet from which an extract is reproduced on the opposite page.

10 2500   532° 06.7'   338 360   29°45' 6H
           8   15.0   26   314   14.6
           338° 21.7'   314   66°E 29°59.4'

A.P. 18°N 26 21.7'W   HA 46°E   Dec 22°38.7'S
29°28.3' - 62   29°45.0   A₂ N 130.2 E.
    - 5.4'   29°23.4   - 90.0
29°23.4'   21.6 TOWARDS   40.2

12 01 22   D.   02°06.3'   24   42°42.7'
            01.   15.0   2   14.9'
            22   5.5'   22°E   62°57.6'
                   02°26.7'

AP 18°N 24°26.7'W   HA 22°E   Dec 22°39.5'
44°08.5 Δ = -87 44°00.6'   A₂ N 151.2 E
    - 79   42°57.0   - 90.0
44°00.6' Position Lat 1°02.6 Away, bearing 61.2°

AP 19°N 24°21.7'W   HA 46   Dec 22°38.7'S
28°47.9' (-63)   A₂ 130.7
    - 5.4   29°59.5'   - 90.0
28°44.5   28°44.5'   40.7
                   1°15.0 Toward

22 59 50   GHA ϒ 46 43.8 SHA 281°44 40°32'   18 14
    - 26   14 50   61°34.8   -71.9
22 59 24   6.0   360 00.0   40°30.1 RIGEL
           61°34.8'   343°18.8
                       18 21.2

AP 18°N 25°18.8'   LHA 42°E   DEC 8°14'S
41°03.8 (-54)   Log 2958   A₂ N 118.5°E
    - 7.6   - 90.0
40°56.2   Int 26.1 miles AWAY   28.5

10 16 27 (2) 10   332°00.2' 360   0 32°19.1' (9H)
    - 22   335   3°30.0   309   14.2'   3010
10 16 05   309   1.3'   51   32°33.3'
AP 16°N 26°31.5N   HA 51 E   Dec 22°45
26°57.8 - 54   126.3
    - 8.3
26 49.5

1325   90°00.0'   38 51.2'   50°54'   3025
1 59.7   51 08.8   22°45.9   14.8
1 15.0   38°51.2   16 04 3   51°08.8'
38°14.7   Noon Lat 8th 16°04.3'N

17 48 10   16   61°58.5'   88   17°21.1' 09H
    - 17   147 26 45.0'   25   12.7   3047
17 47 53   88°56.8'   63   17°33.8'
AP 16°N 25°56.8W   HA 63°W   Dec 22°46.7
17°19.2' - 44   33.8   A₂ N 120.4 W
    - 7.3   11.9   270.0
17°11.9'   27.9 TOWARDS   149.6°(A)

It can be seen from this extract—which covers his sightings for December 8th—that he was making an unusually large number of calculations of his genuine position as he neared the Cape Verde Islands. The reason for this, one can presume, was firstly because he did not want to run aground and secondly because he dare not take the risk of being sighted from shore and reported in a different position from that which he was claiming to be in. The extract from this genuine plotting sheet clearly shows his noon altitude on December 8th as 16° 04.3′ N., and a logline reading of 3,025 miles.

Crowhurst then turned to a second plotting sheet, on which he made a large number of clearly fictitious calculations. He began by drawing in a "safe" distance to pass off the Cape Verde Islands and then drew in course lines with log distances marked beside them. His intention was evidently to invent positions which would agree with his claimed false log distances. It can be plainly seen from a number of calculations that he then worked backwards from these predetermined positions to find the necessary altitudes for fictitious sun sights. On the right of this plotting sheet he then arranged the results in the normal way for copying up, as shown in the extract below for December 8th:

It can be seen from this extract that Crowhurst has now altered his noon latitude for December 8th to 13° 29.3′ N. and has changed his logline reading to 3,215 miles. This puts the yacht nearly $2\frac{1}{2}$° further south and has added an excess of 190 miles to his log distance.

Crowhurst continued this process throughout the period December 6th to 10th. Presumably at some later date he then transcribed the calculations from the second plotting sheet into his logbook, making one or two further small amendments, and, of course, omitting the reverse calculations. He also added in a commentary for greater credibility. This is how the calculations for December 8th finally appear in Crowhurst's logbook:

There is no doubt that the record run of 243 miles claimed by Crowhurst is false, as, on the first plotting chart, is the table of actual and claimed distances which is reproduced earlier in this book. This is the final and irrefutable evidence of deception.

The amount of work involved in a deception of the magnitude envisaged, apparently, by Crowhurst would be staggering. Beside his normal routine navigation to establish his actual whereabouts he would have all the additional calculations necessary worked backwards, to give the desired positions. These would have to be entered into the logbook and any number of copying errors would doubtless appear. On several occasions when Crowhurst was making false entries in the logbook, he made mistakes in copying which on inspection make nonsense of the results he obtained.

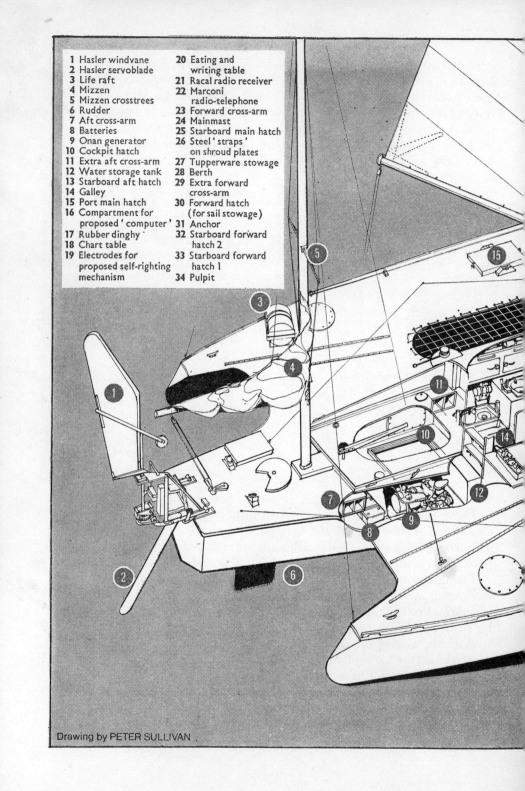

1 Hasler windvane
2 Hasler servoblade
3 Life raft
4 Mizzen
5 Mizzen crosstrees
6 Rudder
7 Aft cross-arm
8 Batteries
9 Onan generator
10 Cockpit hatch
11 Extra aft cross-arm
12 Water storage tank
13 Starboard aft hatch
14 Galley
15 Port main hatch
16 Compartment for proposed 'computer'
17 Rubber dinghy
18 Chart table
19 Electrodes for proposed self-righting mechanism
20 Eating and writing table
21 Racal radio receiver
22 Marconi radio-telephone
23 Forward cross-arm
24 Mainmast
25 Starboard main hatch
26 Steel 'straps' on shroud plates
27 Tupperware stowage
28 Berth
29 Extra forward cross-arm
30 Forward hatch (for sail stowage)
31 Anchor
32 Starboard forward hatch 2
33 Starboard forward hatch 1
34 Pulpit

Drawing by PETER SULLIVAN

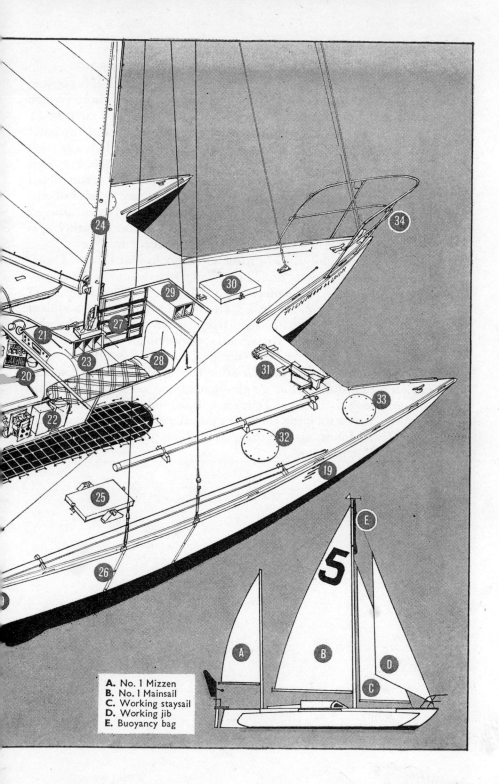

A. No. 1 Mizzen
B. No. 1 Mainsail
C. Working staysail
D. Working jib
E. Buoyancy bag

Provided he relied on the sun only, and used the rather crude method of finding the longitude previously described, it is possible the fabrication could have been achieved for the whole voyage without too much work, but the entries in the logbook concerning weather would also have to tie in with distances sailed. Crowhurst took the necessary reports for the areas concerned obviously with this in mind, as has already been explained in this book. Provided suspicion had not been aroused, a cursory glance at a completed set of fraudulent logbooks might fail to detect any signs of deception. In Crowhurst's case, however, suspicion had been aroused and once the logbooks had been put under close scrutiny it is unlikely that the deception would have succeeded.

It would certainly appear from his logbooks that Donald Crowhurst was a sufficiently skilled navigator to have made the round-the-world voyage, and there is no doubt he learned a lot about the theory of navigation in his attempts to make the fraudulent voyage. The fact that he sailed over 16,000 miles single-handed must be considered a remarkable achievement in itself—three years ago it would have been considered magnificent. Even before he put ashore at Rio Salado after 8,155 miles, Crowhurst had sailed a multihull further single-handed and non-stop, than anyone save one rival. Nigel Tetley is still the only man to have gone further. It is a sobering thought that after the Chichesters, Roses and Knox-Johnstons anything less than 30,000 miles is now thought insignificant.

Appendix 2

The Design of Teignmouth Electron

by John Eastwood

The great tragedy of the *Teignmouth Electron* project from a marine engineering point of view was that there was insufficient time to develop and test many advanced features of Crowhurst's original conception. Some of the ideas — particularly those concerning the basic structure of the boat — were incorporated in the design, and appear to have performed well; the difficulties Crowhurst encountered on the voyage mostly involved aspects of equipment and fitting-out of a superficial nature that would have been cured if there had been adequate trials. I would like to discuss some of the principles we were working towards, because it would be a pity if the use of a trimaran for this kind of project were discredited because of the partial failure on this one voyage.

Teignmouth Electron was based on standard Piver-designed "Victress" class hulls and crossarms, which provided an over-all length of 41 feet, a waterline length (centre hull) of 38 feet, and a beam of 22 feet. But the remainder of the boat was designed specifically for Crowhurst's requirements, and departed in many respects from the standard specification. The main intention was to provide greater structural strength for the taxing conditions of the Southern Ocean, even if at some expense to space and comfort. Some of the changes were fundamental—such as dispensing with the large cabin and wheelhouse of the normal "Victress". Others were simply a matter of strengthening and upgrading at vulnerable points.

The hulls themselves were made by normal series-production methods by Cox Marine of Brightlingsea, Essex, from $\frac{3}{8}$-inch marine plywood ($\frac{1}{2}$-inch on the bottom of the main hull) glued to fir frames and sheathed in glass fibre. At key points—along the keels, chines, stems and transoms and deck-to-hull joints—the sheathing was trebled in thickness by the addition of several extra layers of glass fibre, to give greater strength.

In the standard "Victress", the hulls are connected together by two box-section crossarms, made from $\frac{1}{2}$-inch and $\frac{5}{8}$-inch plywood. Crowhurst wanted two additional crossarms, which I thought was sensible for a voyage of this kind. For these, we used a similar cross-section to the standard aft crossarm, and they were each accommodated about four feet forward of the standard beam positions. Extra bulkheads were required to provide attachments for these beams, and two watertight collision bulkheads were included in each hull. This multiplicity of bulkheads gave great strength, but resulted in an unusually large number of hatches—four in each wing hull and three in the centre hull—because of the reduction of access to storage compartments.

The attachments of the crossarms to the bulkheads was made far stronger than usual. The number of bolts was trebled and instead of using washers, the load was spread by passing the bolts through continuous strips of heavy gauge stainless steel glued to the timber.

Yet another device was used for adding lateral rigidity. In a trimaran, the stresses from the rigging tend to bend the extremities of the crossarms upwards. Since plywood is more liable to deterioration under repeated compression than under repeated extension, it follows that the upper surface of the box-section crossarms is more in need of strengthening than the lower surface. We found a simple method of achieving this. The deck, to which the upper surface of the crossarms is glued, was doubled in thickness—two layers of $\frac{3}{8}$-inch ply were used instead of the usual single layer. An additional bonus in this extra layer of decking was that all joints could be staggered. We also took the precaution of avoiding high stress points in the decks by generously radiusing all corners at such places as the junctions between wings and hulls.

Crowhurst proposed a novel method for fastening the rigging shrouds to the hulls. Each shroud plate, made from stainless steel, was extended from the deck, down the outside of the hull, under the keel, and back up the other side, where it formed the complementary shroud plate. Thus the shrouds, in effect, were fixed to stainless steel straps encircling the entire hull. Crowhurst was also very insistent on a very close fit between the shroud plates and the fork of the rigging screws, and between the holes of the shroud plates and the clevis pins. This would minimise any tendency for the pin to bend, and would reduce the various stresses as much as possible—an important consideration when a boat is likely to be subject to extreme conditions.

The masts of *Teignmouth Electron*, made of aluminium alloy, were supplied by International Yacht Equipment Ltd. The main mast was 38 feet—some four feet less than on the standard "Victress". (One of the several reasons for reducing the height was the weight of the buoyancy bag, which Crowhurst wanted to fix to the masthead.) A larger mast section was used than on the standard "Victress", and all shrouds and stays were increased one size.

The mizzen mast was reduced in height accordingly. In retrospect, I think this may have been a mistake. One of the problems that Crowhurst encountered was the boat's moderate performance into the wind, and there is reason to believe it would have behaved better with a greater sail area aft. There were, however, a number of other possible explanations for this fault: the mainsail and mizzen may have been cut too full, and also the presence of the bulky buoyancy bag cannot have helped. I would also have liked to have had time to experiment with increasing the area of the fins.

Crowhurst carried a wardrobe of 15 sails, which were:

1	Ghoster Genoa	468 sq ft
1	Reaching Staysail	267 sq ft
2	Yankee Jibs	244 sq ft
2	Large Jibs	328 sq ft
2	Working Staysails	123 sq ft
1	Working Jib	123 sq ft
1	Storm Jib	61 sq ft

1 Trysail	61 sq ft
1 No. 1 Mainsail	278 sq ft
1 No. 2 Mainsail	182 sq ft
1 No. 1 Mizzen	90 sq ft
1 No. 2 Mizzen	56 sq ft

He had doubled up on most of his headsails for use as twin running sails. This is the well-known device of setting identical sails on either beam of the boat, and connecting their sheets to the tiller to provide self-steering. For self-steering while running, Crowhurst had also been considering another scheme which I have not seen used elsewhere. The idea was to trail a warp (or a rope with a bucket on it) and connect this through a variable-ratio linkage to the rudder shaft. This would be set to operate the rudder in such a way as to keep the boat and the warp in a straight line. It seemed a quite feasible plan, but to get the ratios quite right would have required more time for experimentation than Crowhurst could allow. For normal use, the boat was provided with a standard Hasler self-steering gear.

Manual steering was by tiller, operated from an open cockpit. The positioning of this involved some difficulty, as the rudder itself was aft of the mizzen, while the ideal position for the cockpit was forward of the mizzen. We therefore had to make a linkage via two shafts. (This unusual arrangement made many people believe, incorrectly, that *Teignmouth Electron* was a yawl and not a ketch.) There was the additional facility of manual steering by wheel mounted inside the aft cabin bulkhead. It was positioned so that it could be operated with the cabin totally closed, or from a seat that could be clipped to the companion ladder with the helmsman's head just protruding through the main hatch.

There were a number of other sailing aids inside the cabin, including a Hengist-Horsa wind speed and direction indicator, which displays information on electrical dials from a masthead vane and spinner. It had been Crowhurst's intention also to couple this information about the wind into his projected electronic alarm and switching system. Any abrupt changes in the wind would trigger off alarms or would electrically release the sheet cleats.

The main principles of Crowhurst's electronic safety devices have been described in the body of this book. They contained some good ideas, as well as others of doubtful practicality, and it is a pity that Crowhurst was able to finish so little of his planned system. The buoyancy bag arrangement clearly needed more sophisticated development than was possible in the circumstances, but there was nothing inherently unworkable about it. Crowhurst had found neat solutions for many of the problems — such as the positioning of banks of electrodes in such a way that they could distinguish between normal splashing from waves and permanent immersion in a capsize. This part of the arrangement was completed before *Teignmouth Electron* set sail, but not the firing mechanism for inflating the bag.

Other of Crowhurst's proposed devices — such as electrical sensing of excessive bilge-water — might also have been of use on the voyage. But his idea of putting stress-gauges in the rigging was, I thought, a rather marginal refinement. However, since virtually none of it was completed we cannot know precisely how much value Crowhurst's technological innovations would have had for the practical yachtsman.

My own view is that, despite the result of the *Teignmouth Electron* project, a trimaran conceived along these lines would be an excellent vehicle for long-distance single-handed cruising, providing there was a sufficient period for development and tuning. It should not be forgotten that *Teignmouth Electron* twice covered more than 8,000 miles without stopping, and that the two trimarans in the Round-the-World race performed on average just as well as the monohulls.

INDEX

Index

307